TEACHING
PRIMARY LITERACY
WITH ICT

Learning and Teaching with Information and Communications Technology

Series editors: Tony Adams and Sue Brindley

The role of ICT in the curriculum is much more than simply a passing trend. It provides a real opportunity for teachers of all phases and subjects to rethink fundamental pedagogical issues alongside the approaches to learning that pupils need to apply in classrooms. In this way it foregrounds the ways in which teachers can match in school the opportunities for learning provided in home and community. The series is firmly rooted in practice and also explores the theoretical underpinning of the ways in which curriculum content and skills can be developed by the effective integration of ICT in schooling. It addresses the educational needs of the early years, the primary phase and secondary subject areas. The books are appropriate for pre-service teacher training and continuing professional development as well as for those pursuing higher degrees in education.

Published and forthcoming titles:

R. Barton (ed.): *Learning and Teaching Science with ICT*
M. Hayes (ed.): *ICT in the Early Years*
A. Loveless and B. Dore (eds): *ICT in the Primary School*
M. Monteith (ed.): *Teaching Primary Literacy with ICT*

TEACHING PRIMARY LITERACY WITH ICT

Edited by
Moira Monteith

Open University Press
Buckingham · Philadelphia

KH

Open University Press
Celtic Court
22 Ballmoor
Buckingham
MK18 1XW

email: enquiries@openup.co.uk
world wide web: www.openup.co.uk

and
325 Chestnut Street
Philadelphia, PA 19106, USA

First Published 2002

A catalogue record of this book is available from the British Library

ISBN 0 335 21246 8 pbk   0 335 21047 3 hbk

Library of Congress Cataloging-in-Publication Data
Teaching primary literacy with ICT / [edited by] Moira Monteith.
        p. cm.
    Includes bibliographical references and index.
    ISBN 0-335-21047-3 — ISBN 0-335-21246-8 (pbk.)
        1. Language arts (Elementary)—Computer-assisted instruction.
    2. Computers and literacy.   3. Educational technology.
    I. Monteith, Moira.

    LB1576.7 .T44 2002
    372.6'044—dc21
                                                                    2001056001

Typeset by Graphicraft Limited, Hong Kong
Printed in Great Britain by Biddles Limited, Guildford and Kings Lynn

11/22/04

CONTENTS

LIST OF CONTRIBUTORS

Richard Bennett is the ICT Coordinator for the School of Education at Chester College of Higher Education. He teaches on undergraduate, postgraduate and in-service courses in teacher education. He is currently conducting research into the development of teachers' ICT skills. He is a registered Ofsted inspector and a former advisory teacher and primary headteacher.

Jon Callow is a lecturer in literacy education at the University of Western Sydney, Australia. His experience includes classroom teaching from primary to secondary level, working as a literacy consultant with schools in low socioeconomic areas and adult education in Europe. His current interests include language and critical literacy in both written and multi-media texts, and the use of technology in teaching and learning. His edited text *Image Matters: Visual Texts in the Classroom* (PETA 1999) explores the theoretical and practical aspects of visual literacy for teachers and students in educational contexts.

Lyn Dawes has worked in schools and in teacher education. She has a strong interest in the use of ICT to support collaborative work, especially speaking and listening. She is co-author with Neil Mercer and Rupert Wegerif of *Thinking Together*, a teacher's pack of resources for developing thinking skills at Key Stage 2 (http://www.thinkingtogether.org.uk). Lyn now works for the British Educational Communications & Technology Agency (BECTa).

Carol Fine works as a principal lecturer in ICT at Kingston University. She has contributed to a number of books and publications in this field. Her main area of expertise is in designing, writing and delivering courses to enable teacher trainees and teachers to integrate the use of ICT into their subject teaching. She is presently researching the emergence of ICT as a National Curriculum subject in the last 20 years.

Bob Fox is a senior lecturer in the Faculty of Education and Psychology, University College Worcester. He has written extensively on the use of ICT in education, both as regards literacy and also numeracy. He is currently involved in a national project for developing new guidelines for the use of ICT during the Literacy Hour. His research interests focus on the use of ICT by primary schoolchildren.

Julian Grenier is Acting Head of Centre at Woodlands Park Nursery Centre in Tottenham, North London. He has been involved in a series of research projects at the Nursery Centre on the theme of raising levels of parental involvement, including setting up and evaluating a computer-lending project for families. He is currently undertaking an MA in early childhood education and has lectured on ICT at the University of North London and at the Centre for Language in Primary Education. He is a regular contributor to *Nursery World*.

Steve Higgins is a senior lecturer in primary education at the University of Newcastle. He was Project Manager for the TTA-funded project 'Effective Pedagogy Using ICT for Literacy and Numeracy in Primary Schools'. The aim of the research was to help teachers raise pupils' achievements by developing their pedagogy through increasing the range of informed choices about when and where to use ICT and to understand the implications of using these technologies.

Jackie Marsh is a lecturer in education at the University of Sheffield, where she teaches on the M.Ed in literacy and MA early childhood education. Her research interests include the role of popular culture in the literacy curriculum and the development of critical media literacy in the early years. She has published a number of books and papers in the field of early literacy and is a co-editor of the *Journal of Early Childhood Literacy*.

Moira Monteith is currently an educational consultant and was previously a principal lecturer in ICT in education at Sheffield Hallam University, and before that a teacher. She has written and edited a number of books concerned with the use of ICT and with writing and was co-editor of the literacy pack produced by MAPE, an association concerned with the use of ICT in primary schools. Her research has included the observation of word-processing stages by children in Reception and the first years of schooling.

David Moseley is Reader in Applied Psychology at Newcastle University where he is involved in the professional training of teachers and educational psychologists. He is an executive member of the National Literacy Association, for whom he initiated the NLA-Docklands Learning Acceleration Project (1995–7). He then headed a TTA-funded research team to study and support effective teaching methods using ICT in primary schools. His publications include assessment and teaching materials, research reviews and work on emotional literacy.

Henry Pearson is a principal lecturer in the School of Education at Chester College of Higher Education, where he lectures on language and literacy. His publications include *Children Becoming Readers* and *Reading Time*, produced for teachers in the developing world.

Mary Lou Thornbury was born, educated and trained as a teacher in New Zealand and came to work in a London comprehensive. There she was involved in research into children's writing. Later she transferred to work in primary schools and subsequently retrained in computing. After advisory work in schools she lectured on computing in primary education at the University of North London. She now acts as an educational consultant and is continuing her research into computers and the early years.

Alison Tyldesley is a literacy consultant working for Derbyshire Local Education Authority. She has broad experience in both primary literacy developments and in ICT. She taught in the primary sector for over 20 years during which time she had a role as a primary IT advisory teacher. She is currently working towards an MA in language and literacy and has recently contributed to the National Association of Advisers in Computer Education (NAACE) guidance on ICT and Literacy (www.naace.org.uk).

Jean Underwood currently holds the Chair of Psychology at Nottingham Trent University and is a visiting research fellow in the ESRC CREDIT centre, Nottingham University. She is editor of *Computers & Education* and on the editorial board of the *Journal of Information Technology in Teacher Education*. Her research is concerned with the impact of new technologies on teaching and learning. This includes continuing investigations into computer-based cooperative learning with particular reference to gender and task variables, and an evaluation of large-scale tutoring programs (integrated learning systems) in UK schools.

Rupert Wegerif has spent ten years researching children's talk around computers for The Open University. He has published widely on this topic and also designed educational software to support pairs and groups learning together within the curriculum. A recent book written with Lyn Dawes and Neil Mercer, *Thinking Together: A Programme of Activities for Developing Thinking Skills at KS2* (Questions Publishing 2000) suggests ways that teachers can improve the quality of children's talk around computers (www.ThinkingTogether.org.uk).

Tatiana Wilson taught in primary schools for ten years before joining the University of Exeter as a lecturer in primary education. She has contributed to a number of books, including *The Poetry Book for Primary Schools, Making Progress in English* and *Differentiation and Diversity in the Primary School.* She is currently researching into cross-curricular English and creativity in literacy teaching and learning.

Katina Zammit lectures in primary education at the University of Western Sydney, Australia. Her background in visual literacy comes from her days as a literacy consultant and primary teacher in disadvantaged schools in the inner suburbs of Sydney. Her interest in visual literacy was initially stimulated by her own and teachers' use of CD-ROM programs in their classrooms. This interest has continued with her research on the intersection and integration of literacy and technology. She is currently involved in the development and trial of a curriculum framework for new learning environments and literacies, designed to support teachers with the integration of a range of literacies into classroom practice.

SERIES EDITORS' PREFACE

The current concerns over literacy are both significant and universal, and are reflected in policy decisions. In England and Wales, especially, the government has introduced the concept of the Literacy Hour in primary schools and this is currently being extended to the first two years of secondary education. Such moves have been largely successful and welcomed by teachers. Alongside such initiatives there are parallel concerns to extend the range of information and communication technology (ICT) expertise and provision throughout the system. The odd thing is that these concerns are being developed largely in isolation from each other. This is reflected to some extent by the view of some practitioners that the 'new technologies' and the traditional values of 'literacy' are in some ways in competition with each other.

Nothing could, of course, be further from the truth. However, such concerns are by no means new. As long ago as the civilization of the ancient Greeks, Plato was warning against the dangers of the new technology in the form of writing: it would destroy the values enshrined in dialogue and lead to a diminution in the faculty of memory. The editor of this volume, Moira Monteith, refers to this in her own chapter ('What has ICT got to do with Literacy?') by quoting from an earlier Open University Press book edited by Daniel Chandler and Stephen Marcus (1989) entitled *Computers and Literacy*, to which the present volume is in many respects a successor.

But during the nearly 20 years between the publication of the two volumes much has changed, not least the evolution of 'new literacies' alongside 'new technologies'. Of course the latter still have an important part to play in the teaching of older literacy skills. Students need to learn to compose both on paper and screen and the necessity of developing their skills in drafting and redrafting becomes ever more important. However, the full potential in these areas presented by ICT is still all too little exploited in schools: computers are sometimes seen as 'intelligent typewriters' rather than as agents which can extend the reading and writing repertoire in all manner of ways, including the potential for collaborative writing both within, and beyond, the conventional classroom.

Reading itself is redefined by ICT: text is no longer linear and static. The act of reading no longer refers simply to words on the page – graphic literacy is a key concept. Hypertext opens up the exciting potential for interaction between text, author and reader. Achieving reading literacy with ICT demands more of the learner in the acquisition of multiple literacy skills.

We have presented elsewhere (SITE 1999, San Antonio, Texas, USA, 1–4 March) on the need to extend beyond traditional 'schooled literacy', or what has been memorably called 'letteracy' by Papert in *The Children's Machine* (1993), to include 'extended literacy' (involving visual and computer literacy awareness) and 'networked literacy' (bringing classrooms across the globe in direct contact with each other through the agency of the Internet), both of which will make the traditional distinction between literacy and oracy ever more irrelevant.

In addition, the concept of 'literacy' itself has to be fundamentally rethought. This has become particularly clear in countries where older forms of literacy were less clearly established than in the developed western world, such as among the Aboriginal communities in Australia or the, until recently, dispossessed 'black communities' in the Republic of South Africa. For example, Professor Douglas Young of the University of Cape Town, in a paper ('Languages, Literacy and Communication') prepared as an advisory document for the South African government developing its language policy, suggests that 'the term "literacy" has expanded to include several different kinds of literacies. "Literacies" stresses the issue of access to the world and to knowledge through development of multiple capacities within all of us to make sense of our worlds through whatever means we have, not only texts and books'. (It is ironic in the present context that our computer, as we write this, has a built-in spell-checker that refuses to recognize the word 'literacies'!)

Young goes on to suggest examples of a range of 'literacies' which include:

- *Cultural literacy*: cultural, social and ideological values that shape our 'reading' of texts.

- *Critical literacy*: the ability to respond critically to the intentions, contents and possible effects of messages and texts on the reader.
- *Visual literacy*: the interpretation of images, signs, pictures and non-verbal (body) language.
- *Media literacy*: the 'reading' of, for example, TV and film as cultural messages.
- *Computer literacy*: the ability to use and access information from computers.

It is significant that such thinking is most prevalent in societies that have begun to develop the new literacies before the older forms of 'print literacy' have been universally established.

The present volume marks a bridging operation. It is well aware of the continuing importance of the literacy traditions of the past and of the significant contribution that can be made by ICT to their teaching and development. But it is also cognizant of the new literacies and has important chapters devoted to these, especially the area of visual literacies. It should be of especial value to those teachers involved in literacy teaching (and that means potentially *all* teachers) at any level of education. Such a book can never be finished: the new literacies, and our awareness of them, are continually evolving and developing, the phenomenon of 'texting', or 'txtng', being but one current example. We feel it appropriate therefore that the current volume should be the first publication in a new series that is planned to embrace the core curriculum areas and it represents a pioneering approach to a theme that will be echoed throughout the whole series.

Anthony Adams and Sue Brindley

INTRODUCTION

Moira Monteith

Language, as ever, gives the tell-tale signs about how our
attitudes are changing . . .

(Humphrys 1999: 8)

Language typifying a social practice such as . . . education
does not change without cause.

(Barnett 1994: 157)

Changes in the language we use reveal attitudinal and social changes. For
example, we are now far less likely to know as many of the words used
about saddling and bridling horses as people did in previous centuries
before cars became so widespread. The words 'literacy' and 'information
and communication technology' (ICT) as used in the title of this book
indicate pivotal change, happening now.

Evolving definitions

'Literacy' is an 'old' word, used before dictionaries could date its beginning,
but young in terms of its general applicability. It appears to have retained
its traditional meaning intact: a literate person remains one who can
read and write. At the same time, a secondary use is evolving: the word
can indicate a level of knowledge or expertise not in literacy but in some
other learning. Here are three recent examples: religious literacy, emotional
literacy and computer literacy: 'Church and family were once the principal
agents of religious literacy' (Simons 2001: 3); 'we are left with a growing
number of children unpractised in making and consolidating friendship,
dealing with conflict, taking risks – all key components in the development

of emotional literacy' (Humphrys 1999: 76); 'computer literacy has become a catch phrase ... but the knowledge acquired [on current computer literacy courses] is so shallow that someone who knew the equivalent amount about reading and writing and books would be called *illiterate* ...' (Papert 1996: 26).

We need to acknowledge that the significance of 'literacy' is widening, even though its secondary meaning need have no specific connection with traditional literacy: for example, 'emotional literacy', as interpreted by Humphrys, cannot come from reading books. At the same time, the primary or core meaning of 'literacy' is still fundamental and vital to its understanding although its meaning is still evolving and we may often use the word 'literacy' with this wider significance in mind. (It is interesting to note that we do not use 'numeracy' or 'science' in this way.) In this book we focus on the traditional view of literacy as learning to read and write, since we are concerned here with primary education from nursery to the age of 11. As the chapters continue, this traditional view of literacy expands to include other versions such as visual and digital literacy, and 'texts' include books, CD-ROMS and material from the Internet.

ICT as used in our title (and in schools) can most effectively be defined by its basis in and connection with inventions such as television, cameras, computers and phones. The words, 'information' and 'technology' have been linked together for some time, certainly as early as 1958, when they were used in the *Harvard Business Review*. 'Information' was the powerful word and was coupled, according to the *Oxford English Dictionary*, with a number of other words as people sought to find an acceptable term. 'Information technology' is the one which has stuck. The next few sentences are in some ways a digression, but need to be included as many people are genuinely puzzled about the ongoing disagreement as to which term and therefore which abbreviation we should use in education. The first edition of the National Curriculum used information technology (IT). Subsequently, several organizations chose to add 'communication' to IT. Some educators have been very ingenious in defining what they consider to be the difference between IT and ICT. There are learned discussions on email groups, in books and at conferences about whether to use IT, ICT or indeed CIT or C&IT! Often the distinctions drawn seem falsely distinguished, but like all verbal changes we shall just have to wait and see what sticks. We use ICT here as that is what the Department for Education and Skills uses currently, and of course the notion of 'communication' fits very well with that of 'literacy'.

The combination of ICT with literacy leads to a potent fusion, both verbally and in practice. We can hardly overestimate their significance for us both as a society and within our individual lives. The authors in this book focus closely on ICT and literacy within the primary school curriculum and in research into teaching and learning. As most of the writers work in England the focus is more often than not English primary schools, but we believe that the book offers a very useful platform for discussion in other countries.

An alternative view

The use of ICT in classrooms has become widespread and organized, yet sometimes seems ineffectual. Both teachers and pupils occasionally wonder what they are doing. It is inevitable perhaps that critics should question the expense and value of the whole enterprise. One example of this alternative viewpoint on current ICT usage has arisen from findings of the Alliance for Childhood (Davies 2000). In this article, Debbie Davies questions the need for ICT (together with all its 'baggage' of equipment, training, Internet access and cost) in primary schools and recommends instead that children receive the necessary training in Year 7 (pupils aged 11 and 12) in secondary school. It is certainly true that there are many problems with using computers and other ICT equipment in schools. However it does seem surprising that some people would prefer to ignore what is happening outside school, so that during the first six years of formal education some children would have nothing to do with computers at all, some would play games only and some would become very adept indeed at using ICT. Educational inequality would flourish in such a situation.

We can sympathize with the teachers and children who have had rather negative experiences of ICT, with little or no technical support and inadequate equipment in school. All our writers are aware of the range of alternative viewpoints concerning the use of ICT in education but are committed to the belief that ICT and literacy are strongly and beneficially connected. The wait-until-later argument is countermanded by the New Zealand research mentioned in Chapter 4. Early ICT use, coupled with continuing use as the children grow, grants particular advantages. Apparently, children who might otherwise be considered as deprived of certain educational advantages can reach and maintain educational standards alongside their peers when they have used ICT from an early age. Clearly the whole area of ICT and literacy needs far more research, particularly during the early years. I believe such research findings would encourage governments to fund primary education more generously than they do at present.

The organization of this book

The book is organized in traditional linear fashion but this does not preclude you from reading it in other ways. You may find the following summary of what I see as important connections between the chapters helpful in choosing your own route, relevant to your own knowledge, experience and practice.

Chapter 1 sets the scene as to the development of both literacy and ICT. We may now be on the threshold of a wholly literate society for the first time in the UK. Well, nearly. *A Fresh Start: Improving Literacy and Numeracy* (DfEE 1999) suggests that the literacy problem in England will be solved by 2054, half a century away. The great majority of individuals have the potential to become literate at school but a fifth of them do not do so. Thus it is important to look at both individual literacy development and that of the whole society. Plenty of books exist to tell us why at a given point schools are not succeeding in enabling all pupils to become literate. In fact, we appear to have improved matters very little over the last 50 years. Although as teachers and advisers we have worked very hard, following one educational leading light after another, still the level of literacy has remained fairly constant, with a fifth of our people disenfranchised from the benefits of a literate society. However mass literacy (even if only of four-fifths of society) has brought about the development of a mass audience and a mass need for communication. In the twenty-first century, literacy is a major goal for governments and commerce, as well as schools and booksellers. It is a global requirement in that virtually all developing countries understand how important literacy is as part of a general development policy. At the same time, when we look around us we are already aware of the effects of living in a networked society.

ICT is not just a range of equipment that will help us drive up literacy standards, but is the latest stage in the development of literacy technology. ICT has embedded within it the prerequisite that users should be prepared for literacy if not already literate. US research findings indicate that skilful teachers are the most likely to develop skilful pupils. This is hardly surprising. We have known for some time that skilled workers are essential for productivity gains. So teachers are of paramount importance in the great literacy push. Information as to good practice and statistical data as to effective practice (both gathered and circulated by means of ICT) will encourage further progress.

In Chapter 2, Steve Higgins and David Moseley illustrate just how useful sharing such information can be. They examine results from a carefully planned and executed research project in primary school classrooms, using ICT for teaching literacy and numeracy. They found that previous 'Publications on the use of ICT in education have traditionally suffered from an excessive optimism' (Moseley *et al.* 1999: Appendix 2, vii) and did not wish to do the same. Their team began with the principle: 'The process of change needs to be evidence based'; so they used research evidence that text-to-speech software can improve reading and spelling, word processing can improve writing, and collaborative talk can improve thinking and reasoning. Very importantly, the project teachers were consulted as to what they wanted to do with ICT, so that the schools were not dealing with an academic agenda only.

The teachers observed in the project did not find the introduction of ICT in lessons very easy. Often their attention was divided and there was less expanded pupil/teacher talk, a plenary review was often omitted and the teachers asked fewer questions. Indeed, a subsequent postal survey found that a year later, although the computers in the schools surveyed were more plentiful and often more powerful, use of them had decreased, possibly owing to the introduction of the Literacy Hour and the teachers' consequent attention on that.

One finding tentatively links with the discussion in Chapter 4, concerning children's use of computers in the early years. In the survey that Higgins and Moseley and their research team undertook before their project began, they found that 'at the school level, Reception classes made greater progress in reading where schools reported higher computer use . . . but not in Year 2 [6 to 7 years] or Year 4 [8 to 9 years]'. This is of course only a tentative pointer but does indicate that computer use by very young children needs more research.

Higher-order literacy skills feature in each chapter, as clearly our education system should aim to provide more than functional literacy. In this case, Higgins and Moseley relate how the research team found evidence that children's comprehension skills were helped when they generated their own questions about a text. Therefore, a number of electronic texts were designed where the children drew up their own sets of questions. This does seem to be a strategy that deserves more discussion and trial by teachers and pupils, not only in terms of electronic texts but as a way of focusing on good literacy practice also.

Alison Tyldesley's chapter is teacher focused, discussing what is needed to help teachers use ICT during the Literacy Hour, a Department for Education and Employment (DfEE) strategy which she explains. The Literacy Hour guidelines accept ICT as a literacy medium and she suggests reconsidering the definition of literacy to include non-linear texts and sound and moving images. She found, like Higgins and Moseley, that teachers have been preoccupied with the management of the curriculum, particularly when new changes such as the literacy and numeracy programmes have been added. As a result, some teachers have tended to neglect the use of computers.

She suggests that emphasis on ICT is more significant in school if it is linked to prestigious classroom practice, and teachers are more likely to use ICT if they can visualize its use within their current planning. She sums up this use as 'Doing simple things well in a new context'. The teachers are confident about what they are doing in terms of literacy and their confidence begins to work with ICT also. For example, the teachers in the six case studies commented that whole-group work employing explanations from digital whiteboards, large computer screens or projected computer screens proved to be very creative in terms of classroom learning. One particular teacher found that giving children a simple 'bland' text on a word processor and asking them to rework it had the most impact on pupils' learning. The group of teachers in the Derbyshire project outlined by Tyldesley indicate one way forward in the significantly creative use of computers in literacy work.

One important point arising from this very practical project is, I think, that the integration of ICT and literacy should not be artificial. This particular aspect, the functional, creative use of ICT, is considered further in the two chapters dealing with software and the numerous comments about program design throughout the book. In Chapter 8, Jackie Marsh suggests that school classes should discuss home use of computers. Home use is not 'artificial' in the sense that children do not play computer games for the sake of using computers or because they were told to. Discussion as to how pupils use computers at home can encourage talk about the range of uses to which we put computers. It also helps us use their knowledge and skills in furthering their literacy attainment.

In Chapter 4, Mary Lou Thornbury and Julian Grenier examine the use of computers with nursery-age children, emphasizing the expressive purpose of play. Central to this chapter are their reflections on a project where nursery children took home laptops and during the same period of time the parents went to a literacy class. The integration of literacy with ICT occurred at two levels: both children and parents working at home and at school. Significantly, the authors found the computer to be ideal for adult/child dialogue as the screen contributes to a sense of shared ownership. The children, in effect, were scaffolded by parents, staff and computer programs. 'Scaffolding' is a term used throughout this book and is defined in this chapter as helping children 'to remain engaged and to think and act at a higher level than would be possible otherwise.' Thornbury and Grenier found other research evidence that community and parental involvement were important factors in raising standards of achievement. They take evidence from a New Zealand re-search project where families who owned computers when children were younger conferred an advantage on children in later achievement in maths and English. Early use of computers also encouraged curiosity and individual responsibility.

They also consider some negative findings, including, for example, the criticism that 'children rarely tried new programs or new levels of difficulty' when left by themselves at a computer. However, the authors' own observation of children using several software packages revealed children with a growing sense of control. Young children started to choose which page of a talking book they would begin with, and which colour of the many on offer they would choose from a paint program. It is a thought-provoking chapter, giving evidence against the view that children should use computers only at a later stage in school, when they are older.

In Chapter 5, Rupert Wegerif and Lyn Dawes reveal how classroom work can be improved in general, as well as in ICT. If we believe that speaking with other people is the way we come to hold opinions, to change our minds, to learn to look at a subject from another point of view, then clearly speaking is integral to our own learning. For many of us, such 'learned' discussions are very much the ideal and do not feature all that often in the hurly-burly of argument and decision-making which is what we hear in 'group work'. Wegerif and Dawes do not begin with 'the ideal' but with the problems teachers themselves have observed. The chapter indicates a way forward based on evidence, whereby discussion can be improved and so can children's learning. As you read it, you find yourself entering into the discussion also, considering points made and comments you might add. From my point of view, I would like to hear more about gender roles in discussion groups, particularly as Jean Underwood in Chapter 7 discusses research findings that girls appear more able than boys in using talk in ways advantageous to their learning.

Wegerif and Dawes consider the proliferation of references to new kinds of literacy – for example, design literacy, network literacy and ICT literacy. They believe there is a convergence between the potential of the new technologies and approaches to learning that stress the discursive construction of knowledge through dialogues. Knowledge is found in communities of practice and learning is involved in becoming one of the community chosen. In school, 'talk is still the main medium for the construction of meaning in classrooms and will probably long remain so'. A focus on spoken language helps solve some of the problems teachers face when using ICT in class. Teachers reported pupils failing in group work, using unfocused net searches, information without understanding and sending inappropriate emails. Wegerif and Dawes suggest that we make the talk effective by agreeing to use ground rules for discussion. As teachers, we remind children before each class activity that high-quality talk is as much an aim as completing the ICT-based task. Wegerif and Dawes suggest that the collaborative function of talk must be emphasized because otherwise children may view computer-led activities, like computer games, as competitive. Jackie Marsh, in Chapter 8, advocates more discussion of computer games within the classroom, so that children can see the benefits and disadvantages of playing these games. Class discussions about collaboration and competitiveness would certainly be evidence-based in such a situation and might aid deeper thought among our pupils about the processes of learning.

Ground rules for talk can improve unfocused net searches. Children can ask themselves the key question: 'How does this information help with our shared purpose?' Tatiana Wilson, in Chapter 11, found that

Internet searches improved when children discussed and completed prepared grids about what they knew, and what they wanted to know, before they started their search. Wegerif and Dawes believe the teacher's crucial role involves explicit teaching of skills which enable 'learners . . . to engage constructively in knowledge-building conversations'.

Like all the authors in this book, Wegerif and Dawes believe that software design is important and they suggest questions we might ask when selecting software to buy or use. In Chapter 6, Richard Bennett and Henry Pearson look in greater detail at the criteria software should meet if it is to satisfy teachers' and pupils' needs. The context in which the software is to be used is in this case helping and encouraging children to read. So they discuss lucidly and at some length the aims and levels of reading. They suggest further questions we should ask of software to ensure that any program meets at least some of our requirements, including the potential for children's independent work and the type of feedback given to pupil and/or teacher. A hundred and seventeen teachers were surveyed about the use of ICT in their teaching of reading. A list of software which teachers used most frequently, or which appeared to answer their needs as they described them, was constructed. Bennett and Pearson provide a very detailed and carefully analysed review of each program using their previously formulated questions.

Overall, in the software reviewed, tasks often appear disappointingly mundane, repetitive and unchallenging. It is puzzling as to why more innovative software for literacy should be lacking. It may even be preferable to use other software, apparently unconnected with reading but which could sustain children's interest more effectively. As Bennett and Pearson say, agreeing with points made in Marsh's chapter, supposedly non-educational computer games sometimes offer challenging problem-solving environments where children observe, question, hypothesize and test. They are disappointed that opportunities for sustained periods of ICT use are less likely to occur at the moment, owing to other curriculum requirements. This comment chimes with the observations made in Chapters 2 and 3. Teachers now want short, focused computer-based activities. Interestingly, Underwood in Chapter 7 recounts one research finding that frequent but shorter periods at a computer might prove advantageous for children's learning.

In Chapter 7, Jean Underwood examines two research projects, one involving the use of an integrated learning system (ILS) for improving reading skills and the other the use of talking books. She believes that 'critical literacy is one of the most demanding but also the most reward-ing activities with which children will be involved'. As she states, people have no natural talent to remember the relationships between abstract visual patterns and their connection to words, so reading and writing need to be taught. She looks at how ICT could help in this process. Use of certain software can give a child the equivalence of 'practice with an adult' and have a positive effect on sight word acquisition. Also, computer supported reading instruction may have beneficial outcomes.

An ILS follows the behaviourist model of learning, involving 'drill and practice' exercises. In this research, the way in which individual schools chose to incorporate the software into their learning programmes appears to have been a critical factor in the effectiveness of the intervention. Children did better if they worked at the ILS more frequently for shorter periods rather than, say, one hour a week. Scores were also improved if it was seen as a whole class activity, rather than some children at a time being withdrawn from class. There may well be implications for general learning outcomes here. Teachers found that children could be very successful at some ILS modules – for instance, word attack. However, their overall grade perhaps hid a relatively poor performance on text comprehension. Although the ILS system 'promoted' pupils to the next level, not all were ready for the more difficult aspects of critical under-standing. They needed more practice in comprehension. The teacher's input was crucial here, in order to see why pupils were not immediately responding to the challenges of new material.

Reading aloud is recognized as one helpful component among proced-ures leading to literacy achievement. Underwood cites evidence to show that talking books do provide supplementary practice for beginning readers. The children observed in her research activated the animated features on CD-ROMs rather than using the pronunciation clips, and they also recalled them more effectively. As teachers, we generally support the use of spoken text in such programs and would frown at the 'over use' of animations. However, as Bob Fox points out in Chapter 9, talking books may indeed be a different genre and the same reading patterns might not apply. Underwood found that girl/girl pairs worked best together and this showed up in story recall. The girls intuitively asked each other for more information and orientation than did other pairings. She also found that children were highly motivated by both sets of software – that is, both 'drill and practice' on the ILS and the more open-ended talking books.

In Chapter 8, Jackie Marsh argues for a measured response to cultural icons, such as Disney or Pokémon characters, which take up so much of children's time. She suggests schools should take more interest in what interests children so much. Tatiana Wilson, in Chapter 11, found that children do want to investigate television characters on the Internet. Moreover they believe that such an interest-led search is a perfectly proper activity during school time. It is true that, as teachers, we need to widen children's literary experience but we can also give them oppor-tunities to work with their own areas of knowledge.

Children seem to prefer commercialized games to educational ones, partly because they tend to be located within children's popular culture which encompasses music, television, film and also sport, clothing, food and so on: 'Our pupils are surrounded outside school by a complex web of intertextual references in which technological developments are central'. Computer games are located within a universe of related products including books, comics and magazines. However, games consoles are more likely to be owned by working-class children and these games are also more likely to be mistrusted by schools.

Marsh points out that texts are 'increasingly complex' whether televisual or printed, definitely non-linear and often multi-modal. Like Tyldesley, she believes that the traditional view of literacy should be expanded to include these. The commercial artefacts that exist in a child's world are linked to form a broad narrative. The consequent intertextuality offers considerable potential for literacy development. The characters involved are often stereotyped, with sexist, racist and violent characteristics but it is surely better to address these issues in school. Children might then engage more critically with the material.

It is quite possible to look at games as narratives, as typically a player negotiates a character through specific terrains which contain challenges. Pupils could sequence sections of the games so that they produce the basic structure of a narrative. Marsh lists a number of ways teachers and children could develop excellent literacy activities arising out of this interest. This way schools can take account of children's home computer literacy skills which contain rich opportunities for dialogue.

I find the viewpoint in Bob Fox's chapter particularly interesting. He takes what might be termed a traditionalist position, in that he considers a love of story and a delight in books both reward and motivation for literacy. This means, however, that he has high standards in view when he comes to consider the value of talking books. He dismisses 'textoids', those talking books which are really just an ICT-style 'talking' version of a story rather than a creation in their own right. He emphasizes the value of play as well as reading and aptly describes animated features as 'attractive nuisances': 'Some of these have an unacknowledged (and probably unmeasurable) value in their capacity to develop anticipation and prediction skills'. I go further and suggest that these features encourage persistence and thoroughness, qualities essential to successful learning. Children like to be sure they've tried every feature, and when they're going through a talking book for the second time they try to remember everything included on each page. 'I think I've done everything,' as one young child said to me. Unlike some teachers and parents, Fox tolerates children's squabbles as to who has the mouse: 'perhaps it is more like sharing a sweet than sharing a comic'. This seems to get to the heart of the matter, I think, and reinforces the viewpoint of Dawes and Wegerif as to guidelines. We need to understand the importance to children of this momentary sense of power and delight as they click the mouse and discuss with them ways they can use computers more fairly.

The deeper level of reading that Fox refers to is indicated in his description of 'dialogic reading', where interacting with the story indicates close parallels with a view of learning based on engaging in talk. Fox suggests we consider talking books as a new literary form, and discuss and evaluate them in class. Children's collective experiences could be pooled. As he says, he's never met a child who didn't like a talking story. If we take up his suggestions and use them as part of our current literacy practice, then perhaps this might help boys like those in Underwood's research to learn to have a love of 'story'.

In Chapter 10, Carol Fine and Mary Lou Thornbury look closely at the philosophy behind software design. As they point out, older software tended to consider the teacher more important whereas now we often expect the software to act as part of the scaffolding structure in a child's literacy learning. The authors examine differing design processes. The first is highly consultative, whereby users' needs are considered. They also reveal how important the introduction of software is to its subsequent use. They comment on a most interesting case study where two groups of teachers viewed a CD-ROM. The second group who were given a list of suggested questions about the software and were able to conduct the evaluation in pairs, were much more positive about the software itself. Clearly, having some intermediary (in this case the list of questions) and being allowed to work collaboratively had considerable effect; the study both illustrates and underlines the impact of the teacher in choosing how to introduce software to pupils.

Fine and Thornbury decide that there are several stages in terms of elucidating the available material on a CD-ROM. The first involves a session of joint attention, where children and teacher together consider the material and decide what they are going to do with it. Subsequently, when children have done some work with the software they can share their knowledge with others. Thoughtful teachers can make remarkable use of poorly designed software but some of the best software might be inadequately used by teachers who have not been trained in the use of analytical tools for establishing what might be the curriculum purposes behind the software. As in Underwood's study, teachers are vital mediators.

Tatiana Wilson started with the aim of seeing whether or not children could transfer strategies for learning which they had gained in the Literacy Hour in searching the Internet. However, she found they had few conscious strategies for learning and were unaware how to manipulate the information they retrieved from the Internet. So, like other contributors, Wilson believes these skills should be taught and given higher emphasis than is given to them at the moment. She employed a model introduced in the training materials of the National Literacy Strategy (NLS), which should be quite applicable in other classrooms. Of course, it needed some modification and it is interesting to see what Wilson thought this should be, after her research. In Chapter 11, she states, very sensibly, that teachers could teach children away from the computer a structure or system they could use for questioning the material they had discovered on Internet searches. She feels it is particularly important that children's Internet work should be contextualized. Wilson introduced a new step: brainstorming key words linked to the questions the children had designed. This is a vital and useful ploy as much of the material on the web is opaque and irrelevant to young (or older) children. She found that the children looked for information about television characters, bearing out Marsh's contention that this would be a successful way to interest children in formulating relevant questions and/or refining their Internet searches.

In Chapter 12, Callow and Zammit believe that people have to be literate in a range of meaning systems or modes of representation in order to fully participate in today's and tomorrow's society. Accordingly, they look at visual literacy. Images play a greater role nowadays in conveying information within educational and technological texts – even written texts are highly visual. So their chapter explores the links between visual and written texts, including picture books and digital and electronic texts. Their first example from the classroom shows children of 5 and 6 looking at pictures of wolves in stories, experimenting with the digital camera to make close, mid-range and distant images of each other and finally deciding to draw close-up pictures of the wolf to show how fierce and frightening it was. The pupils critique an illustration in a satiric book about fairy tales, for child readers. By drawing on a theoretical framework to interpret images, both teachers and children can participate in much richer and more critical readings of a text. By doing this, children can relate such stories to more traditional versions and to Disney versions. This procedure might overcome Bob Fox's criticism that the Disney version seems to be the only one on offer for many children. 'Critical readings' in this manner are clearly not above children's abilities.

The scaffolding support for a class of 11-year-olds comes from deconstructing a website collaboratively. The authors deconstruct a home page about volcanoes to indicate how such scaffolding could take place. They then use a dynamic text where children may interact with visuals which change as the interaction occurs. For this purpose, Callow and Zammit use a screen from a CD-ROM on the topic of machines. They recommend shared viewing activities, agreeing with Fine and Thornbury, so that children can learn how to use, interact and read the visual and written information. We cannot take for granted that any child can read all the different forms within the range of texts available. Providing children with a language to talk about visual texts and engaging children in critiquing them can form the basis of the teaching and learning of multimodal texts.

The main themes of the book thus emphasize the crucial importance of the teacher and/or parent mediating children's use of ICT. Positive use of discussion as to guidelines in learning how to formulate questions is highly important, particularly if we consider dialogue as an essential learning strategy. A new emphasis on the more critical literacy skills we and our pupils need is overdue. We expect this book to further the debate.

References

Barnett, R. (1994) *The Limits of Competence*. Buckingham: Open University Press.

Davies, D. (2000) Fool's gold, *Times Educational Supplement*, 29 September: 5.

DfEE (Department for Education and Employment) (1999) *A Fresh Start: Improving Literacy and Numeracy*. London: HMSO.

Humphrys, J. (1999) *Devil's Advocate*. London: Hutchinson.

Moseley, D., Higgins, S., Bramald, R. *et al.* (1999) *Ways Forward with ICT: Effective Pedagogy using Information and Communications Technology in Literacy and Numeracy in Primary Schools*. Newcastle upon Tyne: University of Newcastle upon Tyne.

Papert, S. (1996) *The Connected Family*. Atlanta, GA: The Longstreet Press.

Simons, J. (2001) Theology at McGill, *McGill Newsletter*, Faculty of Religious Studies, Spring.

1

WHAT HAS ICT GOT TO DO WITH LITERACY?

Moira Monteith

> cultural continuity and individual creativity are comple-
> mentary and interdependent facets of all activity, and hence
> of the developmental learning trajectories of those who
> participate in them.
>
> (Wells 1999: xii)

Introduction

Continuous learning is both an individual and a social activity. Our
continuum of knowledge and learning has arisen almost entirely as a
result of our capacity to speak. Literacy has widened the store of knowledge and hastened its development. We each have our own literacy level
and at the same time belong to a culture steeped in traditional forms,
while simultaneously new aspects of literacy burgeon and fountain and
sometimes disappear. Returning to basics is certainly essential for those
who do not have the basic literacy skills, but those basic skills need a
wider interpretation nowadays. Each stage of literacy technology has
pushed on the heels of the last and information and communication
technology (ICT) is the most recent. I open the debate in this book concerning the current connections between literacy and ICT and suggest
that for the first time we may be moving towards a wholly literate society.
For the purposes of this introductory chapter I will take the definition
of 'literacy' as being 'the ability to read and write' in its traditional sense
(Crystal 1987). Other chapters widen the definition and suggest new
forms of literacy. 'Functional literacy' is a term normally confined to
'adult literacy' and clearly must be a minimum standard aimed at within

our school system; for this I refer to the levels used within Basic Skills and indicated in *A Fresh Start: Improving Literacy and Numeracy* (DfEE 1999a).

We all have a literacy timeline, a sequence of formative language experiences that affect our levels of literacy. Sometimes these experiences overlap; for example, we may be beginning to recognize words and letters (emergent literacy) while we are still broadly learning to speak (perhaps we are learning the syntax or grammar of our speech community). Some experiences cause us to change our current practice and thinking; for example, at some point soon after we reach the age of 2, our talk becomes much more understandable by members outside our immediate family. We give up the noises which make up our own versions of words and which our nearest carers have worked hard at interpreting and begin to use words more understandable by others. We have decided at that very young age that we need to communicate effectively.

I imagine that most of you reading this chapter will have the same overall sequential timeline that I have: learning to speak, read, write and, some years subsequently, to use computers. Of course, we may have used phones, cameras, radios and television much earlier than we used computers, so the world of ICT opened to us in different stages. Today, children growing up have access to a multiplicity of resources: not just phones, cameras and television but also computers, talking books and video games, all of which can be viewed as one wide interconnected experience, unlike the disparate elements they seemed only a few years ago. Literacy must appear in a rather different guise to young children, though no doubt they are able to learn the very important skill of understanding abstract symbols just as well as we did. It remains to be seen how this understanding might be changed by viewing print on a screen (of whatever size or shape) and enjoying its close links with a range of graphics. I have emphasized this timeline so that we might begin to see what is the same and what is different between the literacy of older people and that of the very young, and question our own views of what literacy is and will be. I hope also to put into words my view that ICT does indeed result in a new stage of literacy experience and, significantly, helps us better understand our own and our pupils' learning practices.

The possibility of being literate has existed for only a few thousand years and for the greater majority of people in most societies only for the last century and a half. Most of us will have had some quite recent ancestors who were to all intents and purposes illiterate. To some extent therefore we are discussing a comparatively recent development compared with the capacity for speech. Perhaps, at this point, you would like to consider your own answers to the following questions: What do you remember about learning to speak? Helping someone else learn to speak? Learning to read? Learning to write? Your first experiences using a computer?

The answers to these questions place each of us in a unique position in terms of the details of language and literacy experience and development, but in general ways reveal how we are usually very similar to the rest of humankind. Individual needs and the motivation to be literate are a personal matter and reflect our cultural situation, our education, our work and our social requirements.

Speaking

I don't remember anything about learning to speak. I do remember an occasion when my niece, just over 2 years old, was beginning to speak fluently. She sat among a group of adults, including several young men in their late teens and early twenties and was the focus of everyone's attention. People encouraged her to talk perhaps because she made such delightful mistakes – mistakes in terms of the adults listening. She was corrected, but not at all in the manner in which later her writing would be corrected. The occasion was one of complete encouragement; if people laughed at what she said they did so at the same time as encouraging her to try another phrase. I have since seen similar scenes and heard accounts of others. Adults clearly enjoy talking about young children's talk. This kind of situation accords well with the zone of proximal development (ZPD) as defined by Vygotsky (1978), whereby adults stimulate younger learners by helping them cope with skills or concepts which they would be unable to tackle on their own and yet are only a stage more difficult than their current understanding. This concept was made more understandable in a practical sense when Bruner (1986), Wood (1988) and others used the term 'scaffolding' to explain what adults do in such learning situations. Usually, no one has taught any adults to help small children learn to speak. What we all have in common is that we in our turn previously learned very successfully how to speak. Presumably we instinctively know how to scaffold in this context. There are qualitative differences, however. If a young child converses mainly with other children (as may happen for the youngest children in large families) they often do not make the same progress in speaking as the older siblings do (DES 1975). Also, if children are brutalized and neglected and have few, if any, opportunities to learn how to communicate when young, their later speech development may be affected (Crystal 1987: 263). But on the whole we all learn very effectively in a comparatively short time. After all, human beings have been speaking for thousands of years; our skills of learning to speak and helping others to learn are embedded by now. When we come to literacy, it is a different matter.

Reading and writing

In terms of learning to read, I can remember a half-and-half stage where I sat saying nursery rhymes out loud with a nursery rhyme book on my lap. A visitor said in surprise, 'Can she read?' To which my father replied, 'No, she's just saying the words.' At some point, soon after, I learned to read 'properly' to the point when I realized at school that I could 'read' aloud words whose meaning I did not understand.

I do remember learning to write, though not the preliminary 'pretend' experiences. Many children (and perhaps I was the same) scribble lines such as zigzags on paper and insist this is writing and not drawing or painting. I remember the physical problems of writing rather than any problem about recognizing letters or words: holding chalk, crayon and very thick pencils and trying to make letters and numbers. Even at 5, when I was keen about school, I remember the boring activity of trying to write long lines of a single letter, a a a a a a and so on. Subsequently, when I was 9, I had missed school the week when the class was taught joined-up letters. I did what I could to copy what others were doing by just making linking lines between letters, but somehow they didn't look very good. It took me some months to get back to a position in the top handwriting set and all my learning in this instance was peer supported.

Memories of physical difficulties met while learning to write are common. Many of the children aged 11 or 12 whom I interviewed in one research project spoke of their feelings of inadequacy about writing. When questioned further as to how they knew they were 'no good at writing' they related early memories of their physical clumsiness when learning to write. Such memories of being 'no good at writing' appeared to carry over into contexts where I expected them to know that ideas and descriptions were just as important as forming letters. However, the pupils continued to believe they were no good at writing stories, essays, anything. (Strange, how when we want learners to transfer skills from one learning situation to another we find it is very difficult to do so, whereas a sense of failure moves across with ease.) In my many conversations with children and students over the years it seems that problems with writing are remembered rather than the successful acquisition of skills. Presumably if the skill becomes embedded then we forget the details of its acquisition, though we may remember times when we were praised by teachers or other adults.

Use of ICT could remove some of the residual power remaining from memories of clumsy handwriting. One aspect of word processing that everyone seems agreed upon is its usefulness in 'presentation'. Stories abound of children and students whose motivation has increased considerably after they see their work word-processed rather than the untidy scripts they previously and usually managed to achieve. Unfortunately, as Alison Tyldesley indicates in her chapter, we still seem to encourage children to use computers for 'fine copy' only. If we do grant children early access to word processing and the computers we use need keyboards, this means that early writing then requires other skills. Children would need to recognize the letters on a keyboard, and not just letters in the form of an alphabet. Many teachers complain that children using word processors early on take far longer to type a couple of sentences than they would to write or copy them on paper. This is no doubt true as children (and adult beginners) use the 'hunt and peck' method of picking out letters to form words. Early access to computers would shorten that learning time.

Keyboards can produce other benefits. Some schools use the keyboard layout as an effective reinforcement of the skills needed in the recognition of letters, groups of letters and words. If one of the most important things we learn from reading is its second-order symbolism (Olson quoted Wells 1999: 32), then the keyboard is a concrete example of this. Children who use the keyboard at a young age can enter the world of print and print recognition in a way that earlier generations with clumsily drawn letters could not. It does not appear to matter to them that the letters on a keyboard are laid out differently than the order of the alphabet. And although it is extremely important that we learn the alphabet so that we can use the letters in indexes such as the *Yellow Pages* or a dictionary or other indexes of structured information such as the fields in a database, it may well be useful to see letters in distinctively different orders, so that we understand the symbolic role of letters beyond any one system of categorization.

Teachers can also use children's early typewritten messages as evidence of their writing development (Monteith 1996, 1999). There are clear stages of progression (following the Marie Clay stages in reading readiness) from recognition of a few letters, to most letters, to the initial letter of a word, to other consonants in the word – particularly the end one – to keying in short words such as 'the' and gradually many more words. Since this is a constant progression it means that children can always be praised for their continued development, in the same way as we are encouraged in our early experiences with talk.

With much of the current software available, both word processing packages and CD-ROM reading books, children can recognize the differences and similarities between spoken and written words and sentences. The text remains the same, except that it can be spoken one minute, written the next and listened to just after that. These connections could never have been so obvious before.

Listening

Listening is central to language learning; without the ability to listen young children cannot develop intelligible speech. We need to listen to what others say in order to learn from them, or to learn the cues of conversation, when opportunities arise for us to speak. Lyn Dawes and Rupert Wegerif emphasize in their chapter how we need to listen to others' opinions if our learning and problem-solving as a group is to be successful. People who are learning a language other than their mother tongue often have a positive stage when they remain silent but learn effectively. It is true that we need opportunities to speak in a new language but we also need to feel comfortable listening, particularly when we are trying in the beginning to absorb a wide range of language details and usage. Collaborative learning and effective communication are important aspects of ICT in education and both require the ability to genuinely listen to others.

ICT skills

I began to use computers when my children were young because they were interested in them. I had to learn from my children as well as with them. I cannot remember a comparable learning situation with my own parents. Some parents of that generation may have learned alongside their children, perhaps concerning a particular hobby or skill. However, the majority of children in the pre-computer era did not learn with their parents or teach them. Yet this is often the case today (see Papert 1996). This is an amazing and fundamental change in learning practice. It is connected with ICT rather than with learning skills and in all probability is linked to the short time span between one ICT development and the next.

Finding a new vocabulary

When considering a new subject area in the curriculum, such as ICT, it is perhaps always difficult to decide which are subject-specific skills. Different people and agencies have tried rationalizing the situation. The Teacher Training Agency (TTA) in England, faced with upgrading the ICT skills of entrants into the teaching profession, have had to work out what they consider to be the vital skills to use now (which could, and will, change in the future). One section could be denoted as 'desktop skills':

- Dragging and dropping
- Having more than one application open at a time
- Highlighting
- Knowing how to find the size of a file
- Making selections by clicking
- Moving information between software (e.g. using the clipboard)
- Navigating around the desktop environment
- Printing
- Undoing the last action
- Using menus
- Opening items by double clicking with the mouse

The vocabulary used is highly metaphorical but quite understandable and also specialized. Perhaps only two usages are new: 'mouse' and 'software'. All the others (for example, clipboard) can be defined quite easily and differently from their everyday use yet are linked metaphorically to that use. The skills are closely concerned with the current designs for a computer desktop – that is, with a specific software interface, but lack any content. If we decide the content is to be literacy, we see how very useful these skills can be in writing or reading or presenting material. Nevertheless, the skills which have common-sense words as names do require a new conceptualizing of material and/or activities. For example, 'drag and drop' indicates that the user knows that the particular material needed is at hand and within control, and that some pieces can be moved about at ease. So the combination of 'drag' and 'drop' denotes a quite specific skill, in a specific context.

In current training in ICT for all teachers in England, Wales and Northern Ireland, teachers have been expected to categorize which skills or knowledge belong to ICT and which are subject-based (DfEE 1999b). This is not always easy to define and, moreover, the skills which belong to ICT or another area of learning are not finely balanced. The metaphorical usage may hide this imbalance. An example of this can arise when editing or redrafting using word processing. 'Cut and paste' is an old method of reordering and redrafting material. It probably was not widely practised before the use of paper and scissors but that still makes it an 'old' skill. Writers or editors could change the order of sentences and paragraphs by literally cutting one section out and then moving it elsewhere, to another position within the written piece. 'Cutting or copying and pasting' is an important skill for all ICT users to acquire because we can cut and paste items between a range of software packages. We can cut and paste audio clips, scanned drawings, statistical tables as well as words. Very young children can perform the few actions needed to cut and copy or paste comparatively straightforwardly. However, teachers and researchers have expressed disappointment that when word processing pupils do not seem to want to change more than the spelling and perhaps a word or two here and there. We need to recognize that redrafting for editing purposes is a high-level cognitive skill, and therefore does not run in tandem with the ability to 'cut and paste' on a computer.

Learning skills

The important skills we learn while using ICT may well not be those that appear to be technological. In the first instance, a great deal of what we learn appears to be self-taught. What this means in fact is that we use the various forms of scaffolding available. We ask questions of our friends, teachers, children, parents or we attempt to follow manuals or learning guides, in which case the scaffolding is (we hope) a vital component of the instructions. There is perhaps no other area at the moment where skills, knowledge and information are so readily shared. 'Self-taught' also implies a lack of formal qualifications, what some people might consider as a lack in 'educational property' or no significant stakehold, yet ICT is an area where most of us will accept that certain people have more authority in advising us just because they know more than we do in particular instances.

Metacognitive learning

A metacognitive approach to learning is one of the benefits arising from the use of ICT. By this I mean that we learn about learning rather than a range of particular skills or sets of data. For example, there is the matter of hardware, just getting to know what is there and how to use it. The time and effort we have spent learning to use obsolete hardware is time disappeared. So what we really learn is that our learning quickly becomes obsolescent. We also learn that new skills are not always more difficult than ones we learned previously. In the past, in school for instance, we learned that each year's work was, or was supposed to be, harder than the previous year's. Many ICT users have been extremely pleased to find that searching the Internet and creating web pages (two comparatively recent ICT skills) are actually easier for them to learn than the spreadsheets and databases which they learned to use in previous years. It has been possible over the last decade or so to consider software packages as falling into distinct categories. Databases, spreadsheets, word processing and graphics packages were the stable entities or generic types most people had to learn to use. Now there is the interconnection of these with cameras, mobile phones, televisions, musical keyboards and the Internet. So we learn about 'interoperability and interconnectivity'. The challenging aspect is that it is difficult to 'future proof' our learning for any considerable length of time.

This is not true of course of our other subject areas – in this case literacy. Older people often do know more, in terms of vocabulary and possibly rhetorical skills, and have had more time to read more source material. The individual timeline of learning may well be differentiated according to the different subject areas and their dependence on recent technological advances.

Being literate gives us another view of the world, apart from the fact that it helps us to learn the stored knowledge of our own and other cultures. Gordon Wells cites Vygotsky, Halliday and Olson in support of his view that learning to write is 'a much more abstract task than learning to speak' and,

because of the more abstract nature of written language, both with
respect to its use of a second order symbolism and with respect to
its tendency to make use of words that refer to abstract entities (i.e.
'other wordings'), in learning to read and write, children have to
reconstitute their meaning potential in a new, more abstract mode.
A further important consequence is that, in the process, they begin
to become aware of language itself as a semiotic tool that has its own
structure and organization. This metalinguistic awareness is what
Olson sees as the major cognitive consequence of learning to write.

(Wells 1999: 32)

Adults also have been able to gain knowledge in terms of 'metalinguistic
awareness' by using ICT in their writing. That is, they have become able
to think about language as a whole and writing as complete texts as
opposed to separate conversational utterances or individual written phrases
and sentences. Evidence for this is indicated in the report of the working
group chaired by Sir Claus Moser (DfEE 1999a: 60). The Report quotes
Australian research on the use of ICT for helping adults become literate.
Among other things, it led to 'a greater understanding of what producing written text involves'.

Children and adults who can barely read or write have not gained, in
all probability, that more abstract dimension of learning. It may also be
that learning to become literate enables us to become more numerate:
'most adults who have difficulties with reading and writing are also weak
in numeracy, but very few who are good at reading and writing turn out
to have very poor numeracy' (DfEE 1999a: 4). This function of literacy,
the use of a second-order symbolism, will not disappear even if we do
use ICT for much or even most of our reading material. Therefore we
must ensure that all learners become aware 'of language itself as a . . . tool
that has its own structure and organization' whatever the reading matter
or writing technology we use.

The technology of literacy

ICT is the latest stage in the development of the technology of literacy.
At each stage of this historical development the nature of literacy itself
has changed. The first known written records appear to be lists or inven-
tories. Indeed listing, or keeping information about listed items, remains
one of the main functions of literacy. We have moved from using clay
tablets to stone tablets to various forms of template such as wax, cloth,
papyrus, parchment, paper, slate, sand and now screen. We have exploited
a range of tools: chisel, stylus, printing press, quill, pen with nib, pencil,
crayon, spray can and software. There can be few surfaces in the world
nowadays that have not been written on, with the exception of water,

Table 1.1   The progression of literacy

MS and early print culture	The spread of literacy	Networked society
Books rare	Books widespread	Books special
Authorship not important	Rise of author	Decline of author: writing more collaborative
Clerics as distributors	Rise of publishers	Writers as publishers
Changeable texts	Definitive texts	Changeable texts
Copying important	Concept of plagiarism	Death of copyright
Authority	Individualism	Communality
Reading aloud/listening	Private, silent reading	Participatory reading
Varied orthography	Writing conventions	Challenge to conventions of writing
International (Latin)	National	International

Source: Chandler (1989)

and no doubt someone will manage to do that soon. We worry neither about permanence nor light. We hang poems on trees (whose trunks we also carve) and inscribe our names or initials on cacti and other plants. In places almost without light such as some prison cells and dungeons, people have left their names or some comment just to mark their presence. The mythical importance of naming creatures in religions and racial or tribal histories has given way to the practice of being written on or over. Graffiti is now sprayed on and washed off in ever recycling waves in our cities. There has never been a time before this when we have been surrounded by so much print. The concept of the market has resulted in every possible advertising surface being used. Advertisers' brand names and current political and social slogans are emblazoned on all manner of clothes. All over the world people wear garments carrying words often in a language they do not understand. New photographic and printing technologies allow us to write and project our writing far afield on many surfaces. The difference between those of us who are literate and those who can see words but not read them is all the deeper.

In 1989 Daniel Chandler drew up some reasoned and far-seeing statements about literacy and technology (see Table 1.1). Not many other people have written about the effects of ICT and found their words still as relevant and resonant 13 years later. At the time he wrote, the vast expansion of the Internet had not occurred and the hardware available for general use, both in business and in education, precluded the kind of networks we see today. One of the underlying changes he indicates in this comparative table is the shift in writing. In a networked society, he believes, writing is more collaborative, people can publish their own work easily and this writing does not necessarily abide by the conventions of publishers, academic scholars or school requirements. Most people would agree we have already seen a shift in the language of online communications, particularly emails and text messages on mobile phones. Young people growing up will still be bound by existing writing conventions, for example those used in most printed books and those required by examination and assessment boards, and through them the school curriculum. However, students will see simultaneously the much more casual and informal approach used in email messages and on many websites. No one yet knows what the long-term effects of hypertext will be on our concept and practice of literacy.

Concepts of authorship, copyright and plagiarism may be changing as Chandler has predicted – there are certainly indications that this is happening. Our views of textuality may change also, as texts can be transformed from speech to print to handwriting and back again.

The changing context for the school curriculum

One of the important requirements for personal literacy is that both the individual and their society see the need to be literate. It has seemed a puzzle that extremely rich and highly productive countries such as the USA and the UK have large groups of functionally illiterate adults. There have been countless research projects to discover why children remain virtually illiterate and go on to be illiterate adults. In parallel many programmes for improvement have been undertaken and yet the illiteracy, or semi-literacy, continues. It is important to at least consider the cultural and social context of illiteracy.

Paulo Freire, a dedicated teacher of international renown, was a widely respected innovator in teaching groups of poor, uneducated Brazilians and African-Portuguese speakers to become literate. Indeed many of his concepts have now been accepted into the mainstream of educational thought (see Freire 1987). For example, on the DfEE Standards website, on the first page of the *National Literacy Strategy: Review of Research and other Related Evidence* (DfEE 1999c) (updated 16 April 1999) in the subsection entitled *Policy and Strategic Justification* it stated: 'Literacy is widely seen as promoting valuable ways of thinking about and understanding the world and ourselves'. This is not so different from Freire's view: 'reading the word and learning how to write the word so one can later read it are preceded by learning how to write the world, that is, having the experience of changing the world and touching the world' (1987: 49). He encouraged adult students to write and read about their worlds, so their living experiences became the context for their move into literacy. Freire developed the concept of empowerment that comes with literacy and knowing more about your society and the ways you are governed.

It is easy to understand how countries with a poor educational infrastructure and often inadequate access to schools might have high levels and/or pockets of illiteracy. Freire considered how the USA could continue to have so many illiterates in a country which gave its children years of free education. He concluded that a level of illiteracy was inevitable in such a society, in part because the educational regimen continued to deskill teachers while it simultaneously sought to reproduce 'the dominant ideology' of those in power rather than addressing the linguistic needs of the underprivileged. That view could be dismissed as part of Freire's own radical ideology, but it is worth considering as the UK tries once again to address the literacy problem nationally. Some children clearly have not seen the need to be literate, to be empowered in the manner that Freire described. Is there any likelihood that the English educational system will be more successful this time?

One of the most disturbing findings of the *Review of Research* carried out for the National Literacy Strategy (NLS), was the somehow inbuilt inadequacy of our education system to enable everyone to be literate:

> According to the reviews of evidence undertaken by the National Foundation for Educational Research (NFER), standards in literacy among British primary school children have largely remained stable over the period between 1948 and 1996. Slight changes have often been followed by changes in the opposite direction a few years later. For instance, in the surveys undertaken in England, Wales and Northern Ireland by the Assessment of Performance Unit (APU) between 1979 and 1983 and between 1983 and 1988, the reading attainment of 11 year olds rose slightly; their writing attainment rose slightly between 1979 and 1983 and fell slightly between 1983 and 1988. In surveys undertaken by the NFER, between 1987 and 1991, the average reading attainment of 8 year olds fell by 2.5 standardised points; between 1991 and 1995 the average reading attainment of 8 year olds rose again by almost the same amount.
> (DfEE 1999c)

During the time covered by the review – almost half a century – a major committee of inquiry was commissioned by the government to look at 'all aspects of teaching the use of English' and the report, *A Language for Life* (DES 1975) was published in 1975. Several other high-level working parties took place subsequently and impressive reports and programme changes followed. The National Curriculum was established in 1988. All the excellent and dedicated work during that half a century by skilful teachers, language advisers and researchers just kept us in the same place, with a long 'tail' of children who failed to learn to read and write effectively: 'a distinctive feature of British performance is the existence of a long "tail" of underachievement which is relatively greater than that of other countries' (Brooks *et al.* 1996 quoted in DfEE 1999c).

So we still have inbuilt structural illiteracy in the UK though neither finance nor the educational infrastructure in our society can be blamed

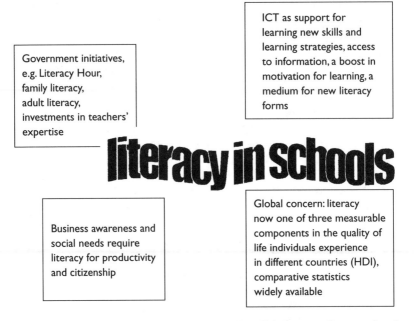

Government initiatives,
e.g. Literacy Hour,
family literacy,
adult literacy,
investments in teachers'
expertise

ICT as support for
learning new skills and
learning strategies, access
to information, a boost in
motivation for learning, a
medium for new literacy
forms

literacy in schools

Business awareness and
social needs require
literacy for productivity
and citizenship

Global concern: literacy
now one of three measurable
components in the quality of
life individuals experience
in different countries (HDI),
comparative statistics
widely available

Figure 1.1 Current contextual factors which will help mass literacy develop

in entirety. If we think of this on an individual level, it seems almost impossible that we should educate our children for over ten years and they should remain functionally illiterate at the end of them. US research quoted in *A Fresh Start* (DfEE 1999a) reckons that an adult on average needs 600 hours of instruction to become literate at a basic level. We have more than enough time of any individual's life to encourage success in literacy while at primary school.

It may be that in a 'networked society' the combination of new skills (both of learning and of ICT), social and industrial pressures and global accountability will destroy illiteracy almost entirely. The universal provision of education, which began in England at the comparatively recent date of 1870, has not so far achieved this. But there is now a congruence of factors which together encourage a belief that we may indeed see mass literacy (see Figure 1.1). I consider these factors to be:

- The language the government uses to express the need for real mass literacy has changed. Full literacy (as opposed to basic or below basic level) is now considered essential for as many people as possible, for economic and social reasons. Perhaps for the first time, the business case for 100 per cent literacy has been made. Productivity is cited as a reason for a literate workforce in both the *Review of Research* (DfEE 1999c) and in *A Fresh Start* (DfEE 1999a). Claus Moser states in the introduction to *A Fresh Start* 'hard economic issues are involved. Improving their basic skills can enable people to earn more, to spend more, to help the economy to grow faster. The benefits to industry and the economy may be hard to calculate, but they must be vast' (DfEE 1999a: 4). In addition, many of our illiterates end up in prison. With wider opportunities available to them before they begin the criminal slide, literacy might help reduce their antisocial behaviour. To do this we would have to tackle the literacy gap, particularly of young men and boys. This set of ideas is forcefully presented in a range of government documents and does, I think, answer Freire's first point.

- UK government initiatives are in place at different levels and aim to both promote and reinforce literacy objectives. The Literacy Hour is sited within the National Curriculum; family literacy policies encourage links between schools and home; adult literacy initiatives are aimed at those people in the community who once were part of the 'long tail' at school or who have immigrated to this country and whose command of the English language is not strong. Adult literacy training within a Basic Skills programme is tied, in many cases, to employment opportunities. Similar sets of strategies are in place in many countries.
- The transforming use of ICT. Thornbury and Grenier, in Chapter 4, have commented on the New Zealand research which indicates that ICT may give children previously hindered by a lack of listening adults in their family or a poverty of books and stories in their background just what they need to keep level with their peers and not fall into the structural fault line of the functionally illiterate. Use of ICT throughout education will give support and encouragement and new sources of information to pupils, students and teachers. A programme of training in ICT has been offered to all teachers now in post. New technologies may provide employment, particularly in communication industries, and employment tends to boost an individual's literacy level. The combination of necessary skills in literacy *and* in ICT may help the continuance and broadening of literacy development.
- Globally, literacy is now one of the three indicators of the Human Development Index (HDI). Some comparative indices do not place the UK in a very favourable light, particularly when compared with other post-industrial countries (DfEE 1999a: 9). However, the effect of statistics, in the form of league tables and studies arising from them, will have an impact on educational practices.

Scaffolding the education system

Scaffolding as a principle of learning is not confined to adults teaching children. We all need some scaffolding help when learning skills, concepts or subjects new to us. We have accepted the notion of lifelong learning and the concept of 'learning institutions' is now almost a truism. However, scaffolding has not in itself produced mass literacy even though it has been highly successful in ensuring that we all speak. The four factors outlined in the previous section together can alter the context in which children are being taught in both developed and developing societies. ICT is versatile. It can be used as the scaffolding to encourage further learning, as the medium through which such learning takes place and can even provide the motivating factor for some people to learn in the first place. It is likely that ICT will alter children's capacity for study and their access to information which, with the benefit of teaching, they will be able to change into knowledge.

Scaffolding for us as teachers may be a little difficult to accept. We know we are not very good at taking what we learn (and enthuse about) in the context of a short course, for example, and then applying this knowledge within our classrooms (Passey and Ridgeway 1992). Debate among teachers, therefore, may be one of the most important areas to stimulate and encourage. Owen (2000) a government statistician in Washington, USA, cites evidence to support his statement: 'that good teaching is a key factor in how well students learn':

> A 1991 study of 1,000 school districts illustrated that investments in teachers' expertise resulted in greater gains in students' achievement than did any other type of investment . . . More recently, a study in Tennessee showed that students who had good teachers for three years in a row demonstrated a significant increase in their performance on state assessments, whereas students with poor teachers declined in their performance . . . in North Carolina and Connecticut, researchers found that concentrated efforts to improve teaching were a primary reason for consistent gains in students' reading achievement . . .

It is important that teachers are given time and funding to develop new skills and hone old ones. Information about learning developments and projects is easily available via the Internet and from more traditional sources. Programmes such as the Literacy Hour in England might appear and indeed be deskilling in the sense that teachers are given instructions that require implementation (though teachers are not entirely bound by these instructions). But the use of ICT, even if teachers at the moment appear to be firefighting almost as often as teaching (as Steve Higgins and David Moseley observe in Chapter 2), is on the whole a new skill for the majority of primary teachers. It will encourage new ways of communicating and learning and together with current contextual factors could bring about much wider literacy in the population as a whole.

References

Bruner, J. (1986) *Actual Minds, Possible Worlds*. Cambridge, MA: Harvard University Press.

Chandler, D. (1989) Computers and literacy, in D. Chandler and S. Marcus (eds) *Computers and Literacy*. Milton Keynes: Open University Press.

Clay, M. (1979) *The Early Detection of Reading Difficulties*. London: Heinemann.

Crystal, D. (1987) *The Cambridge Encyclopedia of Language*. Cambridge: Cambridge University Press.

DES (Department of Education and Science) (1975) *A Language for Life*. London: HMSO.

DfEE (Department for Education and Employment) (1999a) *A Fresh Start: Improving Literacy and Numeracy*. London: HMSO.

DfEE (Department for Education and Employment) (1999b) *The Use of Information and Communications Technology in Subject Teaching: NOF-Funded Training – Expected Outcomes for Teachers*. London: HMSO.

DfEE (Department for Education and Employment) (1999c) *National Literacy Strategy: Review of Research and Other Related Evidence*, www.standards.dfee.gov.uk/library/research/b5/policy/lit

Freire, P. (1987) *Reading the Word and the World*. London: Routledge & Kegan Paul.

Human Development Index (HDI) www.undp.org/hdro/

Monteith, M. (1996) Combining literacies: the use of 'individual time' for word processing for young children, in B. Neate (ed.) *Literacy Saves Lives*. Shepreth: UKRA.

Monteith, M. (1999) Computer literacy, in J. Marsh and E. Hallet (eds) (1999) *Desirable Literacies*. London: Paul Chapman.

Owen, E. (2000) Co-operation and Teachers: Professional Career Curriculum, Evaluation and Promotion. Paper presented at ATEE Conference, Barcelona, August.

Papert, S. (1996) *The Connected Family*. Atlanta, GA: The Longstreet Press.

Passey, D. and Ridgeway, J. (1992) *Effective In-Service Education for Teachers in Information Technology: A Set of Case Studies and Notes for their Use*. Newcastle upon Tyne: Northern Micromedia.

Vygotsky, L. (1978) *Mind in Society*. Cambridge, MA: Harvard University Press.

Wood, D. (1988) *How Children Think and Learn*. Oxford: Blackwell.

Wells, G. (1999) *Dialogic Inquiry: Towards a Sociocultural Practice and Theory of Education*. Cambridge: Cambridge University Press.

2

RAISING ACHIEVEMENT IN LITERACY THROUGH ICT

Steve Higgins and
David Moseley

Introduction

We intend in this chapter to describe aspects of a research project under-taken by a team at Newcastle University relevant to improving the teach-ing and learning of literacy in primary classrooms (Moseley *et al.* 1999). It is an important challenge to educators to identify how information and communication technology (ICT) can be used effectively across the curriculum as technical progress races forward. We hope our approach to collaborative research will be helpful to teachers trying to address similar issues, and to those who support them in literacy, in ICT or in profes-sional development more broadly.

Our brief was to work with teachers and to support them in raising standards by finding ways in which selective use of ICT could complement if not enhance their already effective practice. We did not try to identify the added value of a particular ICT-based system, or to show that one approach is better than another. We took into account how teachers were already working, their own ICT skills, their attitudes towards ICT and their general approaches to teaching. Then, through 11 customized classroom projects we supported the teachers in making more effective use of ICT as a tool for the development of literacy. The results were impressive, showing that effective teachers can make excellent use of ICT, but not showing that ICT can be effective on its own.

We provide background to our research project and the rationale for our work, showing how the research literature we reviewed informed our collection and sharing of data. We look in more detail at the development projects in ICT and literacy which we undertook and some of the issues we encountered. We outline ways in which teachers' thinking, attitudes and beliefs may influence their use of and effectiveness with ICT and we offer suggestions for building on the research evidence that we, and many others, have gathered.

The project

The project, *Ways Forward with ICT: Effective Pedagogy*[1] *using Information and Communications Technology in Literacy and Numeracy in Primary Schools* was funded by the Teacher Training Agency (TTA). It focused on primary children (age 4 to 11 years) in schools in England. The aim was to help teachers make more effective choices about when, when not and how to use ICT in their teaching of literacy and numeracy. In this chapter we are concerned only with the area of literacy.

The aims of the TTA/ICT project meant we were guided by theory and research on effective teaching and learning and on teacher development, as well as by research focused on the use of ICT in primary education. In addition we had to find practical solutions which would work in particular contexts with the equipment and classrooms that we found.

The context

The context then and now is one of opportunities and challenges. There is unprecedented public support for the use of ICT in schools, driven by the view that ICT skills will be needed by tomorrow's workforce and also promoted as a means of raising standards (BECTA 2000). However there was (and still is) virtually no evidence to justify the expenditure needed to replace paper and pencil by computer for daily reading and writing activities in primary schools. The British Educational Communications & Technology Agency (BECTA) found no significant correlation between level of resourcing for ICT and either reading or mathematics grades at Key Stage 1 in 1999, and at Key Stage 2 no correlation coefficient exceeded 0.07, showing that ICT curriculum resourcing was at least 99.5 per cent independent of pupil performance. The finding that only 52 per cent of schools with 'very good' ICT curriculum resourcing achieved above the national average in English when compared with schools of a similar type and social context can hardly justify the spiralling cost of ICT-based instruction when there is a shortage of books in schools. The reported statistical link between poor ICT curriculum resourcing and poor exam performance in 70 schools (2.6 per cent of the sample) was not shown to be a causal one and could be explained by other factors known to influence learning outcomes.

For many pupils at the start of our study, access to ICT tended to be in the context of a weekly skills-based ICT lesson rather than in the more regular use of ICT as a well integrated resource across the curriculum. This in itself made it extremely unlikely that pupils would have enough school experience of using ICT as an aid to literacy for it to impact on their test performance. Many children had better access to computers at home than at school, while others had little or no opportunity to acquire ICT skills in either setting.

Nevertheless, there was a growing body of evidence that regular and systematic use of talking books and talking word processors could help develop literacy skills, as well as the encouraging results from the National Literacy Association (NLA) Docklands Learning Acceleration Project (Scott *et al.* 1997). In that project 15 low-achieving schools were provided with class sets of Acorn Pocketbook computers and 10 schools also received 10 multimedia computers for intensive use by Year 3 pupils as part of a more general literacy intervention supported by two teachers and a technician. Although the results were variable across schools, over the two years of the project the rate of reading progress rose to a nationally average level. A key factor seemed to be the high quality of training and support offered by the project team.

Among the challenges to be faced was what Scott *et al.* (1997: 52) described as 'the innate conservatism of many teachers who had been operating personal systems of working for many years'. On the basis of experience in the London Docklands schools, we expected some teachers to have negative attitudes towards computers or to have beliefs about teaching and learning which clashed with what they saw as a mechanistic or dehumanizing approach. Perhaps rightly, some teachers do see a threat to their professionalism in the prospect of what may appeal to politicians as the low-cost option of automatized e-learning.

It is an open question as to whether massive investment in ICT in primary schools will benefit or harm our children. How will teachers and pupils use the technology and how far will software and hardware producers make available child-friendly and educationally valuable products? An international organization called the Alliance for Childhood has recently raised doubts, calling for 'An immediate moratorium on the further introduction of computers in early childhood and elementary education, except for special cases of students with disabilities' (Cordes and Miller 2000: 98). This position has little empirical evidence to support it, but rightly points to the fact that 'No one has established how to use technology in ways that actually improve education – let alone how to do it in a cost-effective way' (Cordes and Miller 2000: 79).

If possible benefits are to be realized, the process of change will need to be evidence-based, appropriately adapted to local conditions and well managed. ICT can be hard to integrate effectively into teaching and learning in primary schools. Also, our reading of the history of educational change and technological innovation clearly indicates that results cannot be guaranteed. Our experience before and during the TTA/ICT project showed that a considerable amount of time and personal support is required, not least through providing opportunities to learn from other teachers and schools involved in similar development work.

We couldn't have chosen a more challenging time to investigate the contribution ICT can make to raising standards. During the two years of our project the National Literacy Strategy (NLS) was trialled and unrolled, but made little reference to the use of ICT. In the second year the government started to provide substantial financial investment through the National Grid for Learning. Our project ran alongside these developing initiatives, but was just too early to capitalize on the possibilities offered by the Internet or the injection of money to support training.

The project design

There were four main stages in the project:

1 A postcard survey of pupil computer usage in 2053 schools was carried out by the Performance Indicators in Primary Schools project (PIPS) at Durham University and yielded a 66 per cent return rate. PIPS is a professional monitoring project open to all primary schools. The relative pupil performance or value added data that they gather identifies improvements in reading, number and attitude made over the previous year (in Reception) and over the previous two years (in Year 2 and Year 4). This information made it possible to examine the relationship between pupils' attainment in literacy and computer usage.

2 Seven hundred and forty Reception, Year 2 and Year 4 teachers in urban and rural areas whose classes had made at least average learning gains were identified and surveyed by questionnaire. This yielded a 34 per cent return rate and provided background information about ICT provision, use and attitudes. Eighty-five teachers asked for further involvement with the project.

3 Thirty-one teachers (selected largely in terms of accessibility) were observed teaching literacy as they normally would, as well as in lessons where they had specifically planned to make use of ICT. They were also interviewed and took part in an exploration of their personal constructs of teaching and learning. Analysis of these data and from our reading of existing research was used to plan practical interventions with 20 of these teachers. Eleven interventions had a literacy focus.

4 Project staff supported and monitored development work for two terms, through visits, training sessions and telephone or email contact. The

impact on pupil learning was measured using standardized and criterion-referenced tests.

The initial brief postcard survey provided interesting results. It was conducted in Autumn 1997 and the majority of schools reported that each pupil used a computer once per week. Differences in this use showed that, at the school level, Reception classes made greater progress in reading where schools reported higher computer use. The amount of use correlated positively with reading achievement and value-added in reception ($p < 0.05$), but not in Year 2 or Year 4.

The questionnaire provided more detailed information. When we started the project this was the typical picture in the schools we surveyed:

- 1 or 2 computers per class
- 31 per cent had no access to machines with hard disks
- 35 per cent unable to access CD-ROMs
- Only 10 per cent of schools had access to the Internet
- 7 per cent made use of integrated learning systems (ILS) but less than 2 per cent had ILS on six or more machines

A year later we updated the survey and this indicated rapid change in some areas, particularly Internet access: 37 per cent of schools were now connected (usually one computer, probably in the office or possibly the library). More importantly, however, daily use of computers in class had declined – some of the teachers we worked with reported that this was due to the introduction of the Literacy Hour and what they felt was appropriate in the light of the NLS guidelines.

Preliminary observations also provided valuable information in other areas. In terms of links with pupil attainment in literacy we found that teachers who had longer plenaries in literacy were more effective; they also praised pupils more in lessons and had a higher proportion of pupils on task. In terms of ICT, the more effective teachers were likely to plan and provide different ICT activities for pupils with special educational needs, and pupils in these classes talked to each other more when they were at the computer. While many of these results were unsurprising and were found in other research, they confirmed a number of approaches that we were planning. However, a comparison of literacy lessons with and without ICT gave us food for thought about how to use research evidence effectively in supporting teachers in raising pupils' attainment.

Practical challenges

We observed two literacy lessons taken by 31 teachers, one presented as typical and one in which the teacher planned to make use of ICT. We wanted to see whether the inclusion of ICT activities affected the way lessons were conducted. What we found suggested that many teachers did not find it easy to incorporate, let alone integrate, ICT activities into their lessons. Organizationally, we saw significantly less use of group work in lessons in which ICT activities were included. We found that teachers provided less feedback to pupils during these 'literacy-plus ICT' lessons and carried out significantly less marking of pupils' work. It seemed that when the teacher's attention was divided, the lesson became less interactive for the whole class. In most cases the teacher acted as helper for the children using computers, typically spending half of the time available with those children. Because of this, the quality of teacher–pupil talk with the class as a whole seemed negatively affected, in that the teacher was less likely to ask pupils to expand on their answers and to engage in extended talk to develop understanding. Plenary review sessions were sometimes omitted and when they did take place teachers asked fewer questions.

Clearly the picture painted above is based on averages and there were exceptions to the rule. For example, one highly skilled teacher with a class of 35 Year 3/4 pupils organized (with the help of two learning support assistants and the school secretary) a range of absorbing differentiated activities in which pupils showed themselves completely at ease with technological aids of every description, including the fax machine they used to communicate with a local farmer. When technical or operational difficulties arose these were typically sorted out by peer assistance rather than by calling on the teacher, who spent much of her time providing feedback to individuals, pairs and groups and checking work. With this teacher the request to incorporate ICT in the activities meant no significant change from her normal practice. The class had access to four computers (two outside the classroom), which were used mainly for word processing and multimedia story creation and for information retrieval in connection with project work. Here the quality of written work and artwork on display was impressive and it was clear throughout the school that the expressive arts (including music and drama) were highly valued as imaginative ways of engaging pupils.

Our preliminary research also indicated that there were a number of logistical problems to overcome. These were the main issues that teachers identified. Lack of time was seen as a serious hurdle. This was both time for teachers to learn how to use new computers or new software and time for pupils to learn the skills they need to focus on subject objectives. The amount of equipment in schools was also problematic. In our view, the number of computers was insufficient to impact on individual pupils' learning. Most classes had limited access to larger numbers of machines – for example, timetabled once a week in the computer suite in the small number of schools where these were available. Finally there were also issues about reliability and technical support. Even where ICT coordinators were effectively used as unpaid technicians there were still support issues, particularly on networks of computers. In terms of resources, financial constraints meant that solutions were difficult and purchasing software or even new ink cartridges were issues for many schools.

We concluded there is a two-pronged skills issue: the ICT skills that pupils need to develop in order to achieve subject objectives, and the ICT skills teachers need in preparing for effective learning. For example, pupils must be able to cut and paste when redrafting and teachers must be able to reformat text and graphics quickly and efficiently when preparing pages for pupils to use.

As we were interested in literacy, numeracy and ICT we needed to take into account the attitudes of the teachers we were working with towards these subject areas. We knew that some of our teachers had agreed to participate because they saw opportunities for professional development in areas of existing interest and competence, while others were seeking to improve in areas where they felt less confident.

It happened that teachers who enjoyed literacy and language teaching tended to be less convinced about, and less skilled in, using ICT than those who enjoyed teaching maths. For example, Year 2 and Year 4 teachers who preferred teaching English to teaching maths rated themselves as being less competent in cutting and pasting and in using spell-checkers than those who preferred maths to English. Moreover, teachers who preferred literacy and language work were more likely to use computers as recreational resources (as a reward, as part of free-choice activities or as time-fillers) than for purposeful learning. This recreational usage was negatively correlated with value-added scores and therefore unlikely to be effective. Clearly we needed to help some teachers see the potential benefits of new ways of working with existing software or of introducing new applications, while others were quick to suggest creative ideas for quite ambitious projects.

Existing research evidence

We also looked at existing research evidence. Most published reports describe interventions, often testing learning theory from a psychological perspective. Few report on pupil attainment using standardized tests. There were some indications however:

- Text-to-speech can improve reading and spelling, as can speech input, though technically and practically more complex at this point in time (see e.g. Clifford and Miles 1993; Hartas and Moseley 1993; Medwell 1998).
- Word processors can improve writing (Snyder 1993).
- Collaborative talk using ICT can improve thinking and reasoning, suggesting that the pedagogy is as important as the technology (Wegerif *et al.* 1998).

The development projects

To address the issues surrounding pupils' skills, we worked with classes on clusters of computers in schools (where available), in local authority centres, or at the university to ensure that pupils had the skills they needed to use software to achieve literacy objectives. This teaching took place outside the Literacy Hour and as preparation for the project work.

We now consider specific projects we undertook with teachers. The first thing to emphasize is that we negotiated with the teachers about the area of the project (literacy or numeracy) and then worked together to identify a specific focus appropriate for their classes and their skills, confidence and enthusiasms. Our subsequent work on teachers' thinking (Higgins and Moseley 2001) indicates that this process is important in making an effective match between teachers, their teaching contexts and the contribution that ICT can make to their pupils.

Presenting texts with PowerPoint

The teacher, an ICT coordinator, was encouraged by her headteacher to use PowerPoint (part of Microsoft Office) to present texts to the whole class of Year 2 pupils. For one presentation a group of pupils wrote and illustrated a story which became the focus for the next week's shared text. PowerPoint was used to print mini-versions (which appealed to the pupils – enjoyment of 'mini-books' is typical of that age group) as well as class versions. It also provided word lists and cloze passages for sentence-level work when the story was saved as an outline in rich text format (RTF). This was clearly not something you could undertake every week, but a possible development once or twice a term, perhaps shared between classes or schools. The engagement of the pupils as the text is presented on screen, even without display equipment, was noticeable and the teacher believed it was an effective way to focus children's attention on the text.

Developing comprehension skills through questions

In another school the headteacher and staff had a high level of commitment to using ICT to help pupils learn. They had two suites of computers, one with an ILS. Throughout the project they continued to develop use of new resources such as an interactive whiteboard.

We worked with them to extend the use of text-to-speech support in reading and writing. The reading activities were designed to develop comprehension skills and could be used in both paper and electronic form. After piloting the activities, the work was undertaken by three teachers, first in the classroom, using an overhead projector and worksheet presentation, and then in a new computer suite. The reading materials consisted of non-fiction texts from the FunFax series (courtesy of Henderson Publishing), put into TextEase (Softease Publishing) so that the pupils could read the text, get support from text-to-speech and additional support from definitions added as a glossary. There was also a set of prompted question generation activities, based on short rhymes, where the pupils had not only to answer questions but to generate and discuss their own questions about the text. Our reading of research about reciprocal teaching (Palincsar and Brown 1984; Rosenshine and Meister 1994) indicated that this approach to question generation would be a powerful technique to develop reading comprehension.

Supporting literacy in Year 4 and Year 2

We worked with two classes in another school, again basing ideas for development on research work, but negotiating with teachers to find appropriate starting points. In the first case we used a multimedia program, Hyperstudio (TAG Learning Ltd), as a catalyst for teacher and pupils working on omissive apostrophes – *don't, can't, won't*. The Year 4 pupils worked as a class and in groups to create an interactive multimedia presentation, in this case a Hyperstudio stack, to teach other children how to use apostrophes correctly. The literacy work was in understanding the somewhat illogical rules and exceptions for such punctuation in English. The project appealed to the class teacher because she liked to develop the pupils' ICT skills in ways which gave them more control over the computer.

In the other class we used a painting program, KidPix (The Learning Company), for children in Year 2 to illustrate their writing. It's a good example of the tensions between research and practice. Research shows (Norris *et al.* 1998) that if children draw pictures first, the quality of their writing improves. But how do you manage this in a class of 30 and prevent some children from spending all their time on pictures, never writing a word, particularly within the constraints of the Literacy Hour? Our teacher's solution was to use some of her ICT curriculum time for children to create the illustrations during the week so that they could benefit from the stimulus of their own drawing and painting.

Improving spelling and reading in Year 2 with text-to-speech

The area where we believe research evidence is particularly strong is in the use of text-to-speech to support reading and spelling. In one school we took a structured programme of work, based on research and development done in Somerset, Jersey and the North East (Clifford and Miles 1993; Hartas and Moseley 1993; Jersey Advisory Service 1993) where pupils were given a sentence using NLS target vocabulary, on a piece of card. The children read the card, memorized the sentence, turned the card over, then typed it into the computer. The text-to-speech was set to read back each word as it was completed and then each sentence: not a new idea, but an effective one. In terms of our project, the greatest improvement was in reading; for us, this approach was not as successful at developing spelling of NLS target vocabulary.

Developing writing skills with pocketbooks in Year 4

In another project we used pocketbook computers to support writing. They were especially successful at improving the quantity of writing pupils accomplished, particularly as pupils took it in turns to take them home. They appealed equally to boys as well as girls and were successful for both in terms of the impact on output. The teacher found it difficult to respond to the writing because of the amount generated and developed a (paper-based) bulletin board for children to publish their work. We also found that small screens were not conducive to effective redrafting, but were better suited to text input, such as note-taking and writing diaries, as well as getting children (and parents) involved in homework.

This outline of some of the projects gives a brief overview of the activities we undertook with teachers and schools. We hope it also provides a flavour of the range of projects and the collaborative approach we undertook. The full report, published by Newcastle University, and the summary, produced by the TTA, describe the projects further.

Evidence of impact

The pupils in these projects made significant gains on standardized tests in 10 out of the 11 development classes. In literacy the overall average improvement was 5.1 months' progress per month. However, interpreting these results is difficult and we must remember that the teachers knew they were part of a high-profile national project. We cannot attribute the gains solely to the use of ICT. The combination of supported development, feedback to teachers about themselves and their classes and the presentation of their work to peers in workshops and conferences make attributing the gains solely to ICT impossible. While we demonstrated that ICT can be part of raising attainment dramatically, we would urge caution to anyone who does not look at the place of ICT in the social and practical context of classroom teaching and learning. ICT is for most teachers one of many tools with which learning can be constructed. The project teachers chose what to focus on so that learning with ICT would fit in with and enrich other ongoing teaching and learning.

Teachers' thinking and ICT

We knew that the teachers we worked with had different skills in using ICT and had different attitudes and approaches as to where and how it could be effective. Accordingly we undertook a series of activities to help us better understand teachers' thinking in these areas. Distinct patterns emerged from our analyses of this thinking (Moseley *et al.* 1999: Appendix 4; Higgins and Moseley 2001). These patterns were common across the age ranges of pupils, although teachers of younger children preferred a significantly less 'formal' approach.

Taking the sample as a whole there were no clear relationships with the PIPS pupil outcome measures. However, when these patterns were examined by the year group the teachers taught, some associations were apparent. These suggest that while teachers of primary pupils (4–11 years) have similar beliefs about teaching and learning, only some of these beliefs are linked with the progress that their pupils make and this depends on the year groups taught.

In Reception, a degree of scepticism about the value of ICT as well as thinking that computers are not just for play was a positive indicator of pupils' progress. Teachers of Year 2 pupils who valued more open-ended tasks and those who favoured exciting teaching were likely to be more effective. Teachers who valued *pupil empowerment* more than *teacher direction* tended to have positive attitudes towards ICT, although they were selective in how they used it. For teachers of Year 4, the use of ICT for demonstration and purposeful use by pupils were associated with pupil progress.

There are clear implications for professional development generally and for development with ICT in particular. Any such professional development needs to take account of teachers' thinking about teaching and learning generally as well as their skills with, attitude to and use of ICT. These considerations should include the year group taught by the teachers, as predictable patterns are evident even within the primary age range.

Others have argued that effective professional development should include an explicit focus on teachers' learning and development of professional knowledge, opportunities for teachers to examine their thinking and beliefs about teaching and learning, and opportunities for teachers to construct their own knowledge in an environment that supports and encourages risk-taking and reflection (Borko and Putnam 1995). Our data certainly support the view that an understanding of teachers' thinking and beliefs is vital. The investigation described above suggests, however, that taking teachers' thinking and beliefs into account in effective professional development is a complex task. An important component in this process is information about pupils' progress so that beliefs about effective practices generally, and about effective use of ICT in particular, are grounded in the impact that such beliefs and practices have on pupils' learning.

An ongoing process of development

In the project we had an indication that supporting more effective use of ICT needs a long-term approach. New equipment and software become available all the time which require new skills. These developments in turn enable new pedagogical approaches to be developed.

Nearly all the teachers involved in the development work wanted to continue working with the project. They valued the contribution ICT could make to their teaching and wanted to investigate further approaches and ideas. They acknowledged ICT offered them a wider range of strategies and approaches from which an effective teacher could choose in deciding how to meet teaching and learning objectives in literacy. Some teachers felt confident in their own ICT skills, others felt they needed support in skills development. Most felt they would benefit from further support and could identify which area of teaching they wished to develop next using ICT. This applied equally to those who had relatively advanced ICT skills which they used in their teaching as well as to those just beginning to use ICT to support their teaching.

Some areas, for a variety of reasons, we were unable to explore during the project. Sometimes technical difficulties could not be overcome during the lifetime of the project. In particular our proposed developments using the Internet were all problematic. We were disappointed that we could not investigate the contribution that email and the world wide web could make to literacy teaching because of technical difficulties in the schools where such activities were planned. None of the schools had reliable access to the Internet on sufficient machines for a class (or even a large group) to use.

We had hoped to use the Internet as motivation for children to write, publish and evaluate their work. Sites such as KidPub offer an audience for their writing. This creates meaningful purposes for writing activities which children can understand and access, as well as offering opportunities for home-school links.

A number of websites offer up-to-date information about news or current affairs (e.g. BBC or Newswise) with content appropriate for readers of different ages. This capitalizes on the immediacy of information that is available through ICT. The Qualifications and Curriculum Authority (QCA) scheme of work for geography (Unit 7: *Weather Around the World*; and

Unit 16: *What's in the News?*) encourages such an approach, where pupils gather data about weather or relate current affairs to their knowledge of the world. Some sites offer bulletin boards or discussion rooms for pupils to post responses or questions to these items of news. Our intention was to develop an electronic equivalent of a thinking skills approach called 'Community of Enquiry' developed from Philosophy for Children based on these resources (see the Newswise site for further details). We were unable to develop a practical case study illustrating this, due to schools not having adequate or reliable access to the Internet.

The capacity and range of information available through ICT also offers potential to support pupils' reading. Once basic fluency is achieved, the quantity of material read develops higher-order reading skills, as well as developing information processing and retention skills. Information CD-ROMs or appropriate websites offer access to such material where the specific content selected is determined by the interest of the reader. Our intention was to support access to more challenging texts where the enthusiasm of the reader for the content increases their engagement with the text and increases the amount that they read.

One of the reasons this idea could not be developed was because of the teachers' expectations of what was appropriate for literacy teaching, particularly in the light of the NLS framework, as well as expectations about appropriate reading material. Our view is that pupils need to engage with a sufficient quantity of reading materials which develop their interest in further research and reading until they reach a level of fluency or an 'escape velocity' where reading for information is both efficient and satisfying. It may never be realistic with a class of 30 pupils to manage individualized reading materials where the learner chooses the texts. ICT offers the opportunity for a compromise where the interest of the learner shapes at least some of the materials they have access to (whether on screen or printed out). If the material contains unfamiliar words or concepts, an integrated electronic talking thesaurus and dictionary is a powerful aid to learning. In the project we developed non-fiction materials based on the FunFax books where the on-screen text had spoken support for unfamiliar words. These were time-consuming to create and, though the teachers who used them were enthusiastic, the idea was not extended to a wider range of texts.

ICT and effective teaching – a never-ending story?

A goal of enabling teachers to start using ICT as an effective part of their teaching is relatively easily attained. Principles about when (and when not) to use ICT can be established so that ICT supports teaching and learning both effectively and efficiently. The New Opportunities Fund (NOF) for the ICT training of serving teachers goes some way towards beginning to establish such principles (TTA 1998). However, the task of developing teachers' effectiveness through ICT is a long-term goal which needs long-term planning. Developing such effectiveness should become established as a regular part of teachers' professional development. We identified from the research literature on teacher development that teachers themselves play an important part in this process. We therefore encouraged teachers we worked with to identify the subject area that they wanted to support with ICT and negotiated the precise focus of the development which would enable them to use ICT effectively in their classroom teaching. We believe that this was an important factor in their success in raising pupils' attainment. We believe that this identification and negotiation needs to be part of a longer term process of reviewing and improving teaching which can be informed by the wider literature, but which needs to be put into action, or enacted, pragmatically and according to local context and needs. This 'enaction research' should also test out research claims in the robust settings of ordinary classrooms using information about pupils' attainment.

This process will be long term for another reason. Technology shows no signs of standing still. As it develops, new approaches to improve teaching and learning will emerge. This is what makes research and development in ICT and education so exciting and challenging. Finding appropriate matches between technology and educational aims and objectives, balancing these between the short term and long term in a rapidly changing context means there will never be a simple solution. Our project demonstrated clearly that ICT has the potential to help raise children's attainment. It *can* help teachers be more effective. *How* it can help will change as technology and teaching themselves change.

Summary

To use ICT to raise attainment, our team found it essential to identify clear subject objectives which ICT can support, both effectively and efficiently. We also found it vital to understand which skills pupils needed to access the literacy objectives being taught. Matching development approaches in ICT with teachers' skills and aptitudes is challenging and time-consuming, nevertheless we believe that this was an essential ingredient in the success of the project.

Since the project, our work has enabled us to see the potential of ICT training as an opportunity to support more effective teaching. Development work involving ICT can act as a catalyst to bring about change in teachers' thinking and practice in a supportive way. To make this happen it is necessary to give teachers the opportunity to develop ICT skills and understanding and then apply them to the classroom. The change required through using ICT helps teachers make changes in their teaching. This process enables them to make more effective choices about learning objectives and the different teaching approaches, or the pedagogy, that they choose.

It is clear to us that ICT can help teachers be more effective, but teachers need to decide where and how, as the decisions in any particular context, and with any particular class of children, are complex. As technology changes, these choices change. We hope that the information contained in this chapter is helpful in providing suggestions for starting this process.

Note

1 We don't use the word 'pedagogy' much to talk about teaching and learning in the UK. It can be helpful in understanding the difference between approaches to teaching and learning – a pedagogy – and specific techniques or 'didactics' as they would call them in Europe. We were interested in the pedagogy of ICT or how ICT fits into the classroom and not just the specific things it can do when looked at separately. It is this match which makes the issue a complex one.

Software

Hyperstudio (TAG Learning Ltd): multimedia authoring software for children, allowing the creation of interactive presentations.
KidPix (The Learning Company) a child friendly painting (and simple animation) program.
PowerPoint (Microsoft Office): a professional presentation program, designed for business use, but presentations are easily adapted for the classroom where some of the features, such as printing handouts, can be used to create mini versions of texts.
TextEase (Softease Publishing): a program which offers intuitive word processing through to multimedia and even web publishing. The text-to-speech function can be configured to read designated parts of a page as dictionary or thesaurus support.

Websites

The summary and descriptive illustrations were published by the TTA and are available at www.teach-tta.gov.uk/research/pedagogy.htm or from their publications line.
KidPub can be found at www.kidpub.org
Newswise is available through www.dialogueworks.co.uk/
The PIPS website is at http://cem.dur.ac.uk/pips/
The QCA schemes of work are on the DfEE standards site at www.standards.dfee.gov.uk/schemes/geography/

Ways Forward with ICT can be found at www.ncl.ac.uk/education/ttaict/ summary.html or can be ordered direct from the authors c/o Newcastle University.

References

BECTA (British Educational Communications & Technology Agency) (2000) *A Preliminary Report for the DfEE on the Relationship Between ICT and Primary School Standards.* Coventry: BECTA (available on the web at: www.becta.org.uk/news/reports/).

Borko, H. and Putnam, R.T. (1995) Expanding a teacher's knowledge base: a cognitive psychological perspective on professional development, in T.R. Guskey and M. Huberman (eds) *Professional Development in Education; New Paradigms and Practices*, pp. 35–65. New York: Teachers College Press.

Clifford, V. and Miles, M. (1993) Talk back, *Special Children*, 68: 23–5.

Cordes, C. and Miller, E. (eds) (2000) *Fool's Gold: a Critical Look at Computers in Childhood.* College Park, MA: Alliance for Childhood.

Hartas, C. and Moseley, D. (1993) 'Say that again, please': a scheme to boost reading skills using a computer with digitised speech, *Support for Learning*, 8(1): 16–20.

Higgins, S. and Moseley, D. (2001) Teachers' thinking about ICT and learning: beliefs and outcomes, *Teacher Development*, 5.

Jersey Advisory Service (1993) *The Jersey Computer Assisted Reading Development Programme.* Jersey, CI: Jersey Advisory Service.

Medwell, J. (1998) The talking books project: some further insights into the use of talking books to develop reading, *Reading*, April: 3–8.

Moseley, D., Higgins, S., Bramald, R. *et al.* (1999) *Ways Forward with ICT: Effective Pedagogy using Information and Communications Technology in Literacy and Numeracy in Primary Schools.* Newcastle upon Tyne: University of Newcastle upon Tyne.

Norris, E., Mokhtari, K. and Reichard, C. (1998) Children's use of drawing as a pre-writing strategy (research note), *Journal of Research in Reading*, 21(1): 69–74.

Palincsar, A.S. and Brown, A.L. (1984) Reciprocal teaching of comprehension fostering and comprehension monitoring activities, *Cognition and Instruction*, 2: 117–75.

Rosenshine, B. and Meister, C. (1994) Reciprocal teaching: a review of the research, *Review of Educational Research*, 64: 479–530.

Scott, D., Hurry, J., Hey, V. and Smith, M. (1997) *Report of the Evaluation of the National Literacy Association (NLA) Docklands Learning Acceleration Project.* London: University of London Institute of Education.

Snyder, I. (1993) Writing with word processors: a research overview, *Educational Research*, 35: 49–68.

TTA (Teacher Training Agency) (1998) Teachers' Annex A1 (England, Northern Ireland & Wales) *The Use Of ICT in Subject Teaching: Expected Outcomes For Teachers In England, Northern Ireland & Wales.* London: DfEE.

Wegerif, R.N., Mercer, N. and Dawes, L. (1998) Integrating pedagogy and software design to support discussion in the primary curriculum, *Journal of Computer Assisted Learning*, 14: 199–211.

3

A REFLECTIVE VIEW OF THE ENGLISH NATIONAL LITERACY STRATEGY

Alison Tyldesley

It is useful to ask why information and communication technology (ICT) should be used in a structured teaching situation such as the Literacy Hour. The work of six teachers considered in this chapter reveals some answers to this question. Using ICT involved a change of approach which was stimulating, motivating and challenging. The teachers became increasingly confident and enthusiastic about ICT use as the project progressed and they were able to analyse which aspects of ICT use impacted on their pupils' learning.

The Literacy Hour is part of the National Literacy Strategy (NLS) introduced by the English government. Its aim is to improve literacy standards. All primary teachers in England are aware of the essential requirements of the approach which includes a structured and focused Literacy Hour each day in every primary classroom and the use of a Literacy Framework which details explicit literacy objectives for each year group. The NLS has been in place since September 1998. Early indications are that the strategy is having a very positive effect on national primary test results.

It is necessary to have a brief overview of the structure of the Literacy Hour in order to make sense of these six case studies. The hour has four sections which are given approximate timings (DfEE 1998). Whole-class teaching includes 'shared reading' and 'shared writing' followed by 'word and sentence level' teaching (approximately 30 minutes). A period of independent work (approximately 20 minutes) follows after the whole-class session. The teacher works with one ability group during this period on either 'guided reading' or 'guided writing'. The aim of guided work is to develop pupils' independence. 'Guided reading' involves a structured reading session led by the class teacher in which pupils have their own copies of a text. 'Guided writing' usually involves pupils writing independently but with support and intervention of the teacher. The objectives of the lesson are returned to in the plenary session which is the last section of the Literacy Hour (approximately 10 minutes). The plenary is a chance for the teacher to assess and evaluate and for pupils to reflect and receive feedback on their learning.

The contribution ICT can make to literacy teaching and learning has been affected by the curricular changes introduced for the Literacy Hour. Simultaneously, government funding has been available to support training for teachers in the use of ICT. New equipment and resources are available to schools through a National Grid for Learning. Both Literacy and ICT have been given a high profile by the government.

It has been argued that the role of ICT was largely ignored in the NLS Framework. Barker and Franklin, writing in *Focus on Literacy* remark that 'It is interesting to note that apart from a few passing mentions of word-processing and CD-ROMS, there is surprisingly little reference [to ICT] in the National Literacy Strategy Framework' (MAPE 1998). It is true that there are few explicit references to ICT either in the Framework document or training materials, although ICT is implicitly recognized as a contemporary literacy medium. Certainly, the NLS needs to take into account what it means to be literate in the twenty-first century. The definition of literacy may need to be expanded to take account of the role of non-linear texts and those including sound and moving images.

ICT has two distinct roles within the Literacy Framework. It is a literacy medium; for example, a reading medium, an authoring tool, and a presentational tool. It also has a role in developing non-ICT-specific literacy skills; for example, software can be used to teach or reinforce the learning of spelling rules.

Yet the context for using ICT as a tool to develop literacy is, in England, a more problematic one in many ways than in countries where there has been less centralized curriculum innovation. The introduction of something as radical as the Literacy Hour is bound to preoccupy teachers with management and resource issues. The four distinct sections of the Literacy Hour have caused teachers to reassess how ICT can be used. It is not possible to give pupils access to computers for a sustained period during the Literacy Hour. Using computers, with all their potential for technical hitches, can produce another resource burden. The Literacy Hour has encouraged huge changes in teaching. It can also be argued that using computers causes pedagogical change (Monteith 1993). In a context of innovation, yet another change can cause 'initiative overload'. Many objectives in the Framework do not make explicit reference to ICT use, so the temptation is to ignore ICT as a possible literacy tool. ICT may be seen therefore as both a resource burden and a challenging change agent. The short-term response from many primary teachers is to neglect ICT use for the time being.

Primary schools have had over a decade to come to terms with new technology, particularly computer use. However, new pressures may have caused a return to teachers' first reactions in dealing with new tools. I have observed that computers have ended up gathering dust during the Literacy Hour. Their only role has been as part of a rotation of drill work during the 'independent work' section of the Literacy Hour or pupils have used the word processor to type up a 'best' copy of writing.

The aim of this small-scale project was to persuade teachers to move away from either ignoring ICT during the Literacy Hour or using it in the ways described above. We aimed to produce manageable examples of how computers can be used within the context of the Literacy Hour. The focus was on using ICT as a tool to develop writing. This was to counter-act the bias towards teaching reading in the first year of NLS implementation. We also aimed to help teachers in their efforts to raise pupils' attainment in writing by supporting them in using ICT as an effective teaching and learning tool. The teachers had the support of an initial training course and my advisory visits as a local education authority (LEA)[1] literacy consultant. The effectiveness of the intervention was evaluated by the teachers themselves in terms of their observations of pupils' attitudes and their assessment of learning. There was no external evaluation or testing. At the end of the project the teachers summarized their judgement on the impact of the work on their pupils.

The NLS Framework for teaching starts with the words, 'Literacy is at the heart of the drive to raise standards in schools' (DfEE 1998: 2). These opening words emphasize the importance the government places upon the NLS as a tool to raise standards. The main focus of primary teachers in England is to improve teaching and through this to raise standards of attainment. This focus results from policies such as the NLS and a national emphasis on improving test results. However, many teachers still do not see ICT as a key tool in raising attainment. Our starting point was to consider ways literacy teaching could be extended by the use of ICT. We examined current research evidence as to where ICT can enhance teaching and learning in classrooms. We identified key points taken from the Teacher Training Agency (TTA) research project (Moseley *et al.* 1999) and described in Chapter 2 of this book:

- ICT can present ideas in a concrete or dynamic way (e.g. taking an existing text and changing the characters or setting, moving letters on screen to demonstrate use of suffixes or prefixes).

- Feedback can be provided to pupils as they are working (e.g. through speech feedback or interactive spell-checkers).
- Information can be easily changed, improved, reworked and represented. This allows reflection and the altering of mistakes or reworking of ideas quickly and flexibly.

With these points in mind our project began. Six schools interested in using ICT more productively within literacy teaching participated in the project. Teachers in each school documented the way computers were supporting their teaching of literacy within the daily structure of the Literacy Hour. ICT was one of a range of strategies and approaches used during the Literacy Hour.

The project started with a one-day training course. This provided teachers with knowledge of suitable strategies and approaches which would work within the Literacy Hour structure. Suggestions were presented as to how simple open-ended computer programs could be used. Teachers then developed these in ways that would be relevant for their own situations and year groups. The training also made explicit central principles for using ICT when the focus of the work is the teaching and learning of literacy, not developing ICT skills. The principles included these points:

- ICT should be used as a resource to teach the NLS objectives for literacy, not the objectives for ICT capability.
- ICT should only be selected as a resource if it is at least as effective as alternatives.
- Activities with ICT need to be based on clear learning objectives from the National Literacy Framework at word, sentence or text level.
- Feedback and assessment should be included.

The practical question of how ICT use can be managed in a very structured teaching situation was addressed, and various suggestions outlined. ICT has a more significant place in the classroom if it is seen as linked to the main teaching objectives and as part of general activities.

Strategies for using simple word processors were outlined; for example, providing printed versions of texts so that pupils could work on a similar task at or away from the computer. Suggestions were made for differentiating ICT activities. An example of this would be giving a writing task at different levels of difficulty. One group of pupils would be provided with prepared texts to modify, another group would expand a text in order to develop their own version and a final group would design and create their own texts.

The structure of the Literacy Hour can mean that the significance of ICT as a whole-class teaching tool is ignored. A computer can be used as an electronic whiteboard and interactions can take place in front of all the pupils. This develops the potential of ICT as a tool that can present ideas dynamically and engage and motivate pupils. A small number of open-ended programs can be used for creative and reinforcement activities. Pupils become familiar with these programs and more independent in their use. Examples could include a word processor with speech feedback and a desk-top publisher. The click and drop or cut, copy and paste facilities on word processors can be used to allow text to be sequenced, sorted or matched.

Short snappy tasks are the most effective within the structure of the Literacy Hour. Examples of these might include producing captions, lists, poems, posters and recipes or extending and changing existing texts. Long text-entering activities are the least useful way of using computers within the Literacy Hour. However, that should not exclude other occasions when pupils can engage in longer activities. Modelling the development of extended writing by editing writing and then working on printouts at various stages is an excellent use of a word processor. There are well-documented benefits of using ICT for changing and improving work. Writing can be quickly and effectively changed without the need for laborious recopying.

Speech feedback software can be used. This could include talking books and word processors with text-to-speech facilities. The benefits have been highlighted by recent research (see Moseley *et al.* 1999: viii). In early years settings, using speech support can help phonological awareness to develop. At a later stage a word processor with speech facilities can help with redrafting and checking writing composition. Speech support can help older pupils or more fluent readers by reading 'spell-check' examples or by helping with the reading of unfamiliar words. Reinforcement activities can be used to support the learning of spellings or grammatical rules. Finally there needs to be access to different types of text including those with sound, moving images and a non-linear structure.

The guidelines and suggestions above were discussed and agreed with the teachers. They were then introduced to the facilities of open-ended programs that would support them in their literacy teaching during the Literacy Hour. The teachers were asked to document an example of ICT use each school term over a year. The resulting case studies were presented to local teachers at after-school training sessions and were also collated and presented as a booklet each term to allow for wider dissemination.

Each school had recently been given Internet and email access, but none of the teachers used them. These newer technologies were ignored, partly because technical difficulties still hindered them from running reliably, but also because teachers were not confident in their use.

Case study 1

The first case study involved a teacher of 6-year-olds. She aimed to provide support in developing early writing skills within the context of the Literacy Hour. Many pupils could not write independently. The current 'shared text' was a Big Book version of a traditional story, which had been entered into a word processor. All pupils had access to a printed version of the text.

The literacy objective was to enable pupils to sequence and retell an existing text. The program enabled objects to be easily picked up, dropped and dragged. The children suggested which key incidents should be chosen from the story and set up on the screen. Text snippets became 'objects' enabling children to sequence key incidents from the text. Focused discussion encouraged the children's learning. The teacher noted a greater tendency in the group using the computer to engage in discussion (around the screen) than groups engaged in paper-based activities. More able groups could use text-entering facilities to extend the description of key incidents. The activity was embedded into general class work as some groups did the same activity cutting and sequencing sentences on paper.

In the second term of the project this teacher used a 'patterned' story as a model for the children's own writing. The shared text was a simple but effective repetitive story in which the phrase 'dark, dark' is reiterated. The teacher chose to use a talking word processor which could support the children in rereading and improving their writing. She set up a word-processing screen as a writing frame. It contained some text which could not be altered and text boxes in which new words were added. This enabled the children to 'innovate' on the original text with a minimal need to enter text. One of the difficulties with using a word processor with young children is the length of time needed to complete a word-processing task. In this case new stories were quickly created with the same patterned structure as the original. Each page had the same structure until the final page when 'dark, dark' was deleted and replaced. Use of the word processor made the children more aware of the patterned and repetitive nature of the original story. It supported fast and professional 'publishing'. Writing was given a clear purpose and two class books were produced that could be compared and reread alongside the original text.

In the third term of the project the teacher continued developing the same two ideas, using a click and drop facility for sequencing text and setting up supportive 'writing frames' into which a small amount of text could be added.

The key impact of increased use of ICT in this classroom was on focused discussion around the computer screen, which enabled pupils to link their oral utterances more firmly with their written expression.

Case study 2

This teacher taught in a small village primary school with a class of mixed 7- and 8-year-olds. This mix of age groups posed particular difficulties as not only did two year groups have to be considered when planning, but also the needs of two National Curriculum key stages. The aim of work in the first term was to write book reviews for a specified audience and to use ICT to bring these to a published form. The class read and enjoyed a number of humorous books by Babette Cole. The children then looked at various formats for book reviews and decided to create their own.

The teacher scribed the children's ideas. Then she used the computer as an electronic board so that all the children could see the advantages of composing writing using a word processor. The children sat on the carpet where they could all see the computer screen. During independent work the speech facility available on the word processor was very useful as children corrected mistakes after hearing the computer read their work out loud.

Poetry was the focus in the second term of the project. The objective was to use simple poetry structures so that the children could substitute their own ideas and write new lines. In 'shared reading' the class read various poems and discussed rhyme, rhythm and structure. A poem about colours was used as a model for writing. The teacher demonstrated using the structure of the poem as a basis for creating new verse. Interestingly, she also made use of the 'word list' facility on the word processor. A list of rhyming words was brainstormed by the class and typed into the word processor. This was quickly transferred into a 'word list' becoming a customised list of vocabulary for pupils to insert into their writing. The list was used as a support by children writing on paper and those word-processing. The list appeared on the word-processing screen and speech feedback could be set so that pupils could hear the words read out loud and insert them into their writing.

By the third term the teacher confidently used the computer as a whole-class instructional and presentational tool. She modelled changing texts in front of her class. A traditional story was edited and the setting and characters changed. The teacher demonstrated this and then the pupils created their own texts both on and off screen. The strategy of using an existing text and modifying aspects of the text worked extremely well with a word processor. This teacher saw the benefit of creating a bank of short electronic texts which could be easily modified and reworked.

The key change for this teacher was using a computer as a tool for whole-class demonstration. She reported that pupils' views of writing shifted as a result of wider-scale changes being made to an existing text. The provisional nature of text on a word processor made children aware that words are not like 'bricks in a wall' that cannot be moved or changed.

Case study 3

The third teacher worked in a large urban primary school with 9-year-olds. The objective of their work in the first term was to write poetry, experimenting with different styles and structures. The class considered various shape poems and discussed why and how they were written. During 'independent work' pairs of children designed their own poems using a word processor.

The activity was very motivating and the children had some very original ideas. One pupil wrote a humorous 'bed' poem in the shape of a bed expressing a recognizable human feeling: 'I love my bed, I would stay in it all day if I could'. In an 'Umbrella' poem there was a handle moving down the page which read: 'Protecting people's heads'. A pyramid poem was particularly powerful with the choice of vocabulary enhanced by its presentation in a triangular shape. The poetry writing worked well as a short, sharp activity during the 20 minutes of independent working time.

During the second term the class worked on writing newspaper-style reports. The objective was to use ICT to draft and lay out the reports. In 'shared reading' the class read a short novel. After the class had read the book and discussed it at length, groups completed tasks based on different aspects of the novel. Two groups worked on describing and comparing the different characters in the book; one group wrote a book review; another took the viewpoint of the main character and wrote his story; a fifth group worked on computers, turning the story into a newspaper article.

There were three computers in the classroom. Software which creates newspaper pages was used on an older style desktop machine. Features of the program were discussed in the 'guided writing' part of the lesson. First the group word-processed the beginning of an article, discussing the language features and structure of a news report. The children then worked individually on each computer and produced their own newspaper articles. Editing and proofreading were carried out at the end of the writing process. The children were extremely pleased with their work. Their articles were read out during the plenary session and compared with the book reviews, the character portraits and the first person narratives.

This teacher organized the Literacy Hour so that over a period of time each group used the computer. However, groups did not all carry out the same task. Later in the term a different group wrote a newspaper article based on the story of Boudicca, a queen who fought against the Romans. A more sophisticated word-processing program which gave the children more opportunity to develop their understanding of text layout and font styles was used.

In the third term the emphasis changed. The word processor was used not just for presentation but also as a provisional tool that could give feedback to the pupils as they worked. The teacher produced a bland, simple text with no descriptive details of characters or setting. The children's task was to improve this text by adding to it and modifying it to create a more effective piece of writing.

The pupils responded well to manipulating text and became effective users of the speech feedback facility. The teacher reported that the idea of taking an existing simple text and reworking it had made the most impact on pupils' learning, enabling them to focus on the provisional nature of writing.

Case study 4

This teacher worked in a small junior school at the edge of a town and was very committed to using ICT effectively even though, at the start of the project, there was only one computer in her classroom. Her pupils were 8- and 9-year-olds and as soon as they joined her class they were trained to become confident computer users. Other staff at the school were less committed to ICT use. The teacher was determined that computers would continue to be used during the Literacy Hour as well as at other times during the school week. Over a five-week period she tried to ensure that each group participated in an ICT activity. Each computer activity was managed by taking the group concerned through the necessary procedures before the Literacy Hour started. Two children per day worked on the computer activity while the rest of the group completed their set activities. There was usually a very similar task both on and off screen.

During the first term the teacher developed some short computer activities for use. The aim was to concentrate on simple tasks which would increase the children's confidence and familiarity with word processing. The tasks involved some investigation into spelling conventions or punctuation rules and a number of different literacy objectives were covered.

For the first task a passage from a text already discussed in 'shared reading' was word-processed. The children then worked in pairs and highlighted all verbs in red. A great deal of discussion was generated as the passage contained a number of verbs in different forms such as the infinitive *to sing*, past tense forms such as *was*, *came* and so on, and present participles such as *thumping*, *spreading* and *panting*. The teacher was able to listen to the ensuing discussions which helped her to plan future activities. The plenary sessions were used to extend and consolidate learning.

The teacher also prepared lists of words. The objective was to encourage understanding of the segmentation of words into constituent phonemes. The children sorted words into seven different vowel phoneme groups and then added further words to the list. Examples included words with the 'er' phoneme spelt 'er', 'ur' or 'ir', according to usage in different words. The word processor which was used had a drag and drop facility, making this kind of spelling investigation quick and easy. The speech feedback was used so that pupils could check that they were not choosing words only for their visual pattern.

A further investigation took place with lists of roots and suffixes. The drag and drop facility was used to create words. The objective of the activity was to spell accurately words with double consonants. Another task involved children being given a list of verbs to put into the past tense. There were three possible spellings: 'ed', 'double consonant and ed' and 'y changed to i and ed'. The word processor highlighted wrongly-spelt words (e.g.: 'stoped' in yellow) and this meant that children had their attention drawn to errors and they could work out the rule more easily for themselves.

During the second term the objective was to write alliterative poems and to use ICT to bring these to a published form. The teacher modelled the activity the children would complete during independent working time. For this activity the teacher prepared templates and these provided a stimulus for writing during 'independent work'. The children were asked to write a four-line poem using as much alliteration as possible. The letter used had to be the initial letter of the animal illustrated. The poem could be 'nonsense' verse, drawing on a wide range of vocabulary to add interest to the finished work.

Using a word processor helped draw children's attention to the need to discriminate in their choice of vocabulary. The templates helped to fire the children's imagination and contributed to the effect of the layout of the poems. These pupils were all familiar with editing and using a spell-checker and this helped with the production of a higher-quality piece of writing. During the plenary session seating was slightly rearranged so that everyone could see the screen and the poems could be read and commented on.

Work in the third term involved a student on teaching practice who continued some of the earlier work and produced tailor-made word-level activities.

Increased motivation was the key impact reported by this teacher. The Literacy Hours were planned so that one group always had access to computer activities. She could observe the difference in concentration between groups engaged in work using ICT and those using pen and pencil. The ICT groups engaged in purposeful discussion and stayed on task for longer. This teacher increased the children's interest in literacy work and was very effective in using one computer to maximum advantage.

Case study 5

The teacher in this case study worked in a junior school in a small town. The school had a computer suite which had not previously been used during the Literacy Hour. She wished to experiment in using the computer suite during literacy teaching with 9-year-olds. The suite included 15 desktop machines. The children were able to work in pairs on a task.

During the first term the theme was persuasive writing. The computer suite was used during the second week of a four-week block of teaching and its inclusion at this stage worked well. The focus of the writing was to persuade parents that it would be a good idea to introduce a new pet into the family. The computer was used as a 'shared writing' tool with all pupils grouped round the screen. A writing frame was already loaded. The children suggested which sentences might be typed in using the plan drawn up on the previous day. The teacher acted as scribe and the children came up and typed in their suggestions. The emphasis was on a draft copy so that spelling and punctuation did not interfere with the flow of ideas. Being able to insert, delete and modify the text as they went along enhanced the 'shared writing' session.

During 'independent work' the lowest ability group sequenced sentences they had encountered previously. Sentences had been entered on a program that enabled them to click, move and drop pieces of text. They had the help of a non-teaching assistant to read and remind them of the structure of persuasive writing. They were not hampered by handwriting and spelling difficulties and could concentrate on the sense and sequence of the text.

One group used the writing frame demonstrated during 'shared writing' to help them structure their persuasive writing. The two most able groups produced their own persuasive text. Phrases in an on screen word list could be used for support but did not have to be. Speech feedback enabled appropriate choices to be made.

During the second term the computer suite was used to create letters linked to a history topic on the Second World War. Pupils wrote letters in the role of evacuees writing to their parents. Letter templates were set up. The teacher found there were two main advantages in using computers: the benefit of improved presentation and the support offered by speech feedback for the less able pupils.

The teacher returned to the theme of non-fiction writing in the third term. The pupils accessed a CD-ROM encyclopedia to research information about sport. Strategies for scanning text from electronic resources were modelled during whole-class teaching. The pupils were shown how to navigate their way through a multimedia text. The non-linear, interactive structure of the encyclopedia was demonstrated and pupils were shown how to jump to and fro through the resource by using hypertext links. The skills of scanning and skimming were the key literacy focus. An ICT reference activity was ideal for encouraging these skills. The fact that pupils were only allowed short, sharp interactions with the CD-ROM meant that they had to focus on accessing the relevant information quickly.

The next step was to create notes by locating key phrases, headings and sentences and to summarize the text. This teacher created effective strategies for using the computer suite during the Literacy Hour. The suite had previously not been timetabled for use during this intensive teaching period. However, all teachers at this school were now aware of the potential and effectiveness of whole-class instruction using ICT to model key literacy skills.

Case study 6

This teacher worked in a small primary school at the edge of a small, isolated town. The pupils were 10 and 11 years old. The teacher worked with three ability groups. There were three computers with word processors in the classroom.

The literacy objective in the first term was to write from another viewpoint; for example, retelling an incident in letter form. During the week all the children wrote letters from the point of view of a character in a book. Three pairs of children worked on the computer during 'independent work'. The teacher set up the word processors with a letter format and the children wrote during two independent sessions. She also prepared an on screen word list in a word-processing program. This included a list of connectives to help the children structure their writing.

Preparing a word list to use with a word processor supports pupils without over-influencing their writing. Children's word processors often have the facility for the teacher to produce a word list (see Case study 2). These can act as a checklist by reminding pupils of aspects of content to be included. They can contain words and phrases that pupils might find difficult to spell. They can also provide grammatical prompts by providing connective words and phrases that will lead to more complex sentence structures. The speech feedback facility can be used within word lists. This can offer extra support for pupils who would otherwise find the vocabulary difficult to read and enable them to make more sophisticated vocabulary choices.

Editing and spell-checking were carried out at the end of the writing. These were skills the children had been taught at other times. Not all the children had access to the computer for writing their letters. The rest of the group wrote letters in their books and had access to the computer on another occasion for a similar activity. In the plenary session the class discussed the difference between handwritten and word-processed letters.

In the second term the literacy objective was to prepare a short section of a story as a script using stage directions and details of location and setting. Extracts from a novel were read in 'shared reading' sessions. The class then looked at a variety of play scripts and analysed the layout, including items such as setting/location, stage directions, the use of brackets, bold type and italics.

In a 'shared writing' session the teacher modelled changing a short extract from the novel into a script, listing the characters, making notes about the setting and looking for clues about how the characters might act.

In an 'independent work' session the children chose a favourite story and rewrote a short section from it as a script. Two children from each group worked on computers. Similar word-processing facilities were used. The children chose font style, size and colour of text, and edited their work adding bold type, italics and so on. They used spell-checkers and saved and printed their work. Most of the class completed handwritten scripts but had access to the computer for another task later in the term. To test the writing for clarity, children worked with a response partner, read each other's scripts and then made appropriate alterations.

In the plenary session the class discussed the advantages and disadvantages of using either ICT or pen and paper. It was decided that word processors produced a more professional-looking result. However, in these instances using the computer took longer and therefore these scripts were shorter. As children develop better ICT skills this would not necessarily be the case.

By the third term the teacher had started to use the computer as a whole-class teaching tool to demonstrate writing instructions. Children were able to work independently in pairs and small groups to write their own instructions on how to use new computer programs recently introduced to the school. Their grasp of editing facilities had moved on and they chose a greater range of presentational features including alignment, italics, bold type and underlining. In the plenary session the children shared and tested out each other's instructions, making sure they were clearly set out and easy to follow.

These children had used word-processing programs widely, both within and outside the Literacy Hour, and had become competent in their use. They used this tool well, accessing spelling and speech support and using editing and presentational facilities to a high level of competence. Using word processors well influenced the pupils' view of writing. They became aware of the advantages of the editing and presentational features of word processing. The teacher reported that spelling and speech feedback had a positive effect on progress.

Conclusion

This project did not set out to assess pupils' progress as a result of increased use of ICT. However, teachers reported that certain features of the planned activities contributed significantly to pupils' learning. The feature that all teachers noted was the impact of increased use of ICT as a presentational tool. They noted that their use of ICT in this way helped to focus pupils' attention during whole-class teaching. Several teachers noted that ICT provided support for less able pupils through speech feedback and word lists. It also provided a challenge for more able pupils by setting expectations that work should be produced to publication standard. Two teachers in particular reported that children in their class changed their view of writing as a result of using a word processor. Pupils began to see writing as 'provisional' and were motivated to add, extend, rearrange, delete and reshape their writing. This was a real boon as often improving writing in classrooms is little more than 'copying up neatly'. One teacher reported the value of a computer-based activity for generating purposeful and focused discussion.

The teachers involved in this project developed simple uses for computers in classrooms. They ignored the more sophisticated uses of ICT and returned to the effective use of open-ended applications clearly linked to the tight learning objectives of the NLS. Their work did not break new ground. However, in a time of great change it can be important to return to doing simple things well in a new context.

The most significant change of practice generated by this project was using computers as a whole-class or whole-group teaching aid. All the teachers began to experiment with whole-class teaching using ICT. They began to demonstrate and explain literacy objectives to their whole class using a computer screen. In the past, ICT use has sometimes been sidelined as an extension or reward activity for one or two pupils and teacher intervention was missing. Using a computer for whole-class or group teaching reverses this tendency. The increasing availability of computer suites in schools supports whole-class teaching. Banks of machines can be used to support a whole-class approach with the chance for immediate application of learning for all pupils. Computers with larger screens or interactive whiteboards can be used in a similar way with the teacher demonstrating, interacting and explaining key points. Computers are powerful and effective tools. They become even more powerful when the teacher provides a learning interface between pupils and machines.

Note

1 The LEA retains some overall responsibility for schools although many of its functions have in recent years been devolved to school managers. School improvement involving both pressure and support remains a function of the LEA.

References

DfEE (Department for Education and Employment) (1998) *National Literacy Strategy Framework*. London: HMSO.

MAPE (1998) *MAPE Focus on Literacy Pack*. Northampton: MAPE Publications.

Monteith, M. (ed.) (1993) *Computers and Language*. Exeter: Intellect.

Moseley, D., Higgins, S., Bramald, R. *et al.* (1999) *Ways Forward with ICT: Effective Pedagogy using Information and Communications Technology in Literacy and Numeracy in Primary Schools*. Newcastle upon Tyne: University of Newcastle upon Tyne.

4

JOINT ATTENTION: ADULTS AND CHILDREN PLAYING WITH COMPUTERS

Mary Lou Thornbury

and Julian Grenier

Si l'école n'a pas adhère a la révolution numérique, vous pouvez laisser vos enfants pianoter sur l'ordinateur familial. (If the school has not joined the digital revolution, you can let your children play (or tinkle) on the family computer.)
Le Figaro, 21 August 2000

Introduction

How do we find a language that expresses the relationship of young children to computers? Are the children playing or working? In the French, children 'tinkling' on the keyboard images the operation of the computer, in a language semantically musical, as an aesthetic rather than technical activity, subverting the instrumental to expressive purposes. In English the alternative language of skills and training was expressed by a politician who said: 'Children [have] to learn keyboard skills in school, since whatever they are to do in life they are going to come in contact with the microchip. We have to train the young people of today for the jobs of tomorrow' (Baker 1993: 192). This chapter asserts the expressive purpose of play with computers by early years children.

In this chapter we reflect on the learning of children at the computer, scaffolded by parents or centre staff, and then on the way the children move on in their learning, scaffolded by those features of computer programs which provide feedback and reinforcement. We have exemplified their learning of story and their attention to text using talking books and the development of oracy using a paint program alongside other software. This occurred in the context of parallel learning by the parents in their literacy class.

Children learning with adults

The idea that children's early learning takes place in the context of their society and that it is mediated through their relationships with adults and other children is central to this chapter. Research by Monteith (2000) showed the engagement of parents and children using the computer together; the parents 'really enjoyed working' with the computer and said that it gave them 'a shared interest'. A project on the assessment of preschool children found that: 'Research in child care is confirming earlier studies of home environments which emphasised the long term positive effects for children of responsive and reciprocal relationships in early learning environments' (Carr 1998).

A longitudinal study in Sweden (Broberg *et al.* 1997) found evidence that the quality of adult–child interactions in an early childhood setting was a strong predictor for success at 8 years. American research (Rattner and Stettner 1991) confirmed that these relationships have a positive influence on attention span and persistence at cognitive tasks. Persistence is a key factor in later learning and this is based on dispositions developed within consistent relationships, particularly in the preschool years.

Persistence is the chief characteristic of those children who might be called 'autodidacts'. The first poem of one such child (Laura, aged 6) begins:

> My skin is as smooth
> as polished wood.
> When my mother strokes me
> she sands me
> with her hands.

Laura honed her poems on a computer; she received encouragement in that she was allowed to stay up later if she was writing on the computer. So she wrote:

> I would take sleep
> out of the world.
> I would put rings
> around my eyes
> so they never close.

Another child, a 7-year-old described in a study conducted by the British Film Institute (Sanger *et al.* 1997) showed an advanced interest in film, an awareness of issues of certification, a memory for producers, dates and styles, and an interest in the construction of special effects.

Both these children had access to their technological interests through their parents. These children are at one end of a spectrum of children's scaffolded learning and though not every child will become a little poet or film buff they exemplify the role adults can play in children's learning. By scaffolding, we mean providing the kinds of support which enable a learner to remain engaged and to think and act at a higher level than would be possible otherwise. This support would include anticipating frustrations and providing just enough help to prevent a child being over-whelmed by failure, while also encouraging the child to take appropriate risks. The adult may need to journey with the child beyond both of their current knowledge bases. The atmosphere is characterized by joint atten-tion and discussion of the enterprise, in a relaxed and culturally sensitive manner. There is a tangible spirit of enquiry (Whalley 2001).

For our research we obtained two laptop computers for an early child-hood centre. We considered they would be easy to take home, as demon-strated in the Docklands Project (Scott *et al.* 1997; Monteith 2000). We also felt that laptops were more suited to young children since they have less distance between the screen and the keyboard. Many children at keyboards in school sit with their heads tipped back, trying to see the screen when their eyes should be as near as possible and on the same level to it. With the laptops they would be naturally on the same level or even looking down. Parents could use the computers with their children as an aid to learning, bringing children and adults together in a joint enterprise. We found the computer ideal for adult–child dialogue as the screen contributes to a sense of shared ownership.

Access and achievement

The purpose of our initiative was to give access to technology in an inner-city setting. We took note of some research that supported the use of computers in raising achievement and giving children access to the tools of our society. The Docklands Project in London showed positive results with children in an area of social disadvantage, using computers in the teaching of maths and English. The findings on parental involvement were applicable to our study, however the programmed learning content was not relevant to our initiative and the children were at primary school level. The Docklands Project concluded:

> Parental involvement in changing the culture of teaching and learning in inner-city schools was an important ingredient. The project

undoubtedly contributed to its encouragement and the most successful schools were the ones which harnessed parental support most
effectively. The project team also contributed in various ways to
raising literacy standards by supporting work in the communities
from which the children came. In other words, community and
parental involvement in the schooling of inner-city children is an
important factor in raising standards of achievement.

(Scott et al. 1997: 32)

In our nursery there was already in place a literacy class for parents and
this was the vehicle for the introduction of the new computers. Hence
we built on dimensions which already existed in our early years setting.

Substantial longitudinal research in New Zealand (Carr 1998) found
that the home ownership of computers reversed achievement trends for
poorer children. The families who owned computers when their children
were younger conferred an advantage on the children in terms of later
achievement in maths and English in the early years of schooling. This
was regardless of family income; indeed, the advantages were more marked
for children from low income families. This finding contrasts with results
from research where no early information and communication technology (ICT) initiative was involved. Economic decline of inner-city areas,
and the parallel decline in children's achievement, was the subject of a
local authority report on children's achievement in the London Borough
of Ealing (Ealing Education Services 1998), an area of great ethnic and
social diversity, rather like our own. The report showed a strong association between the performance of Reception pupils (children in their first
year of schooling) and their social background. The deterministic role
of advantage was seen to increase as advantaged children migrated to
'better' schools.

Thus the possibility of making our early years setting advantageous
along the lines of the Headstart initiative in America (Hopper and Lawler
1997) also offered the opportunity of reversing those trends in which
children from socioeconomically deprived backgrounds are condemned
to decline in achievement relative to the more privileged.

In the Headstart initiative, Lawler set up projects where the children
commanded items to appear on the screen and then manipulated them.
One situation described occurs where the author's daughter plays with a
microworld programmed in LOGO by her brother and sister. There was
no way that a significant other, parent or sibling, could be absent from
this scenario. If the child wanted a 'sun' in the picture she would have to
ask for the letter string that brought it up; somebody had to give her the
string of letters which she would match to the letters on the keyboard.
Once she had learned the functions of the strings she inevitably learned
the letter strings as words in the process of making more and more
complicated worlds on the screen.

Computers in the early years setting

Another New Zealand study (Wylie and Thompson 1998) followed up and compared the progress of children from four early years settings. On most key indicators the progress made by those who had used computers at home since before the age of 5 was in advance of those who had no computer or who had recently acquired one. Quantitative analysis of children aged 6 revealed that: 'At age 5, having had a computer was an advantage for literacy but acquiring one at age 6 gave no such advantage (or any advantage was not yet measurable)' (p. 95). There were advantages too in terms of other qualities, namely curiosity and individual responsibility as well as social skills.

The introduction of the two new laptops into our early childhood setting involved as many of the interested adults as possible. One nursery teacher in the course of postgraduate study made a series of observations of young children's behaviour at the stand-alone computers already in the classrooms. These observations revealed the children's attentiveness and cognitive advances. Playing at the computer had not been 'random' time-filling, but was consistent with the learning promoted by other activities. The teacher wrote:

> Some staff feel very negative about it, that there are some children
> just sitting round watching and others stay on the computer for
> too long. But when I looked more closely, I found that lots of the
> children who were watching were learning too. P spent a long
> time watching two children pointing to the words in *Just Grandma
> and Me*, and then later I saw him matching the words on the
> screen to what he was reading with the computer. Another child
> who has Down's syndrome was ordering objects by size on
> another program, even though some staff felt he was randomly
> pressing the keys. I saw lots of children making decisions, talking
> about their choices and learning actively.

The whole staff were involved in regular discussions exploring the possibilities of using computers to foster learning dispositions, including curiosity, attentiveness and sociability.

However, the potential for computers to appear to go against the grain of an institution's approach to children's learning has been demonstrated in a report from the Westminster Children's Society Nurseries (O'Sullivan 1999). A year-long observational study of the introduction of computers into nursery settings reported that the children showed no transfer of attentiveness to other learning. The report concluded that the children 'had to have an adult with them'. Statements that 'it is easy to confuse a child's concentration with mesmerisation' were balanced by the summary advice that: 'Adults have to be involved in order for children's knowledge of the computer or another curriculum area through a program to develop. When using the computer alone children tended to play their favourite CD-games and repeat the same ability level. They rarely tried new programs or new levels of difficulty'. This implies that the nursery had started off with a mental model of the computer as tutor, a tool that required no adult initiation, reaction or response. But it also demonstrates the fact that the staff had moved on and had become aware of the role of an adult in relation to learning with the computer.

Further strictures are rehearsed in Jane Healy's (1999) book, *Failure to Connect*. In a review of the book, Haughton (1999) warns that 'Very young children who use computers are being exposed to a kind of training that may change the way their brains work and impair their ability to learn'. Some of Healy's criticisms of computer use are summarized as:

- Just because children are performing tasks that look technologically sophisticated does not mean they are learning anything important.
- Parents and teachers are often beguiled by the heady mix of fun-packed, fast-paced graphics.
- Much 'educational' software is crowded with extraneous and time-consuming effects that accomplish little beyond distracting children and distancing them from 'real' learning. Very few pieces of software 'teach' anything.

Parents with children using computers at home

In our study, we began by offering to loan the laptops to the parents in the literacy class. These parents came twice a week to the nursery for literacy support. They also worked one day a week in the nursery developing materials and learning how to develop language skills with children. The teacher went through the language of the computer and we introduced them briefly to the programs.

The parents received the computers with a mixture of worry and excitement:

I heard you can't really break them.

When you first said about taking a computer home, I thought 'Uh-oh', but it's been easy to use.

One mother described her first use of the computer:

We had the program, Speaking for Myself [Black 1997]. It is a program with Makton sign language to facilitate communication with children who have Down's syndrome. The first time we borrowed it my son was quite interested in it but he found coordinating the mouse difficult as he has poor fine motor skills. He was interested in the tunes and the pictures flashing; he knew some of the words but he needs more practice.

We had opened up possibilities. But much more was needed in terms of peripherals and availability. One parent used the CD-ROM herself when her child was sleeping, so as to get to know the computer better. Another parent said:

> Whenever I switch the computer on she doesn't want to go to bed early; she's always watching it and I find it very, very interesting and educational for her. We show her the ABC, the computer says the word and it also writes the spelling of it and that helps her. She loves moving the mouse. Whenever I show her what to do she doesn't want me to show her so I always leave her. She loves it by herself when she is doing the game Eggs and Ham.

This parent's daughter was already sufficiently familiar with the Eggs and Ham program to engage with it, supported by the program itself.

At the end of the year, one parent of a child with a specific language disorder still revealed her lack of confidence: 'He [her son] enjoyed it but he wanted to do it on his own, you know, and I was a bit scared that he could touch something and I didn't know what would happen, so after that I didn't take it home any more'. However, she planned to compensate for her own lack of skills: 'I've already decided that I'm going to do a course on computers. I've really wanted to, so that we could have a bit of time together on the computer, because when we borrow the props from the literacy room we have a really good time together, playing'.

Another parent said, 'When we first got the computer, it was "Watch out, don't do this, don't do that" but now I'm not like that because the computer's not as scary as I thought'. She also wanted 'More teaching of what I could do on it. And more teaching of what the children can do as well. I could be a novelist!'

How the computer is used at home

The parents in our study realized that they wanted skills both for themselves and for their children's sake. As Margaret Lally states: '[We] have increasingly recognised the need for children to see adults using their skills and knowledge' (Lally 1991: 134).

The New Zealand research showed that children benefited from using computers at home, but it is not clear in the report (Wylie and Thompson 1998) whether the computers had been bought for them. The children were probably using computers belonging to parents and older siblings. If so, they had a model of the computer's purpose and use as well as a model of how to care for it.

One parent in our centre had, over the course of the year, become very confident in her own computer skills:

Actually we only took it [the laptop] home once or twice; since then I've [acquired] a computer myself. We had been thinking about it for a while, because his [her son's] older brother uses computers at school and J uses computers here and as life goes on, a lot of it will be computerized. I feel that by having a computer at home you have more opportunity to be able to do things.

This parent was very aware of her children's learning. She had experienced very little schooling herself and gained her skills only when she joined the literacy group at the nursery. As a result when she commented on how her children used the computer she observed details of her son's learning, such as the identification of initial letters.

The following comment shows how family members interact in this learning; in this case they were using a commercial program, BARNEY:

To start off with at level one it will show you the letters and you have to match them. And he'll pick the letters out. It'll show you the letter, then he's got three different letters to choose from, so he matches them. Now he can actually do it without seeing the letters first so he knows some of his alphabet. He's only 4 but he knows some of his alphabet; that's a lot to do with his older brother because he'll encourage him.

Another parent's report revealed that once children became familiar with talking books they start to make choices about which page they wish to start with and whether they want to hear the story or interact with it. This family is bilingual in Punjabi and English and the son was 4 years, 6 months at the time of our study.

Mother: He listened and changed the page as well.
Interviewer: And could he read some of the words as well?
Mother: Yes, yes, repeated them, not properly but some words he repeated.
Interviewer: Which words are the ones he repeated?
Mother: Like 'mum's going to a beach'.
Interviewer: So words like 'beach'.
Mother: 'Beach' and 'tree' and 'sand'. He enjoys that story.

This early opportunity for making choices and experimenting is the experiential basis for a disposition to curiosity and experimentation. This child also used the computer at home with his brothers and cousins in ways that were conditioned by their more adult expectations of the technology. The family believed the computer was a tool for introducing the child to learning tasks: they used it to give him an advantage.

Interviewer: What did W do with it?
Mother: Read the story and typewriter as well. Write name and some words in English like 'book' and write a letter as well.

Interviewer: So he knows his letters and when he got the computer he knew what the letters were on the computer?

Mother: He knows alphabetic, A to Z so he knows how to spell little words like 'school' so like typewriter he print those words. I tell him like this when the typewriter is on, spell him 'look', spell him 'book', little bit name of sisters, name of M, name of father, he knows to spell.

Parental styles

Monteith (2000: 81) says that 'parents tend to follow the model of learning provided by the school' but gives the example: 'sometimes, as a mother, she is probably also remembering her own experiences of school' and intervening with her child in that style, as in our example above. Often parents get caught between their own experiences and memories of school and the style promoted by their children's school. When in doubt they fall back on memories of being taught. Katz (1982) says that parental involvement programmes should offer parents: 'insights and various kinds of information whilst encouraging them to accept only what makes sense to them and what is consistent with their own preferences.' Sandra Jowett (Jowett and Baginsky 1991: 42) exemplifies the danger of not making this meeting of minds. She quotes a parent as saying: 'I've learnt that I've been teaching Hugh wrong for years, teaching him the wrong way to do his reading and all sorts. I've just been told it's completely wrong. He's got to do it all over again'.

One mother in our initiative achieved a successful synthesis using the computer with her 4-year-old who has a muscle weakness and poor coordination. She was confident enough to use the programs in a playful way and hence achieved a scaffolding that was relaxed:

> We played 'Dress Teddy' and instead of putting them [items of clothing] in the right places I put them in the wrong places and J said, 'No, that's not right, silly Mummy' and he put it in the right place and I thought, 'That game has encouraged him' because J's poor coordination with his pen and paper skills . . . and for J to use the computer and to dress Teddy for himself is quite difficult for him because his concentration is not very good as well so for him to, sort of, spend ten minutes on something like that is really good.

The software

The two most frequently used programs on the laptops were a painting program and CD-ROM talking books. Children with Down's syndrome had an additional specialist program called Black. There was also a language program intended for young children and those with special needs. This program, ALEX, has an iconic face which can be changed to that of a boy or girl, black or white. The character can do many things like laughing, whistling or pulling faces. It is possible for early readers to use this program through the use of picture symbols. For the parents it demonstrated the responsiveness of the computer and because the program also has the possibility of clicking on words or of keying in words, many of the second language parents used it as much for their own sake as for their children's.

An observer gave one example of ALEX's iconic attraction when the computer was in the room of the youngest children, aged 6 months to 2 years, 6 months:

> Computers encourage joint attention . . . Children as young as
> 11 months were being drawn into the ALEX program. One child
> turned excitedly to his mother and made a series of noises and
> gestured in response to ALEX's noise and expression. His mother
> looked at him, smiled, looked back to the computer and pressed
> a button again. They both watched ALEX intently. This type of
> episode of joint attention and communication is the high-calorie
> supplement to children's developing thinking, communication and
> sense of well-being as they establish their experience of the world.

Painting programs and the learning dispositions

The language of 'learning dispositions' (Meade 1995; Cullen 1998) enables early years teachers to analyse children's learning in terms of their abilities rather than in terms of a universal theory of learning. Paint programs give children another way of exploring their own creativity and expressing these dispositions or intelligences. A paint program is 'passive' software as defined by Finlayson and Cooke (2000: 108): 'In passive usage the computer liberates the user by making the arrangement of tasks much easier and quicker to perform without adding any other contribution or dimension to the task other than a constraining framework . . . it reflects the users' ideas back to them for their consideration, and in such a way can aid the creative thinking process'. They further point out the opportunities for reflectiveness when children are supported in a meaningful activity. Using the computer, children have direct control. When they click on the paintbrush icon in a painting program, they always get the paintbrush. They always get yellow when they click on the yellow box. Young children do not have such a direct, reliable and predictable sensation of control very often. Matthews (1999: 60) writes:

It is often claimed that very young children cannot cope with many choices between, for instance, a range of different colours. Hence, advice is often given to teachers to limit the range of different colours. Our studies of children's selection and use from a palette of several hundred colours on the computer screen seriously challenges such assertions, showing that such ideas are not statements about a universal 'stage' of development but rather effects which are highly media dependent . . . hundreds of colours can be arranged very easily on the computer screen. After a very short time, our sample of children were already showing abilities to select from these.

The painting programs we used also had shapes which provided many starting points for talking about where objects were in relation to others and the relative sizes of objects, quantities, shapes and properties. Children's early experience of these key mathematical concepts while using the computer may be reflected later in their awareness and demonstration of mathematical language.

Painting programs also allow provisional work. Children can try out a paint effect and then click the 'undo' icon if they dislike it. This encourages children to think about what effect they want in an abstract way, and it encourages thinking around the difficult idea of reversibility. Computers in this sense encourage children to take risks, as reflected by the higher scores computer-using 5-year-olds achieved later on at school for 'invented spelling' in the Competent Children Project (Wylie and Thompson 1998).

In paint programs children can make a design, click to shrink it and then duplicate it to create a wallpaper effect. This would be extremely complicated to do in any other way. So young children can take responsibility for their own learning in complex areas like reading or creating intricate and ordered patterns. This type of early experience on the computer may be reflected in the higher scores children achieved for 'curiosity and individual responsibility' in the Competent Children Project.

With paint programs, children make choices and take risks. Once they are familiar with the basic workings of a program, many users will start to experiment even when the outcomes are unclear. Children painting will start clicking on different icons to 'see what happens'. This empowers the 'reflectiveness' mentioned by Finlayson and Cooke (2000).

Analysis of the records of children's talk as they used computers at the nursery revealed that they were using types of talk which challenge and extend children's thinking. These kinds of talk have been described as 'social modes of thinking' (Wegerif and Mercer 1997: 51). The prevalence of collaborative talk in our observational accounts might account for the Competent Children Project's finding that early use of computers enhances children's 'curiosity, communication and social skills'.

Talking books

Denise Mangat studied the children's use of talking books in our nursery setting: 'Talking Books allow young children to find out – as many times as they want – exactly what each word "says". You just click on the word and the computer reads it for you' (Mangat 1999). The children's early literacy was assessed using the Sheffield Early Literacy Development Profile (Nutbrown 1997). This showed that the children had an awareness of environmental print but less book knowledge. After this initial assessment the children were offered regular opportunities to use talking books freely, usually with an adult present. The children were in pairs and, as often happened with the computer, other children would gather round and join in or just observe.

The children were observed using a familiar CD-ROM book which they had been using in class. Mangat discussed with them the features of the book in reading terms to elicit their understanding of the reading process and make it explicit. The children made predictions about the story as well as looking at the words on the screen page and were shown how to highlight individual words. As Jane Medwell (1995: 5) states: 'Most importantly the child can begin to develop a concept of word . . . The child who sees words highlighted as they are read can begin to understand the role of spaces'.

The children discussed individual pages and retold the story to each other, or reminded each other of episodes they enjoyed: 'Look, Denise, have you seen this? He's scared, see . . . I like this page, I've seen it loads of times. Look what happens here – the hot dog falls, see . . . What does it say? Does it say goodbye? [at the end]'. Then the children were introduced to an unknown CD-ROM book and the researcher looked for evidence to see if they had transferred their understanding of story from their previous experiences to this new one. This tested their ICT learning – for example, clicking on symbols for turning pages (this is identified with and replaces a known physical action) or accessing help, highlighting words to hear them spoken (this replaces social behaviour, asking for help from the teacher or peers).

Subsequent assessment established whether the children's knowledge of conventional books had been informed by the use of this computer software – whether there had been a transfer of learning. An improvement was recorded in all the post-intervention scores, indicating a transfer of skills from the talking book to the conventional book.

Learning gains increased in awareness of text, its functions and structure and in the understanding of book conventions. One of the main arguments put forward by educators opposed to using talking books to support reading development is that the animations and interactive features take the focus away from the text and structure of the story: 'Much "educational software" is crowded with extraneous and time-consuming effects that accomplish little beyond distracting from real learning' (Haughton 1999). In Mangat's study, although the children were acutely aware of and enjoyed the interactive features of talking books, they also showed consciousness of the text. This seems to be a function of age and of the children's purposes in approaching the text. For the younger children the focus was on the effects and the 'story' largely told through the graphics. The older children looked more towards the text and clicked on words. Even without any adult intervention, the older children (4 plus) were aware of the role of the text within the story: K is trying to find words; he looks for 'grandma' and locates it after three tries. This was not so apparent for the less experienced children (3-year-olds) although they still observed the purpose of text and commented on it in relation to the title, author and end.

The children referred to particular pages and had a degree of understanding about where they were in the story. They actively made suggestions such as 'Let's turn the page' and qualitative decisions about the contents of the pages, choosing to revisit some in order to retrieve more knowledge, information or enjoyment. Turn-taking was on some occasions organized between the children in their pairs: 'You have a go and then so will I' but this occurred when it was an equal partnership. When one participant had missed a session or another friend had been drawn in to be shown what had been learned the child initiating the exchange had to be persuaded by the teacher to relinquish control of the mouse: G wants to have control and is reluctant to let M take a turn. When M has the mouse G tells her to click on objects and shows her how when she has difficulty. The result of this was sometimes to silence the less experienced participant. This example was balanced by another pair where the more experienced child found a compatible partner: S is constantly discussing what he is doing, for example, 'When I click here, this happens, see?' and he and M decide between them on where they want to look. 'Shall I click on this one?' 'No, do this one.'

Even less experienced children, who had previously appeared to find concentrating during story sessions difficult, were able to immerse themselves in the talking stories for significant periods of time. Medwell (1996) found evidence to suggest that using talking books improved children's reading by supporting their understanding of the way stories work and the structure of text. The combination of text, sound and graphics appears to motivate young children to acquire early literacy skills. This may be especially beneficial for encouraging some boys with their reading. Medwell's research showed that boys achieved greater benefits than girls did when using talking books.

Conclusion

The first debate about introducing computers to the nursery is about children's learning and how we establish an understanding of what learning has taken place. There is a complementarity in addressing the process of learning through an observation of learning dispositions while focusing on subject knowledge. For example, in the literacy study we asked 'What did the children learn about books?' Early childhood learning is not just about processes, as those processes operate in the context of knowledge acquisition – in this case, knowledge of story and book conventions, of letters and words. Furthermore, our observations show the children's ability to learn in parallel: they were simultaneously learning with and about the technology as well as about books.

We have asserted the importance of joint attention for the learning of children and for the establishment of a disposition to learn. Our observations of young children indicated that after a concentrated involvement with a 'significant other' they continued to explore in a way that demonstrated ludic and cognitive control. The computer was therefore facilitating another style of joint attention: a child alone at the computer is not 'solitary', the programmer is there too. As Mercer (1993: 38) states, when pupils use a computer program they are interacting with a 'hidden teacher', namely the program designer. When children have understood the process or plan represented in a program they can work and play, scaffolded by the programmer's intentions. This play is a transitional stage to completely autonomous learning. The computer does not act as a tutor or teacher, but it can continue to support the child when the adult withdraws. This independent learning gives the sense of control which observers identify as characteristic of children's behaviour at the computer. For young children this transitional support is especially helpful.

The other issue raised by our work in the early years setting was that of access. First, if they confer advantage, all parents would want access to computers for their children. Toni Downes (2000: 63) discusses this in relation to the Australian situation: 'In the more affluent communities in this study about 85 per cent of the children in the school had access to a computer in their home, while in the least affluent schools less than 20 per cent of children did'. Figures for England show a similar divide (Scales 1999). By providing the laptops on loan our nursery went some way towards making up for disadvantages in our community, and this provision, in some cases, provided the impetus for parents to buy their own computers. Second, parents and children require access to programs and how to the them. This requires vision ('I could be a novelist!') and plenty of time to play. Suitable programs can encourage the parallel development of children's and parents' literacy skills – skills which the computer makes absolutely indispensable.

Understanding children's programs and using computers for their own purposes will facilitate for our parents their full involvement in what technology can offer. They will be confident models for their own children. It may have been thought that a new generation could be inducted into the 'technological revolution' without reference to their parents, but we have found that a more powerful model of learning is one in which there are intergenerational partners.

Acknowledgement

The authors thank the staff at Woodlands Park Nursery Centre, the children and their parents for their help. Thanks also to Carole Warden, head of the centre, for her support. The project was established as part of ongoing parent–partnership initiatives, with laptops provided by Research Machines.

References

Baker, K. (1993) *The Turbulent Years*. London: Faber & Faber.

Black, B. (1997) Speaking for Myself. Software produced by Inclusive Technology, designed in collaboration with the Down's Syndrome Educational Trust and the Down's Syndrome Association.

Broberg, A.G., Wessels, H., Lamb, M.E. and Hwang, C-P. (1997) Effects of day care on the development of cognitive abilities in 8-year-olds: a longitudinal study, *Developmental Psychology*, 33(1): 62–9.

Carr, M. (1998) *Assessing Children's Experiences in Early Childhood: Final Report to the Ministry of Education*. Wellington: Ministry of Education.

Cullen, J. (1998) Promoting Positive Partnerships. Keynote address to the Early Childhood Development Unit. www.ecd.govt.nz/where/research/4.2.2.html (accessed Feb. 2001).

Downes, T. (2000) Using the computer at home, in M. Monteith (ed.) *IT for Learning Enhancement*. Bristol: Intellect.

Ealing Education Services (1998) *Ealing Education Services Report*. Ealing: Ealing Education Services.

Finlayson, H. and Cooke, D. (2000) The value of passive software in young children's collaborative work, in M. Monteith (ed.) *IT for learning Enhancement*. Bristol: Intellect.

Haughton, E. (1999) Look what they're done to my brain, Ma, *Independent*, 3 June.

Healy, J.M. (1999) *Failure to Connect*. London: Simon & Schuster.

Hopper, M. and Lawler, R.W. (1997) Headstart progress report, in R.W. Lawler (ed.) *Learning with Computers*. Bristol: Intellect.

Jowett, S. and Baginsky, M. (1991) *Building Bridges: Parental Involvement in Schools*. London: NFER-Nelson.

Katz, L. (1982) Contemporary perspectives on the roles of mothers and teachers, *Australian Journal of Early Childhood*, 7(1): 4–15.

Lally, M. (1991) *The Nursery Teacher in Action*. London: Paul Chapman.

Mangat, D. (1999) Using CD-ROM talking books with nursery children. Dissertation submitted for Honours degree, University of North London.

Matthews, J. (1999) *The Art of Childhood and Adolescence: the Construction of Meaning*. London: Falmer Press.

Meade, A. (1995) *Thinking Children*. Wellington: NZCER.

Medwell, J. (1995) Talking Books for Teaching Reading, *Microscope*, 46.

Medwell, J. (1996) Talking books and reading, *Reading*, 30(1): 41–6.

Mercer, N. (1993) Computer based activities in classroom contexts, in P. Scrimshaw (ed.) *Language, Classrooms and Computers*. London: Routledge.

Monteith, M. (2000) The place of learning, in M. Monteith (ed.) *IT for Learning Enhancement*, 2nd edn. Bristol: Intellect.

Nutbrown, C. (1997) *Recognising Early Literacy Development*. London: Paul Chapman.

O'Sullivan, J. (1999) Screen watch, *Nursery World*, March: 15.

Rattner, H.H. and Stettner, L.J. (1991) Thinking and feeling: putting Humpty Dumpty together again, *Merrill-Palmer Quarterly*, 37(1): 1–26.

Sanger, J., Wilson, J., Davies, B. and Whittaker, R. (1997) *Young Children, Videos and Computer Games*. London: Falmer Press.

Scales, J. (1999) Home PCs delete hope for poorest, *Times Educational Supplement*, 22 January.

Scott, D., Hurry, J., Hey, V. and Smith, M. (1997) Developing literacy in inner-city schools, *English in Education*, 32(2).

Wegerif, R. and Mercer, N. (1997) A dialogical framework for researching peer talk, in R. Wegerif and P. Scrimshaw (eds) *Computers and Talk in the Primary Classroom*. Clevedon, OH: Multilingual Matters.

Whalley, M. and the Pen Green Centre Team (2001) *Involving Parents in their Children's Learning*. London: Paul Chapman Publishing Limited.

Wylie, C. and Thompson, J. (1998) *Competent Children at 6: Families, Early Education and Schools*. Wellington: NZCER.

5

TALKING SOLUTIONS: THE ROLE OF ORACY IN THE EFFECTIVE USE OF ICT

Rupert Wegerif and
Lyn Dawes

Introduction

The importance that teachers place on speaking and listening does not arise from any emphasis given to oracy by the National Curriculum. On the contrary the curriculum is primarily built around developing the skills required for reading and writing. But talk is crucial; it is the principal medium through which teaching and learning goes on during much of a child's time in school. Teachers may not teach speaking and listening skills directly, but the way that they value talk is indicated by the range of teaching strategies in which talk is put to use in classrooms. Teachers commonly encourage their pupils to discuss their ideas, to explain their work, to describe events and opinions, to communicate with one another, with other adults and with a wide range of audiences through talk.

Recently the integration of computers into classrooms has created the requirement that pupils develop a range of new skills; new sorts of technological literacy. In classroom contexts, literacy – including its crucial speaking and listening component, and including use of the tools offered by technology – has the purpose of enabling people to communicate in order to achieve understanding and to get things done. Information and communication technology (ICT) offers invaluable facilities for communication. Effective use of ICT – with an emphasis on the C for 'communication' – can allow *learning dialogues* between pupils working in proximity or at a distance. The importance of dialogue in education is that such interaction allows learners to construct knowledge together (Mercer 1995; Wells 1999). We can combine this idea, that of the co-construction of knowledge by learners through dialogue, with an understanding of *learning as community joining* put forward by Lave and Wenger (1991). Lave and Wenger looked at communities of practice in which knowledge is held within the community (such as tailors or midwives) and suggested that for 'newcomers', learning is a process of becoming part of the community through dialogue with its members. Even the 'old timers' in a community can continue to learn; through talk, knowledge is made explicit and understanding is created. Specialized ways of using words are generated and reinforced, and used in contexts which clarify their meaning. Learning in classrooms involves this social change towards becoming an 'insider' in the discourse of the educated community. Education thus provides access to opportunities in the larger society.

In classrooms, learning commonly occurs through interaction, and learning to do things better in any area requires modelling, support and feedback from peers and the more experienced members of the community (Rogoff 1990). When learning new ways with words – essential to literacy – this modelling, support and feedback often takes place through dialogue (Mercer 1995). Perhaps the essential skill in moving into any community of practice, such as that of ICT use in education, is learning how to talk to others in such a way that shared understanding is achieved. This is true whether in dialogue with others face to face or via a videoconference or email debate.

In this chapter, we focus on the tools of speaking and listening which can help us to understand and work towards solving some problems encountered by teachers and learners working with ICT in the classroom. We offer some findings from our classroom-based research into speaking and listening. In doing so we emphasize the profound importance of developing oracy as a basis for enhancing learning across the curriculum. We suggest that a focus on the direct teaching and learning of speaking and listening skills may be of particular importance for pupils using new technology.

Some problems reported by teachers

The provision of multimedia computers in schools has led to children spending more time on activities with computers. Our experience as researchers investigating ICT use in schools suggests that not all that time is always well spent. In this section we examine some problems that teachers encounter when ICT is used to support delivery of the curriculum.

We are not concerned here with such issues as adequate resourcing and technical support. Instead we consider what happens in classrooms once the hardware infrastructure is in place, electronic connections available and the use of ICT is integrated into the timetabled school week. The evidence is based on several studies of ICT use in classrooms undertaken by the authors and their colleagues over the last few years (Wegerif *et al.* 1995; Wegerif and Scrimshaw 1997; Dawes 2000). The quotations used are taken from recent extensive interviews with ICT coordinators and classroom teachers as part of an in-depth study of responses to the UK government's National Grid for Learning initiatives. These interviews were undertaken in secondary, middle and first schools in the town of Milton Keynes. Teachers in the study schools acquired multimedia computers under the National Grid for Learning Standards funding, or were in schools where computer suites had been established. All had received training in the skills required to operate these machines. As well as talking to teachers about their use of ICT, the researchers spent many hours in classrooms working with teachers.

Some problems observed and reported by teachers were:

- group work that does not work;
- unfocused Internet searches;
- information without understanding;
- inappropriate uses of email.

We will describe each of these problems in turn before considering how a focus on talk may help to solve them.

Group work that does not work

Group work or pair work around computers is prevalent in primary schools and is a common practice in most secondary schools. Teachers and ICT managers see this as an efficient use of a still relatively scarce resource, and teachers believe that group work is good for the development of communication skills. Our recent observations of group work around computers in classrooms confirm the findings we, along with colleagues, reported some years ago after an extensive study of talk around computers in schools (Mercer 1993; Wegerif and Scrimshaw 1997; Wegerif and Dawes 1998). Observation showed then and shows now that the quality of communication within pairs and small groups working at computers is often poor. This is a judgement made both by the researchers and by teachers who were shown video recordings made during group work sessions. The problems that we have seen include:

- the most assertive or confident person making all the decisions;
- members of the group denigrating or ridiculing one another's ideas (or one another);

- members of the group listening but never contributing;
- the group disagreeing with each other and unable to resolve the conflict;
- those with home computers becoming impatient with the slowness of others and taking control of the keyboard/mouse;
- disputes about seating arrangements, or who touched the hardware, as the main topics for discussion;
- informal, 'playground' talk used with the computer which was seen as primarily a games machine;
- low group confidence with corresponding low quality of work;
- boys and girls adopting stereotypical gender roles;
- members of the group blaming one another when things did not go the way they planned;
- individuals claiming the entire credit for successful work;
- individuals deciding to leave the group.

Since so much ICT work of all types is undertaken in groups or pairs, these problems with collaboration can be expected to have a considerable effect on the general quality of learning in ICT activities.

Unfocused Internet searches

The teachers interviewed in our study saw the Internet as a potentially marvellous educational resource but they found that asking children to conduct searches for information using the Internet led to problems. Teachers reported that the initial aim of a web search could easily be forgotten because of distracting links. Children were reported as sometimes lacking a sense of what was and what was not relevant, and were easily impressed by even the most obliquely connected material.

Teachers also noted that when left to themselves, even with clear guidance, children frequently used the Internet for leisure pursuits. They speculated that this reflected home use: 'They think they can do what they want to do here like at home, *Simpsons* web page, *EastEnders* web page – things like that'. This tendency to move away from the task was partly the result of the frustrating experience of unproductive searches.

Information without understanding

Children were frequently reported to confuse the finding and printing of information from the web with acquiring knowledge or developing an understanding of the topic. As one teacher said: 'You might find them highlighting the right area, but, you know, you still get a spiel. Some of them have wodges of paper they've printed off. They have no idea what it says'.

There were many concerns expressed about the educational value of web searches. A teacher voiced this concern as a question: 'You could keep students occupied for hours searching the Internet, but is that a valid educational use of time?'

Inappropriate uses of email

Email provides many opportunities to communicate with and learn from others all over the world. Left to work at computers, children may not make the best use of this technology. Teachers expressed frustration with what they saw as their pupils' tendency to go off task:

> They email their mums and dads at work, anyone – they email their friends, you know, 'Hi, Holly I'm sat next to you . . .'

> When I looked at what was happening it was all rubbish. No, about 10 percent was work related, the rest was having a look round. Socializing. Sending each other messages. I found one group, one boy sat next to another, and they were sending each other messages. That's really – as I said to them – that's really sad, you've got to do that rather than just talk. And they were sixth formers, and they both had no time to spare.

Some possible solutions

We have been working for some years now with several middle schools in Milton Keynes to promote effective talk. In the talk-based classrooms of the teachers we work with, ground rules for talking together are established as a basis for all group work. Curriculum areas are approached in a collaborative way. Working with teachers and observing their classrooms has shown us how an explicit focus on developing talk, or oracy, as a medium for shared enquiry can help teachers improve small group work with computers and integrate computer-based activities into the larger teaching and learning process. The following suggestions for good practice are based on these observations.

To outline our suggested 'talking solutions' we will return to each of the four main areas where problems with ICT were experienced:

- group work;
- Internet searches;
- converting information into understanding;
- use of email.

Group work that really does work

In response to the evidence that much group work around computers was of poor quality we worked with teachers to devise lessons to teach children how to work more effectively together. We evaluated the impact of the lessons on group work by using transcripts of talk and also by measuring how well groups solved problems together. The results showed that in classrooms where teachers taught the children the value of ground rules for talk, group work was found to be visibly and measurably improved. It was improved because more groups of children more of the time used language as a tool for building knowledge together.

The intervention programme was based on a characterization of the kind of talk which classroom research indicated was effective for collaborative learning in small groups. Following Barnes (1976) and Mercer (1995) we called this 'exploratory talk'. We developed a teaching programme based around the following characteristic ground rules of exploratory talk:

- all relevant information is shared;
- the group seeks to reach agreement;
- the group takes responsibility for decisions;
- reasons are expected;
- challenges are accepted;
- alternatives are discussed before a decision is taken;
- all in the group are encouraged to speak by other group members.

A full description of our approach to teaching thinking together through talk is now available (Dawes *et al.* 2000). The basic teaching programme, which consists of a series of ten lessons, each designed to last for about one hour, focuses on one or more of the ground rules in each lesson. The development of these lessons was influenced by the work of the National Oracy Project (Norman 1992). Earlier lessons focus on skills such as listening, sharing information and cooperating, while later lessons for example encourage critical argument for and against different cases. The children are given opportunities to practise discussing alternative ideas, giving and asking for reasons and ensuring that all members of the group are invited to contribute. Many of the teachers who worked with us devised further lessons, applying the same approach to different areas of the curriculum.

A key part of the programme is that the children are encouraged, through teacher-led discussion, to create and decide upon their own set of ground rules for talking. The rules are then displayed prominently in the classroom and referred to in cases of uncertainty or dispute. In each class these rules are uniquely phrased, but they nonetheless always show considerable overlap with our list of the ground rules of exploratory talk given above. These rules are used to give a structure for collaborative group work. So, prior to work around the computer, the teacher reminds the children that they have agreed to stick to their class 'talking rules' and the children remind one another of the rules before beginning their shared task. The teacher also reminds the children that engaging in high quality talk is just as much an aim for their work together as is completing the ICT-based task.

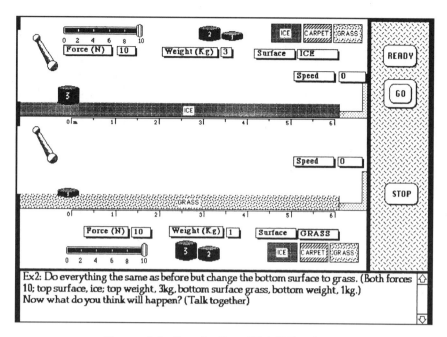

Figure 5.1 Exercise 2 on 'TRACKS' software

Evidence supports the observation made by some of the teachers quoted earlier that children's home use of computers for their own purposes is largely confined to game playing (Selwyn 1998). This may reinforce pupils' perceptions that computer work is competitive – that the aim is either to play against the machine or against each other. Our observations of primary-age children revealed such problems particularly in their use of simulation software. Without the explicit focus on oracy that we are recommending, they tended to make changes and run simulations as if playing a rapid video game, without planning their responses and strategies or discussing the meaning of their findings. To remedy this, it is important that children understand that there are high expectations about how they work together on computers in school time. Clarifying the purpose of their collaboration, and the aims of their talk together, aids such understanding.

Our evaluation of the programme, which included quantitative measures, showed that explicitly teaching ground rules for talking improved the quality of group work around computers (Wegerif *et al.* 1998). Below is an illustration of emerging talk competence that we found in children who had undertaken the talk lessons. This is an example of talk around a science simulation based on the topic of friction, which we called TRACKS (see Figures 5.1 and 5.2). This software was specifically

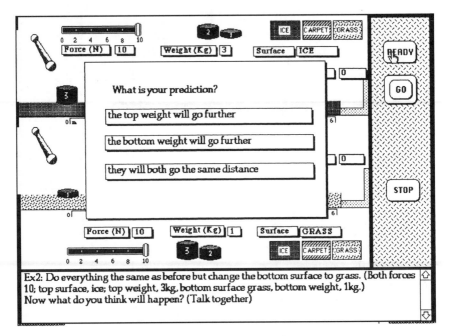

Figure 5.2 Prompt for predictions

designed to work with the talking lessons. One of its unique features is that it prompts the children to talk together about their predictions and their observations. We found that children who had not received talk training ignored these prompts, while those who had agreed on ground rules with their classmates took the opportunity to put them into practice.

In the following transcript, two 9-year-old girls who have had talk training undertake Exercise 2 in TRACKS. This involves comparing the frictional effects on the movement of weights ('pucks') sliding on different surfaces, when struck by a force. The girls are asked by the computer to set the top surface to ice and the bottom to grass and to set the top puck weight to 3kg and the bottom puck weight to 1kg. Both push forces are set to 10 newtons. The computer screen shows a multiple-choice question asking the girls to predict which puck will 'go further' and giving them three possible answers: the top puck, the bottom puck or both the same. (You might like to make your own prediction before reading the transcript!). As you read this transcript, see if you can identify examples of the children putting their ground rules for talk into practice.

Cindy [*reads*]: 'What is your prediction? Top one will go further, bottom one will go further, they will both go the same distance?' What do you think?

Rachel: I think . . . actually this is a bit different . . . I think it might be that one. No I don't. I think the bottom one will still go further.

Cindy: No. I think it's 'they will both go the same distance'.

Rachel: I don't because that's – actually I think that one might go a bit further 'cos this is grass and we tested grass out earlier, um, with the kilogram weight with, um . . .

Cindy: Yeh, I know, but that's lighter isn't it?

Rachel: I know. I still think that.

Cindy: Why?

Rachel: I think the bottom one will go further because it's lighter and grass isn't as bad as the carpet is it? So they're going to have a really smooth one, a middle one and . . .

Cindy: I think they will both go the same distance because that's three kilograms, yes – this is ice – that's grass and that one . . .

Rachel: Yes, but it's ten newton.

Cindy: I know, but they've both got 10 newtons.

Rachel: Yeh, but this one's lighter.

Rachel: Oh, I . . .

Cindy: And that one's grass and that one's ice.

Rachel: I'm sticking with my one.

Cindy: Oh, come on!

   [*Both laugh.*]

Cindy: We're never going to agree then.

Rachel: Oh, OK . . . I still think that but I think that that could actually work if that one is right . . . but I still think that one.

Cindy: So shall we go for the bottom one? Do you agree?

Rachel: Yes.

Cindy [*clicks*]: Go.

Rachel: It might be wrong [*laughs*].

Cindy: I'm right.

Rachel: You're wrong.

   [*The puck on ice starts more slowly than the one on grass but maintains the same speed, while the puck on grass slows down so that the ice puck overtakes.*]

Cindy: I'm wrong, I'm wrong, I'm wrong! Wrong, wrong, wrong!

Rachel: You're wrong, wrong, wrong! Sing a little song about wrong!

Cindy: We're both wrong.

Rachel: No, you are wrong.

   [*Computer dialogue box asks if their prediction was right or wrong and then 'Why do you think that was?'*]

Cindy: OK, why do you think that was?

Rachel: I think that was because you persuaded me to go for the wrong answer.

Cindy: Yours was wrong as well!
Cindy: 'Cos its ice, yeh?
Rachel: Yeh.
Cindy: And the bottom one is grass.

Comment

Cindy thought that both pucks would travel the same distance but Rachel thought that the puck on grass would go further. After discussion Rachel agreed to accept Cindy's suggestion. This combination of weights, surfaces and forces meant that the puck on grass started off faster than the puck on ice because it was lighter, but then the higher coefficient of friction on the grass surface had the effect of slowing the puck to a standstill. Meanwhile the heavier top puck continued to glide along with almost no loss of speed because of the low coefficient of friction for ice. The girls acted as if they were backing different horses at a race. Cindy was excited at first because the bottom puck started faster, but then as the puck slowed down and was overtaken by the top puck Rachel tells her she is wrong.

This exercise provides a motivating context for these pupils to discuss the effects of different surfaces on movement, and to make explicit the idea that the smoother the surface the less friction there will be. Pre- and post-test questions indicated that they understood this concept better after working together with the software. A number of features in the talk indicate the influence of the ground rules for exploratory talk which they had been taught: the desire to reach agreement, the asking of 'why' questions and the expectations of reasons. At the same time there is an attempt at the end to refuse joint responsibility which contradicts one of the ground rules. However these children are learners, not just of physics, but of exploratory talk as a means of negotiating ideas with one another.

Reports on ICT use in schools often comment on the power of computers to hold children's attention. We can see this motivating power in this illustration as Cindy and Rachel follow the race of the two pucks. However, fascination does not always translate into learning outcomes. The most effective learning occurs when a group of children are motivated by the interactivity of the computer program, but are able at times to sit back from the computer screen and consider issues together before returning to the computer to press the 'enter' key or click on the mouse (Wegerif *et al.* 1998). Here we achieved this 'sitting back and thinking' effect through the explicit teaching of ground rules for talk, reminding the children of these ground rules before they sat down at the computer, and by using the specially designed software with its talk prompts.

Supportive software

Software design is important. The TRACKS software was specially designed to support discussion. However, with the teaching of ground rules combined with the provision of appropriate supporting material such as worksheets, other software can be used to similar effect (Higgins 2000). We have found that key factors of computer software can support learning through talk.

The most crucial questions to consider when selecting software are:

- Is useful evidence for rational decision making displayed on screen? (Groups require information on which to talk together and base decisions.)
- Are problems sufficiently complex; do choices have 'important' consequences? (Not all problems lead to collaboration, some simply boost the ego of the child who is quick enough or knowledgeable enough to provide the answer.)
- Are there multiple-choice options to facilitate response? (Typing tends to slow down children who have not developed keyboarding skills. Slow typing may create tension within the group.)
- Does the program discourage turn taking? (Turn taking can lead to competitive game playing between children, who alternate turns and attempt to 'win' rather than to understand.)

Focusing Internet searches

The second problem that we observed in classrooms and that teachers reported was that of unfocused searches on the Internet and via hypertexts. The Internet gives access to so much information and so many alternatives that children can be overwhelmed. Working and reasoning together as a group can provide the support needed. An effective search of the Internet is essentially a reasoning exercise in which the searcher or group is faced with choices and asked to make decisions about the best way to go on the available evidence. The distracted, unfocused and poorly prioritized searches reported by teachers are often a product of the difficulties children encounter when asked to work as a group. When we evaluated why searches of the Internet were going astray we found that this was largely due to one or other of the problems of group work we noted earlier. Children were not reasoning about their searching decisions, and very little group thinking was taking place, resulting in confusion, distraction or information overload.

One of the issues here, as Cox (1999: 19) notes, may be that teachers have been encouraged to see their role in working with computers as different from, and less directive than, their normal teaching. The role of the teacher when ICT is integrated into classrooms is often described as that of 'facilitator'. However, as noted in *Connecting Schools, Networking People* (BECTA 1998: 56) 'the potential for enhancing learning drops away steeply' when children and computers are left to their own devices. The critical role of the teacher when the tools of ICT are used remains that of 'defining the boundaries' as Walker (1998: 61) puts it. Direct teacher involvement in the learner–subject–ICT interaction remains the most effective means of realizing the potential of both the technology and the child. We argue that in the talk-focused classroom children who are given explicit guidance about what is expected of them will have access to both information and the means to make meaning from it. Using ICT, children *can* be left to learn for themselves – but with peer support and the structure of the ground rules to enable joint construction of meaning. The crucial task for the teacher is to integrate the talk around the computer with the larger ongoing conversations of the classroom. By this process children working at the computer are still held within the ties and motivating force of a relationship with the teacher and with the class.

Converting information into understanding

Teacher reports that pupils use the Internet to collect information without understanding it echo the more universal complaint raised by T.S. Eliot ([1934] 1986) about the general tendencies of our modern age:

Where is the Life we have lost in living?
Where is the wisdom we have lost in knowledge?
Where is the knowledge we have lost in information?

As Gordon Wells argues (1999: 89), knowledge is not to be found in things or texts but in the activity of understanding. People do not just understand things in a vacuum, they seek to understand things for socially defined purposes as part of ongoing dialogues and relationships. To be converted from information into real understanding, what is found on the Internet needs to be brought into dialogues and integrated into the larger dialogue which is the construction of shared understanding in the classroom.

We have found that a three-part structure to lessons, moving from whole-class work to small group work around computers and then back to whole-class work, is a good way of integrating work with computers into the curriculum. With this structure the teacher can set up issues and aims at the beginning and then return to these in a whole-group plenary session at the end to explore what pupils have learned and ensure that the lesson aims have been achieved. Through this process pupils should become aware that their talk together at the computer, or communication with others through the computer, can make an important contribution to their learning. It is important that talking and thinking are included in the aims given to the class for each activity so that the class knows that discussing issues, ideas and decisions is not an optional extra but a crucial part of what they are meant to be doing. Of course for this to work it is important that clear ground rules for how groups should talk together have already been established in the classroom. In group discussions using the ground rules for exploratory talk outlined above, pupils are prompted to explain, justify and understand and so are led to take possession of ideas and concepts which otherwise may have passed them by. In Internet searches the key question students need to be led to ask each other in different forms is, 'How does this information help with our shared purpose?'

Learning to learn with others using email

Just as the effective use of talk requires explicit ground rules so does the effective use of email and electronic conferencing. Understanding use of email on the model of developing talk as a medium for learning can provide an educational framework for using email links more effectively.

Although teaching ground rules for talking together face to face is an important preliminary to moving into collaborative learning over the Internet, these rules cannot simply be transferred to the new communication medium. As we described, our 'talking lessons' began with lessons to build up trust and to share points of view. In the new context of dialogues over the Internet this ground work for effective communication needs to be revisited using the new medium. An example of an initial 'trust' type exercise to build up a relationship between two classes anywhere in the world, especially for younger children, is for each class to send 'class representatives' or mascots to one another. The purpose of the class representative (usually a toy animal) is to help give the two classes a shared focus and theme for their communications. The toy can be taken on class outings, which can then be described to the partner class. It can be given a 'voice' of its own in email communications. It can go to visit individual homes and say what happened there. It can report on the weather or seasonal festivals. It might even get homesick. It can support effective group talk. At the end of the agreed project time, class representatives are sent home (see the European SchoolNet website at http://www.eun.org/).

There are many examples of exercises sharing points of view over the Internet, from sharing data on the weather to sharing opinions about global current affairs, or presenting local cultural and geographical information for discussion with others (Roerden 1997; Walker 1998; Warschauer 1999). All of these exercises are about expanding the community of enquiry established in one classroom to other classrooms around the world. Once shared ground rules have been established with partner schools, electronic links can be used for the joint construction of knowledge including critical questioning and reasoning. An example might be taking a particular topic to research together in order to develop joint multimedia resources on the web. This approach is found in Margaret Riel's 'circles of learning' (Riel 1996 and www.iearn.org/iearn/circles/lc-home.html). Marlene Scardemalia's work in Canada has shown how effective these networks for constructing shared knowledge can be both in engaging the enthusiasm of students and in improving measures of academic achievement (Scardemalia and Bereiter 1991 and http://csile.oise.on.ca/).

Conclusion

Computers can provide teachers and learners with powerful tools for communicating. The effectiveness of computers as learning tools may for many curriculum areas lie in their ability to support learning dialogues. Used in educational settings, the computer can help to initiate and sustain learning conversations in which meaning is jointly constructed and learners access one another's knowledge and understanding to their mutual benefit. Such dialogue is not necessarily naturally generated by learners working together with ICT. There may be problems caused by a misunderstanding of the purpose of group work, by lack of speaking and listening skills and by software design. But in classrooms focused on oracy in conjunction with ICT, teachers can provide direct help to enable learners to develop the skills they need to communicate effectively with one another. Peer support during learning conversations then becomes possible; the classroom learning community can establish a common awareness of aims for group talk and a determination to tap into the power of productive discussion.

ICT enables classroom access to a wide variety of communities of expertise, providing learners with the opportunity to talk to experts and become 'newcomers' in these communities. This ability to engage in educated dialogue with a wide range of people helps learners to develop factual knowledge, but such enquiry also helps them to develop into independent learners with a toolkit of talk skills at their disposal. It is an exciting idea to consider the vision that learners can expect to participate meaningfully in the discourse of the range of communities shared across the Internet. But it is crucial to the realization of this vision that learners have the ability to engage constructively in knowledge-building conversations. Our research has shown that this is an ability which can be taught explicitly. Teaching speaking and listening skills requires a commitment to a talk-focused classroom, where dialogue is valued and educational talk is fostered. In this context, ICT can be expected to promote learning across the range of curriculum subjects.

References

Barnes, D. (1976) *From Communication to Curriculum*. Harmondsworth: Penguin.
BECTA (British Educational Communications and Technology Agency) (1998) *Connecting Schools, Networking People*. Coventry: BECTA.

Cox, M. (1999) Motivating pupils through the use of ICT, in M. Leask and N. Pachler (eds) (1999) *Learning to Teach Using ICT in the Secondary School.* London: Routledge.

Dawes, L. (2000) First connections: teachers and the National Grid for Learning, *Computers and Education,* January: 235–52.

Dawes, L., Wegerif, R. and Mercer, N. (2000) *Thinking Together: Activities for Key Stage 2 Children and Teachers.* London: Questions Publishing.

Eliot, T.S. ([1934] 1986) Choruses from the Rock, in T.S. Eliot (ed.) *Collected Poems 1906–1962.* London: Faber & Faber.

Higgins, S. (2000) The logical zoombinis, *Teaching Thinking,* 1(1): 12–14.

Lave, J. and Wenger, E. (1991) *Situated Learning: Legitimate Peripheral Participation.* Cambridge: Cambridge University Press.

Mercer, N. (1993) Computer based activities in classroom contexts, in P. Scrimshaw (ed.) *Language, Classroom and Computers.* London: Routledge.

Mercer, N. (1995) *The Guided Construction of Knowledge: Talk Amongst Teachers and Learners.* Clevedon, OH: Multilingual Matters.

Norman, K. (ed.) (1992) *Thinking Voices: The Work of the National Oracy Project.* London: Hodder & Stoughton.

Riel, M. (1996) Cross-classroom-collaboration: communication and education, in T. Koschman (ed.) *CSCL: Theory and Practice of an Emerging Paradigm,* pp. 187–207. Mahwah, NJ: Lawrence Erlbaum Associates.

Roerden, L.P. (1997) *Net Lessons: Web-Based Projects for your Classroom.* Sebastopol, CA: Songline Studios Inc.

Rogoff, B. (1990) *Apprenticeship in Thinking: Cognitive Development in Social Context.* Oxford: Oxford University Press.

Scardemalia, M. and Bereiter, C. (1991) Higher levels of agency for children in knowledge building: a challenge for the design of new knowledge media, *The Journal of the Learning Sciences,* 1(1): 37–68.

Selwyn, N. (1998) The effect of using a home computer on students' educational use of IT, *Computers and Education,* 31(2): 211–27.

Walker, D. (1998) *Education in the Digital Age.* London: Bowerdene.

Warschauer, M. (1999) *Electronic Literacies: Language Culture and Power in Online Education.* Mahwah, NJ: Lawrence Erlbaum Associates.

Wegerif, R. and Dawes, L. (1998) Encouraging exploratory talk around computers, in M. Monteith (ed.) *IT for Learning Enhancement.* Exeter: Intellect Books.

Wegerif, R. and Scrimshaw, P. (eds) (1997) *Computers and Talk in the Primary Classroom.* Clevedon, OH: Multilingual Matters.

Wegerif, R., Collins, J. and Scrimshaw, P. (1995) *CD-ROMs in Primary Schools: Evaluation Summary.* Coventry: National Council for Educational Technology.

Wegerif, R., Mercer, N. and Dawes, L. (1998) Integrating Pedagogy and Software Design to Support Discussion in the Primary Curriculum, *Journal of Computer Assisted Learning,* 14: 199–211.

Wells, G. (1999) *Dialogic Inquiry: Towards a Sociocultural Practice and Theory of Education.* Cambridge: Cambridge University Press.

6
ICT AND READING: WHAT CAN SOFTWARE DO?

Richard Bennett and
Henry Pearson

Introduction

The teaching of reading is permanently the subject of much controversy, and the advent of the computer has added a further dimension to an already long and complex debate about methodology. To the traditional dilemmas – phonics versus look and say and scheme versus real books – we can now add book versus computer.

Though the book and the screen are two very different media, they do have much in common in terms of reading, for they both require the reader to decipher text through either decoding, analogizing, identifying, deducing or predicting words. On the other hand, with all the dynamic advantages that computers offer, particularly their potential for interaction with the operator, it could be that they are an ideal medium through which not only to teach the basic skills of reading but also to lure young learners to the literacy habit. In addition, the computer provides the potential to engage children independently: supporting teachers with some routine tasks and enabling them to focus their attention on more intellectually demanding aspects of the teaching of reading.

However, for software to be useful in the classroom, it would need to satisfy some general criteria:

- to support and complement the content of any official requirements – for example in England the Early Learning Goals, the National Curriculum and the National Literacy Strategy (NLS);

- to be consistent with established thinking about the teaching of reading;
- to have the children's interests at heart.

In this chapter we set out a series of questions which together provide a framework for a more detailed appraisal of reading support software. We then investigate the validity of our questions by using them to evaluate 16 educational software packages designed to support the teaching of reading. Our conclusions suggest that, while existing programs do address some aspects of reading development, the full potential of the interactive multimedia learning environment offered by today's computer systems has yet to be realized.

The questions

Reading aims and levels

The aims embedded in the National Curriculum for England and Wales are to produce children who can read with accuracy, fluency, understanding and enjoyment. Most teachers would probably add that children's reading should be supported by positive attitudes towards the task. It follows that any teaching programme or approach should bear these aims in mind, though whether they can all be addressed at once from the outset, or whether the technical skills required for reading accuracy should be attended to first, is by no means agreed.

In England for example, the recent push for phonic approaches during focused and group reading periods in the Literacy Hour using games, flash card activities, word grids, phoneme spotting and such like, suggests an approach which has as its main objective the teaching of accuracy, especially at word level and particularly through phonic decoding and word identification.

In evaluating computer software designed to teach children to support reading development, it will be useful to ask:

In what ways does the program address the aims for children to read with accuracy, fluency, understanding and enjoyment?

In Table 6.1 we have attempted to summarize what is involved in the four reading aims and how they relate to the levels – word, sentence and text.

Our explanation of accuracy in Table 6.1 suggests that there are five ways of getting words right:

- decoding using phonic or graphic (sub-lexical) information;
- analogizing by making comparisons with other words with similar parts;
- identifying a word as a whole unit;
- deducing from context;

Table 6.1   Aims of teaching reading

Accuracy	Fluency	Understanding	Enjoyment
At level of word: Decoding words (phonic and graphic) Analogizing (word parts) Identifying words (whole word) Deducing in context Predicting words from: syntax and grammar meaning bibliographic cues	*At level of sentence:* Phrasing (grouping of words) Smoothness (flow) Stress (emphasis) Intonation (pitch) Expression (associated with meaning) Pace (variation) Speed	*At level of text:* Meaning in terms of: recognizing words comprehending sentences apprehending text	Pleasure, delight, benefit, entertainment, titillation, amusement, interest, fascination, engrossment, relishment, absorption Also: attitude, confidence, commitment, stamina

- predicting from syntactic, grammatical, semantic or graphic (for example, pictures) information.

These are traditionally known as word attack skills.

The various dimensions of fluency are all associated with reading aloud – the only way in which fluency can be monitored or assessed. We would argue that fluency is principally associated with reading at sentence level, though this is influenced by the flow of the narrative at text level and the extent to which the child is attaching meaning to what is being read. Though understanding is essentially at text level, we suggest that this is additionally supported by readers being able to recognize words, comprehend sentences and apprehend text. To apprehend implies an engagement with text beyond mere understanding of what is read and into the realms of identifying with characters, information, ideas, situations and events in a way which makes the text one's own.

Enjoyment might cover a number of emotions related to a child's engagement with a text. Less noticeably covered in the National Curriculum are other attitudes, especially confidence, commitment and stamina:

- *Confidence*: a belief in success and a faith in one's own abilities which provides a secure foundation for reading skills to develop.
- *Commitment*: might occur at two levels: to the text being read, enabling one to benefit from the experience; to the act of reading in general, exhibited for example by a reader choosing to read and enjoying discussion about reading experiences.

- *Stamina*: necessary when the going gets tough, when the text provides a challenge and when a less determined and committed reader might give up.

Successful readers clearly operate at all three levels (word, sentence, text) simultaneously. For example, in identifying what they describe as effective teaching of literacy, Medwell *et al.* (1998) suggested from their research that activities should be used which require pupils to work at more than one level – word, sentence or text – and that letter sounds were best taught from the context of text rather than in isolation.

In evaluating computer software, we shall ask:

What use is made of reading at the three levels: word, sentence, text?

Context and reading

Necessarily, any programme of reading instruction, whether it be teacher created, publisher devised, Standards and Effectiveness Unit initiated or computer generated, must address the so-called 'basic skills' and equip children to read the words. As suggested above, reading at this level might involve decoding, analogizing, identifying, deducing or predicting words. The NLS identifies four 'searchlights' which are used to assist in the reading of text. Something similar has appeared in the various versions of the National Curriculum. However, subtle differences in emphasis have emerged, as Table 6.2 indicates.

Table 6.2 Cues, searchlights and strategies

DES (1989) National Curriculum 'Available cues'	DfEE (1995) National Curriculum 'Knowledge, skills, understanding'	DfEE (1998) NLS 'Searchlights'	DfEE (1999) National Curriculum 'A range of strategies'
Phonic cues	Phonic knowledge	Phonic knowledge (sounds and spelling)	Phonemic awareness and phonic knowledge
Word shapes	Word recognition and graphic knowledge	Word recognition and graphic knowledge	Word recognition and graphic knowledge
	Grammatical knowledge	Grammatical knowledge	Grammatical awareness
Meaning of passage	Contextual understanding	Knowledge of context	Contextual understanding
Pictures			

The place of context in the reading process is a case in point. Stanovich and Stanovich (1995) claim that good readers use context less for word recognition than poor or young readers, because word recognition at the accomplished level is rapid and automatic. This means that the reader has no need to make use of context to help with deciphering words but instead is able to access meaning directly. Perfetti (1995) argues that while less skilled readers use context to *identify* words, skilled readers use context to *interpret* words. However, young readers are likely to rely quite heavily on context – particularly syntax, meaning and illustrations – to help them decipher text.

Table 6.2 highlights an important shift of emphasis in the use of context when supporting children's early reading development. As can be seen, pictures have ceased to be acknowledged as a legitimate cue, searchlight or strategy in official documents of the 1990s. Perhaps this is consistent with the approach, used by some adults when listening to readers, of covering up the picture to ensure that the children are actually reading the words and not cheating by looking at the pictures.

Protherough (1992) argues that illustrations may even be a hindrance to learning to read and that those susceptible to sight distractions – for example, the less able and boys – may be particularly affected. In addition, Protherough argues that confusion can be caused because the processes of decoding images and text are very different and occur in different parts of the brain. Furthermore, 'If a child does not know a word and looks at the picture, he or she may not know which part of the picture may help in decoding the word. If the child already knows the word, then the picture is only an unnecessary distraction' (1992: 7). Evans (1998: xv) however, argues that 'illustrations have a crucial role to play in enabling children to gain meaning from books' and that they 'work in partnership with print in picture books'.

Since young readers need all the information and assistance they can muster, clearly pictures are an important source of information for them, though less helpful for learning literacy if they allow the book to be read without reference to the text or if the text and illustration are not related. In addition, the multimedia environment created by computers offers opportunities for pictures to be animated. This feature could add further cues to support readers by, for example, animating part of a story. On the other hand, the animation could diminish the child's need to extract meaning from the text or distract attention away from the words. Our evaluation of computer software will need to establish, then, the extent and manner in which context (syntax, meaning and illustration/animation) is used in the teaching of reading skills. We must ask:

How is the teaching of word attack skills related to the use of context?

Phonic knowledge

The other significant point from Table 6.2 is the introduction of phonemic awareness in the latest version of the English National Curriculum. Phonemic awareness, as distinct from general phonic knowledge, is the reader's ability to decipher a word's individually discrete sounds – its phonemes. In the word 'stand' for example, phonemic awareness involves distinguishing five different sounds: s – t – a – n – d. It is suggested that a reader who is able to do this can thus decode any unfamiliar word by recognizing each sound and then blending them together to make a recognizable word. This is the basic principle underlying what is termed a 'synthetic' approach to reading.

Johnston and Watson (1997, 1999a, 1999b) claim success with these synthetic approaches with their emphasis on phonemic awareness at letter level. They found that their approach developed not only reading and spelling, but also rime awareness skills which relate to the vowel sound and latter part of one-syllable words. Goswami (Goswami and Bryant 1990; Goswami 1994, 1999) found advantages in teaching syllables and onset-rime over phonemic awareness training. She claims that an awareness of onset and rime happens spontaneously in children, and that phonemic awareness does not. She has found, for example, that children are better at distinguishing syllables, onset and rime than they are at distinguishing individual sounds, both aurally and when reading. She claims that the ability to manipulate individual phonemes within words is consequent upon learning to read rather than a prerequisite. Goswami also argues that the value of rime is that it stabilizes the pronunciation of the vowel contained in it. This makes it easier for the reader at rime level to recognize the otherwise unpredictable vowel sound: consider 'women', 'donkey', 'monkey', 'both' as opposed to 'top', 'drop', 'pop', or 'hope', 'cope', 'rope'.

Our evaluation of computer programs will therefore need to assess ways in which awareness of phonemes, onset-rime and syllables is developed: whether the approach is essentially synthetic (based on the blending of phonemes in unfamiliar words), or analytic (based on the segmenting of parts of familiar words). We shall ask:

What form of phonic knowledge is explored – phonemes, onset and rime, or syllables? Is the approach essentially synthetic or analytic?

Word recognition

Also important is the reader's ability to read words on sight, either by identifying them as wholes, or by analogizing with other similar words with which they are familiar. For example, a reader may hesitate over the word 'bright', but recognize the '-ight' from the previously known word, 'night'. This information, combined with the sense of the text and the message of the sentence so far is likely to prompt the reading of the word 'bright'. Thus, any reading program will need to assist children's reading by capitalizing on previously-experienced words, either through recognition or by analogy. We must ask:

Is analogy used as a device for helping readers? Are texts used to assist readers with word recognition?

Independence

Since many teachers in England will want to use the computer software during the session in the Literacy Hour set aside for independent work, it could be important to consider the extent to which children are likely to be able to use the program unaided while the teacher is working intensively with a focus group. We might need to consider whether the child is sufficiently well supported in operating the software, whether it is easy to use and accessible and whether it is of optimum difficulty to the level of reading for which it is designed. Finally, is it likely to sustain children's interest? We must ask:

Does the program provide for children to work with independence on their reading? Does it have the potential to sustain children's interest?

Features offered by the software

The interactive nature of modern multimedia computers adds a further dimension to teaching and learning beyond that offered by more traditional text-based resources. We have already discussed the use of animated graphic images to illustrate, entertain or provide additional cues. CD-ROM based software also offers opportunities for extensive use of speech and sound effects. Individual words, letters or groups of letters can be sounded-out under the control of the child, or the software. Software can be programmed to place control in the hands of the learners, by enabling them to interact with text and images. The teacher can be given some control over the content and level of difficulty or pace of progress presented to the learner, or the software itself may be programmed to react to the responses of the learners. Squires and McDougall (1994) present a comprehensive paradigm for the evaluation of educational software, suggesting that the locus of control could be in the hands of the learner, the teacher or the designer of the program. When analysing the use of reading software, the balance of control is therefore an important consideration, as is the quality of feedback provided to the learner and the teacher. We must ask:

Where lies the locus of control? What sort of feedback is provided for learner and teacher?

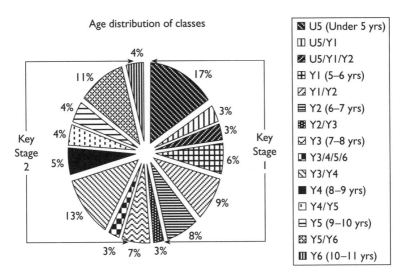

Figure 6.1 Age distribution of the classes taught by questionnaire respondents (n=117)

The evaluation

Background research

We were interested in discovering how teachers attempted to balance the demands of nationally imposed directives for literacy and information and communication technology (ICT) with the needs of the children. The NLS has been in force in England since September 1998. It is not statutory, but most schools have adopted the structured framework which includes a daily Literacy Hour. The detailed framework does not include specific reference to the use of ICT to support the teaching and learning of reading skills but the National Curriculum for English, which is statutory, requires teachers to incorporate ICT resources into their teaching. To ascertain the extent to which teachers were using ICT to support their teaching of literacy, in Autumn 1999 the teachers in 28 primary, junior and infant schools in three local education authorities were invited to complete a simple questionnaire. Returns were received from 117 teachers, with 75 (64 per cent) adding additional comments about the value and difficulties of using ICT in their teaching. They were asked to list up to four pieces of software they used to support their literacy teaching and indicate how and when the software was used. They were also asked to indicate their frequency of access to which type of computer system. The questionnaires were completed anonymously (see Figures 6.1 and 6.2).

Class sizes ranged from 11 children in a vertically grouped language support unit, to 67 under 5s taught by a team of three teachers. Multimedia

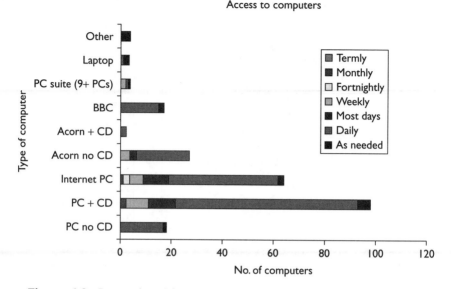

Figure 6.2 Respondents' frequency of access to various computer systems

PCs were the most common computer found in classrooms. In addition, 25 teachers indicated they had weekly access to computer suites of from 5 to 15 Internet-linked PCs.

The software

The software used most often to support literacy activities was the word processor, with language practice and spelling programs also very popular (see Figure 6.3). We were particularly interested in the types of software used by teachers to support early reading development and so focused our attention on those teaching younger children. Although there was substantial use made of word processors, more use was made of specific language practice programs and software designed to support the teaching of phonics (see Figure 6.4).

We also asked teachers to describe an ideal piece of software which would meet their, as yet, unfulfilled needs – for example: 'Something designed to fit in with the NLS, based on high frequency words and self correcting!' (Teacher of under 5 Reception children).

Using the information provided by the survey we selected 16 reading support software packages for evaluation. Our criteria for selection were that the titles should be either those which were most often used by the teachers or which appeared to be designed to address needs which the teachers had identified on their wish lists (see Table 6.3).

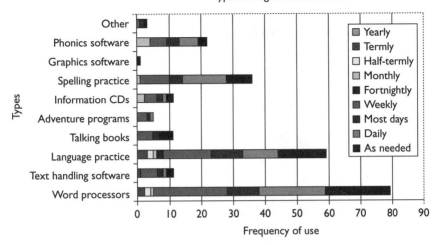

Figure 6.3 Types of software used by respondents, and frequency of use

The evaluation

Having selected the programs, we set out to evaluate the extent to which they addressed the questions we had identified.

In what ways does the program address the aims for children to read with accuracy, fluency, understanding and enjoyment?

All the software titles reviewed placed great emphasis on reading with *accuracy*. Some packages included carefully structured activities to focus on specific skills or strategies aimed at improving accuracy in reading (see Table 6.4).

The programs evaluated offered few opportunities for children to develop *fluency* in their reading, though several titles modelled fluent reading through having text read aloud to the children. One program provided a facility for children to record their voices to enable them to monitor their own reading fluency, but this was limited in scope.

Often, there was little requirement for children to read with *understanding*. In most cases, written words had to be matched either to pictures or to a spoken word, while some activities required the user to identify words containing letter strings or particular sounds. Most programs were highly specific in the lists of words presented, some linking their lists to those in associated structured reading schemes. Only two programs offered a facility for teachers to add their own words. Some 'sentences' were little more than strings of words selected from a highly structured vocabulary. The level of understanding in most word-matching

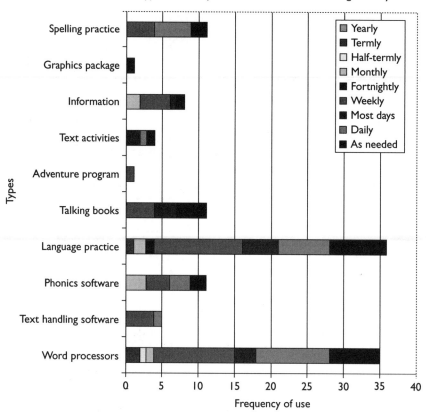

Figure 6.4 Types of software used to support literacy teaching by teachers of 4–7-year-old children

activities was minimal – in some cases the children might not know the meaning of written words they were required to identify (for example, moat, cob, tub), the emphasis clearly being on decoding sounds rather than extracting meaning.

Enjoyment proved more difficult to evaluate. We found some of the tasks to be very repetitive and tedious. After a short while the few animations which were presented became irritating distractions. Our conclusions were that most of the computer-based activities would probably prove to be enjoyable for short periods of time but would pall after prolonged use. To some extent, this view was echoed by some of the teachers' comments. However, we have no definitive evidence of children's views on this issue.

Table 6.3 Literacy software evaluated

Software title	Publisher/supplier
Fuzz Buzz 1	Semerc/Granada/Oxford
Fuzz Buzz 2	Semerc/Granada/Oxford
I Can Read 1	Knowledge Adventure
I Can Read 2	Knowledge Adventure
Learning Ladder	Dorling Kindersley
Letterland 1	Collins
Letterland 2	Collins
Matti Mole's Summer Holiday	Sherston
Primary Literacy 1	Anglia Multimedia
Reader Rabbit 4–6	The Learning Company
Reader Rabbit 6–8	The Learning Company
Rhyme & Analogy A	Oxford/Sherston
Rhyme & Analogy B	Oxford/Sherston
Tizzy's Toyshop	Sherston
Tomorrow's Promise 1	Longman
Tomorrow's Promise 2	Longman

Table 6.4 Strategies used by software to develop accuracy in reading

Strategies used to develop accuracy	No. of programs
Identifying words as whole units	14
Decoding using phonic and graphic information	14
Analogizing by making comparisons with other words	10
Deducing from semantic information	7

Table 6.5 Levels at which activities are pitched in each program

Levels at which activities are pitched	No. of programs
Word level only	6
Word and sentence levels	1
Word and text levels	2
Word, sentence and text levels	7

What use is made of reading at the three levels: word, sentence, text?

Five of the software packages had been designed to relate to the requirements of the NLS and included activities at all three levels. Six programs included only word level activities and others used a combination of word, text and sentence level tasks (see Table 6.5). The emphasis on word level activities could be attributable to the titles selected, which in turn correspond to the educational preferences of the teachers surveyed. However, it might also be that it is easier to program activities in which individual words are correctly identified.

How is the teaching of word attack skills related to the use of context?

Only two programs included text-based story contexts on screen; however, the tasks and problems which were presented seldom linked to the narratives. Two other packages were designed to augment existing published reading schemes. The computer-based activities in these packages were closely related to story contexts with the same characters and scenes appearing in the books and on the screen.

All the titles evaluated included good quality illustrations and some animations to enhance the appearance of the screens. However, in some cases, the images were used merely as attractive backgrounds to the activities and bore little direct relation to the content of the text presented. While one program, for example, used the context of a farm to present a series of activities, the words and sentences were frequently unrelated to the animals or scenes portrayed on the screen. Most programs included activities which required children to match sounds and/or words to images. This was often achieved through the game of Pelmanism, in which children remembered the positions of pairs of matching cards. Only one activity in one program required children to interpret the images on screen, by identifying which of two pencils was bigger, smaller, taller or thinner. There was also surprisingly little use made of animation related to the content of words or phrases. In one activity, images were transformed ('morphed') into their initial letters – for example, an ink pot was transformed into a lower-case letter 'i'. In most cases however, animations were used as rewards for the successful completion of tasks or as supplementary features – for example, to explain what had to be done in an activity. Some activities offered promising opportunities for animation which were not pursued, such as when verbs were illustrated or when words were combined to make composites – for example, hand + cuff.

What form of phonic knowledge is explored – phonemes, onset and rime or syllables? Is the approach essentially synthetic or analytic?

There is extensive use of onset and rime in the word level activities for most of the programs. Activities often required children to link various onsets to rimes to identify or create new words. Other activities were designed to focus attention on syllables – for example, constructing a character's name by rearranging syllables. Some software attempted to develop phonemic awareness, though this was addressed systematically in only one package and then with a very restricted vocabulary.

The majority of phonic activities were analytic, requiring children to break down familiar, known words into segments. This was particularly evident in packages which accompanied reading schemes with controlled vocabularies. A few tasks required children to blend sounds to help them read unfamiliar words, though this would, of course, be dependent on the vocabulary of each child.

It was significant that the titles which had been produced to support published reading schemes were more coherent in their presentation of activities. The other packages often presented activities arbitrarily. This could be supportable if the information presented in the teachers' notes was sufficiently detailed and/or the program could be configured by the teacher to present activities matched to the needs of the children (see the locus of control question, p. 106).

Is analogy used as a device for helping readers? Are texts used to assist readers with word recognition?

Two packages had been designed specifically to present children with sets of words which were related, thereby enabling them to draw and build upon prior knowledge. Similarly, the vocabulary presented in another two was based on structured word lists and so included sets of related words. The activities in another related set of two programs were based on comprehensive, phonically-consistent word lists and so should encourage the children's use of analogy. To a lesser extent, all the other programs included activities which were designed to help children identify words with similar rimes or onsets, though in some cases the number of words was restricted to only two or three in each 'family'.

The programs related to reading schemes included activities aimed at supporting the recognition of words in their controlled vocabularies. The activities in some packages were aimed at helping children improve their sight vocabulary, including activities in which children had to identify particular words within a specified time limit. The Pelmanism word-matching activities which were included in most packages required the recognition of words on sight, though when the child needed to match two written versions of the word it was not necessary for them to be able to read the word in order to match the letter strings; whereas matching written words to pictures did at least require the word to be decoded. The two programs which allowed children to record their own voices appeared to be of limited value, as neither included voice recognition to check on the children's reading accuracy.

Does the program provide for children to work with independence on their reading? Does it have the potential to sustain children's interest?

A large proportion of the teachers who provided written comments in the survey indicated that their greatest concern was over the management of the computer when being used in the classroom with young children. For example, one teacher of 4- to 5-year-old children commented: 'ICT in the early years is of value if an adult is working alongside the children, especially in the autumn term. Familiarity with the programs allows for some independence as the school year progresses but problems do occur when the class teacher is trying to work with another group'. We were disappointed that most of the programs reviewed seemed to require the teacher or an adult continually to guide the children. We would advocate that teachers should monitor children when working at the computer in the same way that they would intervene with any group-based activity. However, teachers do become very frustrated when the children working at a computer are continually seeking assistance with technical or proced-ural problems. Furthermore, very few packages that we reviewed enabled the teacher to select or configure the activities before a session, to address the particular needs of the children. Given the interactive, icon-based, multimedia environments which can be created by today's computers, it ought to be possible for some software to be written for use by the youngest children with minimal adult assistance.

Many teachers commented on the attractiveness of computer software for young children. A teacher of children under 5 said: 'The children enjoy using the programs and gain a lot from them. When they work in pairs they often generate good discussion and ideas. They particularly enjoy the colourful graphics and sounds the software may include'. Even the most mundane activities can be made interesting with the use of stimulating graphics and sound effects. However, we had concerns with several activities which appeared to be tedious and repetitive, such as those which presented a succession of words for identification, with the same background image and the same spoken instruction. Some of the packages, apparently aimed at the home market, attempted to include extrinsic rewards in the form of graphical stickers or points. The use of incentives was presumably to encourage children to persist when the initial attraction of the activity had waned.

Where lies the locus of control? What sort of feedback is provided for learner and teacher?

In all the software evaluated, control was centred on the computer; the program (and hence the designer) decided which words to present to the children and sometimes which activity they should be given next. However, ten programs allowed some element of control to be placed in the hands of the teacher. Of the 16 titles evaluated, 6 could not be configured by the teacher in any way, 6 permitted the teacher or child to select an activity at the start of a session, 2 enabled the teacher to preassign tasks for particular children and 2 enabled the teacher to assign tasks and select or enter word lists for individual children. However, most of the teachers surveyed also made use of word processing and text-based activities which provide more opportunities for the children and teachers to assume control over the activity and hence the learning.

Nine packages allowed the teacher (or parent) to monitor the children's progress though the level of detail provided varied. At the most basic level, five programs displayed a progress chart indicating which activities the child had completed but with no indication as to how well an activity had been accomplished. Four programs provided an indication of progress, with some information about how well each child had tackled the tasks. Two programs also logged the children's errors for later diagnosis.

Discussion

We set out to evaluate the extent to which software used by teachers to support the teaching of reading addressed certain questions related to current educational thinking about literacy. We were anxious to base our evaluations on software which was actually being used by teachers or was aimed at addressing the teaching needs which they had identified. We found that there is a range of software presently available to support reading development. No one piece of software is able to meet all the needs of the reading curriculum which we had identified through our questions; but is this surprising given the complexity of the learning process?

All the titles required the children to read with accuracy, though we had concerns over some activities which could be correctly completed without the need to decode or understand the words. Another concern was that the more sophisticated (and expensive) packages included a wide range of activities, each aimed at reinforcing quite different reading strategies. For these to be used effectively, teachers would have to spend some time familiarizing themselves with the activities in order to be able to select those most appropriate for the needs of their children. The software packages which were more closely related to reading schemes offered the most consistency in the strategies they used, but offered the least flexibility in their use of vocabulary.

The contexts used by the packages would be attractive and appealing to children. However, we felt there was insufficient use made of the multimedia potential of modern computer systems to illustrate or animate the activities. In addition, some of the highly graphical environments offered few clues for the learner in navigating their way through the activities and would require the assistance of an adult.

In 1994, Stephen Heppell lamented: 'If multimedia learning environments are to offer challenge, provide delight and deliver real learning outcomes they must first recognise the emergent capability of learners and respond to the climate of expectation that those learners bring to their computer screens' (p. 158). It would appear from our researches that little has changed. Heppell argues that most educational software does not take account of the sophisticated demands of today's children and does not recognize that supposedly non-educational computer games offer challenging problem-solving environments where children observe, question, hypothezise and test. Although some of the software we reviewed does present reading activities through highly attractive graphical visual and audio contexts, the tasks are often mundane, repetitive and offer little more educational challenge than the programs which were produced when computers first entered the primary school classroom in the early 1980s. One of the reasons could be that the demands placed on teachers by nationally imposed curricula and initiatives such as the NLS have affected their choice of software. The Literacy Hour sets aside only 20 minutes a day for individual or group-based activities and sets out a time-table of activities which allows for little flexibility. Furthermore, there is unremitting pressure for the teacher to move the children on to the next topic. Opportunities to work for sustained periods of time on more intel-lectually demanding and linguistically challenging computer-based activities, such as adventure programs, have been dramatically reduced. Several teachers we surveyed asked for short, focused computer-based activities aimed at meeting the needs of the curriculum in their wish lists:

- Software to assess understanding of issues related to the NLS (teacher of Year 2 children).
- Software which shows progression of skills with a clear and detailed record of work completed and next steps, which is printable (teacher of Year 2 and Year 3 children).
- A simple program to help with punctuation at a variety of levels (teacher of Year 1 and Year 2 children).

In 1995, school inspectors reported that there was a disappointing over-reliance by the teachers of early years children on the use of drill and practice software (Ofsted 1995). Our survey suggests that teachers of young children presently make almost as much use of word processors as they do of practice software. However, it would appear that the most recent changes to the curriculum in primary schools are likely to increase the need for short, focused practice activities. Commercial educational software developers are unlikely to experiment with more open-ended software until the demand is created.

Conclusion

Based on our initial questions, in an ideal world we would like to see literacy software which helps children read with accuracy, fluency, understanding and enjoyment and addresses reading at the three levels of word, sentence, text. We would want children to meet new words in rich and meaningful contexts to ensure the learning of word attack skills is relevant and inherently interesting. We would expect phonic knowledge to be acquired through the development of a range of strategies based on purposeful and enticing scenarios. There should be opportunities for the application of analogy to assist readers with word recognition and we would look for an interesting environment which encourages children to work with confident independence on their reading. There should also be opportunities for the teacher to have control over the content and contexts for the activities and there should be feedback provided for the learner and the teacher.

Our research is by no means exhaustive. We are not in a position to report how typical the software evaluated is of the market as a whole but have based our work on the titles currently being used by teachers in our survey. Our findings indicate that the software reviewed goes some way towards meeting the requirements identified, but as yet we have not found any one program or package which adequately satisfies all our demands. It is perhaps salutary that, up to now, the package which most effectively addresses every one of our stringent criteria is . . . a good book and a well-informed teacher!

References

DES (Department of Education and Science) (1989) *English in the National Curriculum.* London: HMSO.

DfEE (Department for Education and Employment) (1995) *English in the National Curriculum.* London: HMSO.

DfEE (Department for Education and Employment) (1998) *The National Literacy Strategy: A Framework for Teaching.* London: HMSO.

DfEE (Department for Education and Employment) (1999) *English: The National Curriculum for England.* London: HMSO.

Evans, J. (ed.) (1998) *What's in the Picture?* London: Paul Chapman.

Goswami, U. (1994) Phonological skills, analogies and reading development, *Reading*, 28(2): 32–7.

Goswami, U. (1999) Balanced phonics. Conference Paper, Ofsted, 29 March.

Goswami, U. and Bryant, P. (1990) *Phonological Skills and Learning to Read.* Hove: Lawrence Erlbaum Associates.

Heppell, S. (1994) Multimedia and learning: normal children, normal lives and real change, in J. Underwood (ed.) *Computer Based Learning: Potential into Practice.* London: David Fulton.

Johnston, R.S. and Watson, J. (1997) Developing reading, spelling and phonemic awareness skills in primary school children, *Reading*, 31(2): 37–40.

Johnston, R.S. and Watson, J. (1999a) Phonic boom, *Literacy and Learning*, 7: 7–8.

Johnston, R.S. and Watson, J. (1999b) The effectiveness of synthetic phonics teaching compared with analytic phonics, and phoneme and rime awareness training. Conference Paper, Ofsted, 29 March.

Medwell, J., Wray, D., Poulson, L. and Fox, R. (1998) *Effective Teachers of Literacy*. Exeter: University of Exeter and TTA.

Ofsted (Office for Standards in Education) (1995) *Information Technology: A Review of Inspection Findings 1993/4*. London: HMSO.

Perfetti, C. (1995) Cognitive research can inform reading education, *Journal of Research in Reading*, 18(2): 106–15.

Protherough, P. (1992) Not a pretty picture, *Language and Learning*, 9: 5–7.

Squires, D. and McDougall, A. (1994) *Choosing and Using Educational Software*. Brighton: Falmer Press.

Stanovich, K. and Stanovich, P. (1995) How research might inform the debate about early reading acquisition, *Journal of Research in Reading*, 18(2): 87–105.

7

COMPUTER SUPPORT FOR READING DEVELOPMENT

Jean Underwood

Introduction: is reading all there is to literacy?

The focus of this chapter is the role of information and communication technology (ICT) in reading development. Two, possibly three, decades ago I might have posed the question above more succinctly by asking 'How does ICT support literacy?' At that time, to all intents and purposes, literacy and reading were synonymous concepts. This was in part due to the pre-eminence of the reading readiness model of reading development. Reading readiness – the view that there is a threshold of mental maturity that has to be achieved before reading instruction can begin – had profound impacts both on the teaching of reading in schools and on our concept of literacy. Reading readiness of necessity categorized children into those who were ready to read and those who were not. This view of the reading process fits well with a reading pedagogy which emphasizes a carefully sequenced hierarchy of pre-reading and reading skills, and with a task analysis approach to teaching and learning (see Gagne 1970). The model also isolated reading from writing and other language skills – an isolation, which in many teachers' and researchers' eyes, has proved to be unsustainable.

A radically different approach, that of emergent literacy, removed this schism between reading and other language skills. From this perspective, literacy development is based in language and cognitive development and begins well before children actually begin to read. For example, children know what reading and writing are for, and also that the marks on the page convey meaning (Clay 1991).

Today, if we look at the use of ICT in schools, we see that word processing is the most common form of software used but there is also a steady growth in the use of the Internet. Extensive research in the USA confirms that the software which teachers most often name as their most valuable programs for student use are general office applications such as ClarisWorks and Microsoft Works, and web browsers such as Netscape (Becker *et al.* 1999). Studies in the USA show that the use of such software is clearly linked to key pedagogic goals: 'Finding out about ideas and information' was the most commonly reported objective by American teachers, followed by students 'expressing themselves in writing'. Surveys conducted for the Department for Education and Employment (DfEE) confirm that this pattern is repeated in UK schools (DfE 1995; DfEE 1999). Classroom use of ICT is very much in tune with the emergent literacy model and the focus on ICT support for reading *per se* is less widespread than the use of software which ties the act of learning to read to other language activities. Other contributors to this book discuss such software, but the main focus here will be on those programs which are designed to support the reading process.

Foundations of literacy

The study of literacy now encompasses a diverse set of activities such as children's classroom discussions and their awareness of print and its uses. The act of becoming literate presents a very significant challenge. In learning to read and to write children, or late developing adults, must link their oral language with a new, visual system of symbols – marks on a page. Research has clearly shown that literacy is closely linked with children's use of language in a wide range of contexts, such as the home and the playground as well as the classroom. Learning to read is only the beginning of literacy however. Critical literacy – the competent use of language for thinking and expression – should be the end goal, not simple functional literacy (Calfee 1994). Developing critical literacy will prove to be one of the most demanding but potentially one of the most rewarding activities that children will be involved in. Learning to read can be both a pleasure and an opening to economic achievement.

As children enter formal education their language ability is already impressive. Many Year 1 children (5 to 6 years old) will have acquired an extensive vocabulary of 5000 or more words by this time (Chall 1996). They also have a solid command of the mechanics of their native language and can use it to communicate effectively. However, literacy requires explicit as well as implicit knowledge of the language. Thus, despite the fact that most children have the basic capacity to learn to read and write, in most classrooms their performance will be anything but uniform. As Dianne McGuinness (1998) points out, people may have a natural talent to acquire language and vocabulary, but they do not have a natural talent to remember the relationships between abstract visual patterns and their connection to words. This is an important distinction because it implies that while language may be acquired, reading and writing need to be taught. Also, while we may all have a 'language instinct', learning to read and write is influenced by children's language backgrounds. In many schools in the UK, children are working to become literate in a language not readily spoken in their home environment or they are drawn from family backgrounds where books and the act of reading are very limited. The diversity of children's language backgrounds adds significantly to the problems of teaching children to master reading skills.

Why learning to read is not straightforward

Reading has many levels from the orthographic and syntactic, to the formation of propositions and inferences. It is an information processing skill comprising a number of cognitive sub-skills which enable us to acquire purely visual information from a page and convert it into meaning (Underwood and Batt 1996). Spoken words are formed from speech sounds, but among the huge number of possible sounds we humans can make, only a very small subset – the phonemes of any language – are perceived as meaningful. Each phoneme forms a separable identifiable unit of sound, and by changing a phoneme within a word we change the meaning of the word. English, depending on whether it is American English, UK English or another variety, has 43–4 phonemes, which relate to the 26 letters of the alphabet. The written form of words is described in terms of graphemes. Processing the visual form into a speech-based form requires that the graphemes are converted into phonemes, using grapheme to phoneme correspondence (GPC) rules. Applying these rules is only one of a number of key abilities that the beginning reader must acquire and which are identified in Table 7.1.

It is alarming that many of our children fail to acquire this most useful of skills to a level that would allow them to participate fully in our society (see DfEE 1993). Diane McGuinness (1998) argues that this is because we have based our reading programmes, including the much respected Reading Recovery Programme (for an overview and critique see Center *et al.* 1992), on belief rather than knowledge, without recourse to the quality of evidence that would be required in the evaluation of other vital aspects of our lives such as health.

McGuinness argues that the 'phonic v. whole-word' debate that pervades the reading literature is a red herring. Shankweiler (1989) on the other

Table 7.1 Key abilities underpinning early reading

Print awareness	Print carries meaning Reading is directional
Graphic awareness	Recognition of letter details and shapes Letters form words Spaces define words
Phonemic awareness	Ability to hear the separate sounds in words
Awareness of grapheme/ phoneme correspondence	Knowledge that letters and sounds have a relationship; ability to apply that knowledge to decoding unknown words
Morphological awareness	Ability to segment words visually (via graphemes) and aurally (via phonemes), and combine word parts to produce new words
Syntactic awareness	Recognition and use of clauses and sentence level patterns, using within sentence context of words – for example, pronouncing 'lead' in 'He was working with a lead pipe'
Text-structure awareness	Comprehension of relationships between parts of text, including cohesive elements in text and knowledge of text structures, such as an appreciation of storyline

hand argues that text comprehension problems in young children arise from phonological processing difficulties. At 4 years, few children know that words can be broken down into phonemic segments, but by the age of 6 they are beginning to show some level of phonemic awareness. (Nation and Hulme 1997). In alphabetic languages such as English (as opposed to ideographic languages such as Chinese) in which letters represent sounds, phonemic awareness is crucial to learning how to read, and also how to write. Children who are unable to sustain a phonological representation of incoming verbal information will have difficulties in retaining and processing information in verbal working memory (Shankweiler 1989), and this is turn will lead to comprehension failures. Cain *et al.* (1998) concur that there is a well-established relationship between phonological awareness and progress when first learning to read. Indeed, Goswami and Bryant (1990) have shown that phonological training at the level of onset and rime can have positive effects on early readers.

The case for phonics teaching seems well established but the evidence suggests that phonic awareness may be necessary but not sufficient for effective reading. Although phonic methods may work well when we are learning to read languages with a regular orthography such as Finnish or Italian, this is less true for English. The first major hurdle in reading development is providing children with the understanding that there is not a one-to-one correspondence between phonemes and the letters of the alphabet; rather, that printed letters and letter combinations represent the 40 or so phonemes. A second related problem revolves around the number of rules that readers have to learn. Rule-governed systems work very well if the rules are few and the language obeys the rules, but English does not. For example, the 'magic e' rule, which elongates the preceding vowel – MAT to MATE – is broken for words like HAVE which should rhyme with CAVE, if the rule was in operation. Cain *et al.* (1998) argue that reading comprehension difficulties, as opposed to reading accuracy, may not be due to underlying phonological processing difficulties. They have shown that children classed as normal readers but with poor comprehension skills exhibit high-level processing difficulties in inference making, working memory and story structure knowledge. A mastery of good comprehension skills is essential if a child is to achieve a level of critical literacy.

Learning to read in English is a daunting task. Can the use of new technologies help to solve the problem? Is there any evidence that computer-supported learning is an effective strategy in the reading classroom?

Supporting the reading process through ICT

The evidence of learning outcomes from computer-aided learning (CAL) packages mirrors the debate on reading development. There is software to support the development of functional literacy and the basic skills of reading, and also to support wider thinking skills and concept development which fall under the umbrella of critical literacy.

Phonological versus whole-word approaches to reading

Olson and Wise (1992), comparing software based on phonological versus whole-word approaches to reading, found that all children benefited from CAL usage but those using phonologically-based instruction benefited the most. Reitsma (1988) on the other hand found that beginning readers who read text with computer assistance improved as much as a group who were in a reading to an adult situation, even though they made little use of the computer-generated speech. He suggests that accuracy, as demanded in the reading to an adult condition, is not important in the development of sight vocabulary. Rather, it is simply the opportunity for further practice that is most effective. Similarly, Davidson and his colleagues (Davidson 1994; Davidson *et al.* 1996) demonstrated that regular and independent use of such a resource had a positive effect on sight-word acquisition when compared to beginning readers who were not exposed to any supplementary reading instruction. They also found that gains were made in vocabulary not contained in the computerized texts. McKenna (1997) investigated the effectiveness of both whole word pronunciations and exposing children to word analogies in an attempt to encourage independent decoding. Significant gains in word recognition were achieved, but only by those children who had already acquired a limited sight vocabulary. Phonological coaching was not effective but it is suggested that the children in the study may not have been at an appropriate level to have benefited from this form of instruction.

Medwell (1998) looked at two types of talking books: Naughty Stories and the Oxford Reading Tree Level 3 books. Both sets of software appear in parallel print versions and have a similar readability level. The Oxford Reading Tree software is part of a structured reading scheme but the Naughty Stories are a collection of stories without a definitive structure. The first finding of Medwell's research was that using talking books enabled children to retell the story to an adult listener more accurately than simply reading the book alone. However, she also found that children working with the software based on a structured reading scheme were more successful at the task of retelling the story than they were when endeavouring to retell the less structured stories. Medwell argues that this differential performance with the two pieces of software was a result of the simplicity and level of repetition in the Oxford Reading Tree software, compared to the more complex language and storyline of the Naughty Stories software. Medwell noted that her young participants (Key Stage 1) had particular difficulty with the moral theme within the Naughty Stories.

There is therefore some encouragement to the argument that computer-supported reading instruction can have beneficial outcomes. Positive outcomes have been found both for whole word and for phonological approaches to reading. The two studies I present below show that other factors, besides the theory underpinning any reading software, may have profound impacts on learning gains.

Skills tutoring: integrated learning systems

The skills approach model to reading instruction is exemplified by CCC's SuccessMaker reading program, which follows the classic model of guiding learner readers through a hierarchy of pre-reading and reading skills activities. SuccessMaker is an integrated learning system (ILS) that offers individualized tutoring and practice.

An ILS operates on the behaviourist model of learning which uses drill and practice to deliver core curriculum content and skills through individualized tutoring and practice (for a full functional description of an ILS see Brown 1997). Although based on programmed learning, an ILS is brought up to date through the use of the new multimedia technologies, and more importantly through the availability of faster more powerful hardware to support the large data sets and many computations needed to present a differentiated programme of work to students. Individualization is introduced through the use of a computer model of the child's current skills, which are matched to a model of the domain knowledge to be acquired by that child.

SuccessMaker has extensive curriculum modules, delivered and assessed by the management system which can operate independently of teacher or learner control. The program presents variable levels of sub-skills practice through vocabulary enhancement, cloze tests, sentence completion and comprehension activities. Children interact with the software on a one-to-one basis. This closed relationship with the machine is emphasized by the need to use headphones to receive auditory input at key points in the program. As many as 30 children may be working on different problems within one computer room at any one time and this makes the use of headphones essential. The SuccessMaker language package is extensive and provides a differentiated curriculum across Key Stages 1, 2 and 3.

The conclusions drawn here are based upon data collected in two phases over a three-year period. The evaluations began with a short-term Phase 1 (6 months) pilot investigation, which was followed 12 months later by a more sustained, Phase 2 evaluation (12 months). The learning outcomes for reading development from the Phase 1 study presented an inconsistent story (Underwood *et al.* 1994). While attitudes to English were improved by the ILS experience (see Figure 7.1) there were no obvious performance differences between the children working with SuccessMaker and those who were not. When we examined the learning outcomes for all primary and all secondary schools, the ILS and non-ILS groups seemed neither damaged nor enhanced by their ILS or lack of ILS experience. Overall, the results showed that the ILS and control groups made much the same level of progress over the period of the intervention. The pattern of performance when viewed school by school was complex, however. ILS pupils in some schools showed greater gains than their non-ILS peers, while in others the ILS pupils exhibited poorer performances than their peers.

A second round of evaluation was undertaken 12 months later and four primary and four secondary schools took part in the study (Underwood *et al.* 1996). Again, pupil motivation was high: over 80 per cent of children stated that they normally enjoyed their ILS lessons. The findings from this round of testing confirmed those of the earlier study. Once again, for the majority of schools, there was no significant difference in reading gains between ILS and control groups. We had argued in the

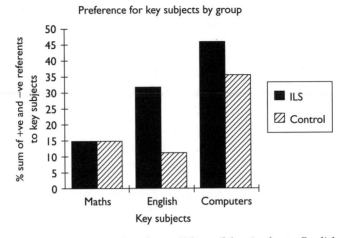

Figure 7.1 Phase 1 ILS and non-ILS pupils' attitudes to English and mathematics

6 month intervention period of Phase 1 that this was too short to produce significant differential performance gains in reading, and this argument was supported by the research literature (Becker 1992). Becker's research led us to predict that effects on reading would occur only after a 12-month trial of the system. We predicted, therefore, that any reading gains would occur in schools that had been part of the Phase 1 trials but this proved incorrect and the positive findings occurred with pupils new to the system. Equally, the one negative finding we recorded for the language programme was in a new primary school.

The disparity in performance across schools was due to the mode of organization of the ILS experience. Two features of the organization appeared to be critical to effective ILS use. The first was that the ILS work was in short daily interactions (15–20 minutes) – that is, the skills development followed a paced practice regime. A longer and less frequent session (one hour per week) proved ineffective not least because children were unable to sustain motivation or attention over these longer periods. A second problem occurred if a school operated a policy of withdrawal of individual children from a class rather than the more prevalent inclusion policy, where all children from a class were involved in working on the ILS. In such schools children had poor attitudes to the ILS experience in comparison to the very positive attitudes expressed by the majority of children in schools where an inclusion policy operated.

Our observation and interview data shed some light on these results. In those schools where differentially positive gains for children using the ILS software occurred, we noted that:

- Children used the software in short, sharp sessions, 15–20 minutes in length, three or more times a week, and were working in a regime of paced practice.
- Children were task focused.
- Teachers made significant interventions in the management of the learning environment – wresting some of the control back from the machine.

In those schools where differentially negative outcomes for children using the ILS software occurred, we noted that:

- Children used the software in hour-long sessions once a week.
- Children were selected as 'in need' of ILS remediation rather than being involved in an activity shared by their peers.
- Children exhibited off-task behaviour. Not surprisingly, behaviour deteriorated after about 30 minutes of intensive work on the ILS. At the one site where the ILS group performed less well than the control group the children were unsupervised and our observations show that their attention to the work in hand was very limited.

The results of the SuccessMaker intervention show some benefits of the language programme at both primary and secondary level but no consistent pattern is discernible. The way in which individual schools chose to incorporate the software into their learning programmes appears to have been a critical factor in the effectiveness of the intervention. The link between positive attitudes to work and measurable learning outcomes was not as clear cut as many might expect. This may in part be due to the fact that positive attitudes to the ILS, particularly for boys, were generated by the lack of writing activities. Boys preferred working with SuccessMaker because they did not have to write stories. The latter activity for many boys was one of the most tedious if not most distressing of all classroom activities.

In one of the few schools where differential learning gains were recorded in favour of the ILS intervention group, teacher intervention may well have been a critical factor in the positive performance outcomes. SuccessMaker manages the work of each child, not by demanding that the child achieves perfect scores, but rather by working on a percentage rate of success, usually set at about 70 per cent. The teachers in the primary school discussed here noted that children were achieving this high rate of success, but when the children were faced with more advanced work their performance deteriorated rapidly. The teachers were rightly puzzled and began to explore the SuccessMaker program in more detail. They discovered that the 70–80 per cent success rate being recorded by their children was due to near perfect performance on four strands of the language programme – strands that focused on word attack skills. All children coped with the fifth activity, which focused on text comprehension, less well than the word skills material. Those children who did particularly poorly on this strand were also the children whose overall language performance fell off when they started work at a more advanced level. This school solved the problem by taking the children back to the earlier text comprehension tasks and not allowing children to advance until they showed skill in this area also. A mastery of good comprehension skills is essential if a child is to achieve a level of critical literacy.

Whole-word reading practice: talking books

The use of talking book software to provide supplementary reading practice is growing rapidly. The second software package discussed here is a disk-based story (a talking book) that exists both in electronic and paper format, designed to provide supplementary reading practice. In this study the talking book was one developed by Brøderbund and based upon Mark Brown's children's story, *Arthur's Teacher Trouble*.

There are a number of reasons for suggesting that educational benefits come through the use of interactive books. Reading storybooks aloud to children is recognized as a crucial component in total literacy development. Indeed, McGuinness (1998) argues that reading aloud is one of the three helpful activities parents can undertake in order to encourage their child's reading development. Interactive books are designed to provide one to one or one to small group support. Their use is also supported by Piaget's notion of learning as an active process, whereby the child constructs their own understanding of the world through interaction with the environment. Interactive books make use of a number of symbol sets to represent information to the learner (i.e. orthographic, pictorial and audio-linguistic). Different symbol systems are processed in different ways, and may be represented differently in memory, and the use of multiple symbol systems in learning media may not only mean that the information has more chance of being absorbed by the learner, with more routes into memory, but also that multiple representations of the same information are generated by the learner. Accordingly, it is more likely that the information will be understood, remembered and recalled by the learner. An educational medium which incorporates text animation, voice with active exploration and online help, as with interactive books, has the potential to bring together in a single instructional environment the advantages afforded to the learner of books, television, computers and teacher–pupil tutoring situations, thereby enhancing comprehension and recall. Additionally, the availability of regular pronunciation of new words may provide more rapid access of sight vocabulary, because it reinforces the link between the marks on the page (graphemes) and the sounds they represent (phonemes).

On the other hand, there may be limited educational gains with the use of interactive books, because much of the animation is not central to the story and may therefore act as a distraction. For example, the text may have little correspondence with illustrations that attract the user's attention. We designed a research study to observe which features of the display gained the reader's attention, and which features were remembered.

The electronic version of the story has a number of modes of use. The children, or the teacher, can elect a non-interactive mode in which the story is read to the children. In the interactive mode the text of each page of the talking book is spoken aloud and then children can 'interact', via mouse input, with the page. This of course includes the option to have the whole text, or a single word, orally represented. The children have other choices, however. The talking book presents an illustration to accompany each paragraph (that is, each 'page' of text), and the components of illustrations may be animated on demand by clicking the mouse when the pointer is in certain parts of the screen. Animated illustrations can develop the depth of the story, and in some instances are congruent with the story, but they can also act as distractions from the principal storyline. An example of a congruent animation would be when Arthur (the hero – a small rodent 'schoolboy') first meets his stern new teacher, Mr Ratburn. Clicking on Arthur produces a 'thought bubble' which clearly articulates Arthur's anxiety about being in this new teacher's class. However, in the same scene children can click on a poster of a baseball player on the school wall and that player will then hit a home run. This is highly amusing but irrelevant to the main plot of this story. The reading level of this text is suitable for Year 4 children (aged 8 and 9 years). The motivating and entertaining characteristics of talking books lend themselves to individual or group reading (see Miller *et al.* 1994).

In contrast to the ILS study in which children worked individually at a machine, in this investigation we worked with pairs of children using the CD-ROM *Arthur's Teacher Trouble* (Underwood and Underwood 1998). Again a traditional pre-test, intervention, post-test design was used but there was no control group. The purpose of this study was not to compare the effectiveness of traditional and non-traditional teaching methods but to investigate what happens when children interact with a rich electronic language resource.

Sixty-two 8-year-old children (31 boys and 31 girls) took part in the study. No member of the sample was considered by their teacher to have learning difficulties, and all had English as their first language.

The children were allocated to pairs on the basis of their reading ages according to McLeod's GAP Reading Comprehension Test (McLeod 1970). The members of each pair had similar recorded reading ability. The children were to use the computer program in one of three dyadic groups: boy/boy, boy/girl or girl/girl, and these three sets of pairs were also matched on reading age. Each pair of children was observed individually, and their interactions with the screen and with each other recorded. One week after work with the storybook had finished, a story comprehension test lasting 30 minutes was administered. The items in the test asked about the story plot, the characters described in the story and the actions of objects that could be animated by clicking on them. Five weeks after working with the software the children were invited to write a short story about Arthur. This story was used to assess their free recall of the events in the CD-ROM storybook. Learning gains, measured by the comprehension task and the free recall (story writing) task, were related to dialogue interaction measures taken from the pairs as they worked through the electronic book.

The first thing of note from this study is that children activated animated features more often than they requested word pronunciations. This confirms the findings of Miller *et al.* (1994), McKenna (1997) and Lewin (1998) who have all shown an underuse of the replay and audio-feedback facilities available in talking books. Many of the animations that so intrigued the children were not related to the text, but the children's recall of these features was superior to their recall of both characters and storyline. The children perceived working with the CD-ROM as a thoroughly enjoyable activity but not an activity directed towards aiding their reading development.

What were the predictors of learning gains? Only pre-intervention reading ability predicted performance on the comprehension test. In the stories written by the children there was a difference in the number of story events recalled by the different gender pairings. Girl/girl pairs outperformed the other pairs, including the girl/boy pairs. As the stories were written individually it might be expected that girls should perform equally well during the story-writing exercise, regardless of the identity of their partner while they were working with the CD-ROM storybook. An analysis of the dialogue between the children in each pair, while working through the pages of the storybook, revealed that pairs of girls showed more tension release by joking and laughing than did the other pairs. Pairs of girls also asked each other for information and orientation more than did the other pairs. Thus, girls working with girls developed a collaborative working relationship which made the task both enjoyable but also focused attention on the educational activity.

Children enjoyed working with the storybook a great deal but both their use of the storybook and their learning were strongly related to those interactive features, such as dancing cookies and the paper aeroplane, which were not central to the main story. Their screen interactions were mainly with these animated features. There were more clicks on these parts of the screen display than on other aspects, and this was reflected in their performance on the comprehension test. Performance on the story recall task, in which the children could write about any aspect of the storybook that they chose, did not show this superiority for recall of irrelevant features. In their own stories about Arthur the children recounted far more story events than descriptions of the animated features. The robust recall of story events during free recall was especially noticeable in the stories written by girls who had been in girl/girl pairs. Furthermore, when girls worked on the storybook with boys their free recall was on a par with that of the boys. Accounting for this effect is not straightforward. The stories were written by individual children working in a quiet classroom. The CD-ROM storybook interactions were completed several weeks previously, and yet some aspect of the paired interaction appears to be associated with recall of the storybook. Analysis of the interactions between the pairs provided a clue as to why girls' memories were influenced by their working partner. Pairs of girls joked and laughed more than other pairs, and were also more likely to ask each other for information than the other pairs. They were more relaxed about working with a partner, they regarded their partner as a source of advice and information, and this had an outcome in their superior recall of the storybook.

Although our investigations with talking books were not directed at performance outcomes we did find that children were extracting meaning from these multimedia presentations. There is some evidence to show that talking books do provide supplementary practice for beginning readers. Clay (1993) argues that such practice positively affects sight-word acquisition irrespective of which word pronunciations are requested and how often, but the texts must be appropriate for a child's current developmental stage.

Teachers' responses to talking books, however, were equivocal. They noted the positive responses of the children to the software but felt that more direct skills teaching would be helpful. In particular, they wanted audio feedback to provide segmented pronunciations at the level of onset and rime (Lewin 1998).

Discussion

Our experiences have shown that children found both of these disparate approaches to language development highly motivating. This is unsurprising for the talking book software, based as it is on a concept of 'edutainment', but the high levels of motivation when using an essentially drill and practice software such as an ILS may surprise some.

Children using the two software packages, the ILS structured sub-skills tutoring program and the talking books whole-word free reading, did show learning gains. The comparative level of gain for each of these teaching strategies cannot be assessed from these data, however. In the case of the ILS, on the whole, children benefited as much from using the ILS as they did from normal classroom teaching. There was little or no evidence to show that they received a differential advantage from using the software in situations other than where the teacher had taken an active role in setting the learning agenda. The mode of employment of the ILS proved highly significant, and in schools where the rule of 'little and often' was not followed children's learning deteriorated below the level of that of their peers in 'normal' classrooms. Such software cannot be 'shoehorned' into the normal timetable structure. Unless a school adapts to the paced practice regime there will be a negative impact on learning.

In the case of the talking book, serendipitous learning took place when children used the software. Medwell (1998) has shown that the use of such software can provide a surrogate adult in the reading process. We found, however, that the social grouping of children, in which peer facilitation occurs, can also aid the learning process.

The message from these two studies is clear, but not simple. Motivation does lead to learning. Learning does occur, but differential performance gains compared to more traditional teaching are not assured. Second, these studies show that current debates about whole-word versus phonological skills teaching can be overshadowed by characteristics of the software other than the mode of teaching. Such variables might include organizational choices and constraints such as length of session, selection of participants and the grouping strategies that teachers make.

Acknowledgements

I wish to thank the children and teachers in the many schools who contributed to this research. This work was supported by grants from DfEE/NCET and the ESRC Centre for Research in Development, Instruction and Training.

Software

'Arthur's Teacher Trouble': Living Books, Brøderbund.
Naughty Stories: Sherston.
Oxford Reading Tree: Level 3.
SuccessMaker: Computer Curriculum Corporation.

References

Becker, H.J. (1992) Computer-based ILSs in the elementary and middle grades: a critical review and synthesis of evaluation reports, *Journal of Educational Computing Research*, 8: 1–42.

Becker, H.J., Ravitz, J.L. and Wong, Y.T. (1999) *Teacher and Teacher-Directed Student Use of Computers and Software*. CRITO, University of California, www.crito.uci.edu/tlc/findings/computeruse/html/startpage.htm

Brown, J. (1997) When is a system an ILS? in J. Underwood and J. Brown (eds) *Integrated Learning Systems in UK Schools*. London: Heinemann.

Cain, K., Oakhill, J. and Bryant, P. (1998) Phonological skills and comprehension failure: a test of the phonological processing deficit hypothesis, *Reading and Writing*, 8: 1–26.

Calfee, R.C. (1994) Critical literacy: reading and writing for a new millennium, in N.J. Ellsworth, C.N. Hedley and A.N. Barratta (eds) *Literacy: A Redefinition*. Mahwah, NJ: Lawrence Erlbaum Associates.

Center, T., Wheldall, K. and Freeman, L. (1992) Evaluating the effectiveness of Reading Recovery: a critique, *Educational Psychology*, 12: 263–74.

Chall, J. (1996) *Learning to Read: The Great Debate*. New York: McGraw-Hill.

Clay, M.M. (1991) Child development, in J. Flood, J.M. Jensen, D. Lapp and J.R. Squire (eds) *Handbook of Research on Teaching the English Language Arts*. New York: Macmillan.

Clay, M.M. (1993) *An Observation Survey Of Early Literacy Achievement*. Auckland: Heinemann.

Davidson, J. (1994) The evaluation of computer-delivered natural speech in the teaching of reading, *Computers and Education*, 22: 181–5.

Davidson, J., Elcock, J. and Noyes, P. (1996) A preliminary study of the effect of computer-assisted practice on reading attainment, *Journal of Research in Reading*, 19, 102–10.

DfE (Department for Education) (1995) *Statistical Bulletin 3/95: Survey of Information Technology in Schools*. London: HMSO.

DfEE (Department for Education and Employment) (1993) *Key Stages 1 and 3: UK National Curriculum Assessment for 1992 and 1993*. London: HMSO.

DfEE (Department for Education and Employment) (1999) *Information and Communications Technology (ICT) in Schools*. http://www.dfee.gov.uk/ict/results.htm (accessed).

Gagne, R.M. (1970) *The Conditions of Learning*. New York: Holt, Rinehart & Winston.

Goswami, U. and Bryant, P. (1990) *Phonological Skills and Learning to Read*. Hove: Lawrence Erlbaum Associates.

Lewin, C. (1998) Talking book design: what do practitioners want? *Computers and Education*, 30: 88–94.

MacLeod, J. (1970) *GAP Reading Comprehension*. London: Heinemann.

McGuinness, D. (1998) *Why Children Can't Read*. Harmondsworth: Penguin.

McKenna, M.C. (1997) *Electronic Texts and The Transformation of Beginning Reading: Technological Transformations in a Post-Typographical World*. Mahwah, NJ: Lawrence Erlbaum Associates.

Medwell, J. (1998) The Talking Books Project: some further insights into the use of talking books to develop reading, *Reading*, 32: 3–8.

Miller, L., Blackstock, J. and Miller, R. (1994) An exploratory study into the use of CD-ROM storybooks, *Computers and Education*, 22: 187–204.

Nation, K. and Hulme, C. (1997) Phonemic segmentation, not onset-rime segmentation, predicts early reading and spelling skills, *Reading Research Quarterly*, 32: 154–67.

Olson, R.K. and Wise, B.W. (1992) Reading on the computer with orthographic and speech feedback: an overview of the Colorado remediation project, *Reading and Writing*, 4: 107–44.

Reitsma, P. (1988) Reading practice for beginners: effects of guided reading, reading-while-listening, and independent reading with computer based speech feedback, *Reading Research Quarterly*, 23: 219–35.

Shankweiler, D. (1989) How problems of comprehension are related to difficulties in word reading, in D. Shankweiler and I.Y. Liberman (eds) *Phonology and Reading Disability: Solving the Reading Puzzle*. Ann Abor, MI: University of Michigan Press.

Underwood, G. and Batt, V. (1996) *Reading and Understanding*. Oxford: Basil Blackwell.

Underwood, G. and Underwood, J.D.M. (1998) Children's interactions and learning outcomes with interactive talking books, *Computers and Education*, 30: 95–102.

Underwood, J., Cavendish, S., Dowling, S., Fogelman, K. and Lawson, T. (1994) *Integrated Learning Systems in U.K. Schools*, Coventry: NCET.

Underwood, J., Cavendish, S., Dowling, S. and Lawson, T. (1996) *Integrated Learning Systems: A Study of Sustainable Gains in U.K. Schools*. Coventry: NCET.

8

POPULAR CULTURE, COMPUTER GAMES AND THE PRIMARY LITERACY CURRICULUM

Jackie Marsh

Introduction

One damp and windy spring morning, I sat in an infant classroom during school breaktime. In this multilingual, inner-city school, children were allowed to stay in classrooms at breaktime if they so wished. There was a constant traffic of children entering the room, huddling furtively in a corner and then rushing outside again. Curious, I went over to a group who were staring intensely at a pile of cards one child held in his hand. They were Pokémon cards, related to a popular computer program of the same name. Much wheeling and dealing went on that breaktime and at the end of it there were a few tears as some children decided they wanted to retrieve cards they had previously swopped. The deputy headteacher had had enough. 'I've banned them from my classroom. They were OK at first, but they are just causing so much aggro', she told me. She is not alone in her reaction. Many reports have surfaced of primary schools banning these trading cards (Burkeman 2000; *TES* 2000). Yet, it seems that much could be gained within the school environment from exploiting children's obvious fascination for these Japanese-inspired computer characters.

This chapter argues for a measured response to cultural icons which populate so many children's lives. It will explore the cultural worlds of children and, in particular, the way in which computer games are located so firmly within this universe. The chapter outlines how children's out of school experiences with computers are often very different from the kinds of computer literacy experiences they are offered in nurseries and schools. The chapter concludes by exploring how primary teachers can exploit children's interest in popular computer games in order to develop language and literacy skills. The aim is to determine how children's fascination with popular computer games can inform the literacy curriculum and is not concerned primarily with the development of computer literacy skills themselves, although of course they will be integral to the work suggested here.

Paradigm shift?

Several studies have sought to identify the ways in which literacy practices are changing in an increasingly technologized world (see Tuman 1992). It seems that, in these first few years of the twenty-first century, we are in the midst of a paradigm shift in the ways in which we communicate, a shift as important as that of the movement from speech to writing or the invention of the printing press which led to widespread literacy development in the last few centuries of the second millennium. There is a need to re-examine the literacy curriculum offered in nurseries and schools to ensure that it enables children to meet the demands placed upon them by increasingly complex texts, whether televisual or printed. One of the ways in which traditional notions of literacy are being transformed is in the insistence that we should not focus simply on children's encounters with print-based texts. Kress (1998) has detailed how the nature of texts has changed and suggests that children are now less frequently presented with linear modes of representation. Instead, print is juxtaposed with images and hyperlinks disrupt the usual linear sequences of text. Some have lamented these changes, seeing in them a threat to traditional notions of literacy:

> As we perfect our lateral sweeps in every direction, flying from node to node, we are also pulling away from language. Language, that is, understood as a process more profound than a mere signal system. We are losing our grip, collectively, on the logic of complex utterance, on syntax; we are abandoning the rhythmic, poetic undercurrents of expression, and losing touch with the etymological variety that has always pointed back towards coinages and, implicitly, the historical perspective.
>
> (Birkerts 1998: 24)

But as traditionalists cling on to long-established notions of what it means to be literate, it is evident that practices are changing. Children engage regularly with texts that are multi-modal in nature, whether print-based or televisual. One could argue that the reading and linguistic skills demanded by televisual, multi-modal texts are, in fact, more demanding than books, but it is futile to journey down this road of textual hierarchy and competition. Rather, we should accept that different genres demand different reading skills and spend time exploring which skills are developed by specific genres, and how such skills can be transferred across genre boundaries.

Computer games can be recognized as multi-modal texts in a number of ways. They present a narrative to young children, a narrative in which players are positioned both as consumer and producer as they take on the actions of characters within the games (Kinder 1991). The games juxtapose images with text, although the amount of text presented to children differs from game to game, with some containing minimal printed text. In addition, children have to read the visual images, both static and moving, in order to understand the rules of the game and succeed in it. Playing computer games demands particular reading skills, some of which overlap with those used in interactions with printed texts. This point will be explored later in the chapter.

The computer games with which children most frequently engage are positioned as pleasurable texts, rather than educational. Educational computer games are those designed with a specific instructive purpose and many focus on skills training related to schooled notions of literacy. For example, some educational games are designed to introduce children to phoneme–grapheme correspondence, or to develop users' abilities to recognize and spell key words. Some programs are calculated to appeal directly to concerned parents, with claims that the games improve children's attainment in the National Curriculum blazoned on the packaging. However, there is some evidence that children increasingly disengage from educational computer games as they get older, preferring more commercially successful games (Funk and Buchman 1995). These commercialized games, which form the focus of this chapter, are often located within children's popular culture. The next section explores briefly the nature of this culture before moving on to look in more detail at young children's use of popular computer games and the kinds of literacy skills they promote.

Popular culture

Culture is a difficult term to define accurately, and there have been numerous attempts over the years (Eagleton 2000). One of the most useful definitions is that of the sociologist Peterson, who suggested that culture is a set of beliefs, norms, values and expressive symbols belonging to a group of people in any given society (Jenks 1993). 'Popular culture', or 'mass culture' are terms used to refer to the beliefs, values and practices shared by large numbers of people. However, the term 'popular culture' does not simply refer to numbers; it is also associated with those aspects of culture which are enjoyed by the mass populace; culture which is not sited within the 'high' arts. Thus classical music, opera and fine art are often positioned on one side of the cultural divide and football, bingo and popular music on the other. The divisions within children's cultural interests are not as distinct, although there are particular books, television programmes and other artefacts which are obviously placed within popular culture. The beliefs, practices and objects that constitute children's popular culture are vast and varied and include music, television and film, sport, toys, books, comics and magazines, computers and related merchandise, clothing, hair accessories, jewellery, oral rhymes, jokes, wordplay and food (Marsh and Millard 2000). This diverse range of resources provides the shared artefacts of children's cultural lives. Children develop relationships with peers based on common understandings about these artefacts and thus establish shared meanings based on collective discourses.

Children's popular culture in the developed world is bound up intimately with the media. Characters and narratives from television programmes, films and videos are related to toys, books and a range of consumer goods. Fast-food chains offer figures from these programmes and films in their 'happy meals' and so children are surrounded by a complex web of intertextual references. Technological developments are central to this cultural iconography as television, video, computers and digital products offer a range of leisure pursuits for children. This has led to much consternation in the adult world, with many lamenting the loss of traditional pursuits: 'the rise of electronic media seems to have undermined the traditional healthy preoccupations of street play, peer conversation and just wandering in the garden long associated with a happy childhood' (Kline 1993: 12).

This romanticized construction of childhood which lingers in the memories of some people bears little relation to the hardships suffered by many children in pre- and post-war Britain. It is just such a romanticized vision of childhood which leads some critics of popular culture to insist that media texts have a corrupting influence on children (Postman 1983). However, Springhall (1998) has demonstrated forcefully how many adults have always reacted in hysterical ways to the popular culture of children and teenagers. He has traced a series of 'moral panics' over popular culture from 'penny dreadfuls' at the turn of the nineteenth century through to gangster movies, comics, video games and rap in the twentieth century. This mistrust of popular culture is often based on a fear of an unknown world, a world which appears to be very different from that experienced by adult observers. As Springhall (1998: 161) suggests: 'The frightened would like to disinvent the new technology that has created the domestic video-cassette recorder or the home computer and return society to an imaginary, non-violent popular culture, a mythical golden-age of tranquil juvenile pastimes'.

Moral panics engendered by commercialized computer games are fed by the frenzy of the tabloid press, which often sensationalizes the issues. This media hype, coupled with a lack of familiarity with the games themselves, leads many teachers to feel that such games are unsuitable material for the classroom. Indeed, a number of them are, but some can be usefully put to work in order to meet broader curriculum aims. However, it is important to address the oppressive and commercially exploitative discourses which are often embedded within popular games programs before using them within the classroom. The following section examines computer games children play and some of the criticisms made about them.

Computer games and their critics

There has been a range of work suggesting that there is a 'Nintendo generation' of children (Green *et al.* 1998; Luke 2000) who have grown up surrounded by, and engaged with, a range of computer games and related products. Clearly, many children in the developed world are familiar with computer games, whether or not they own them (Sanger *et al.* 1997). It is a multi-billion dollar business and a rapidly growing field. The advent of DVD technology brings the possibility of interactive games which combine television, Internet and music in home entertainment systems. However, the significance of these developments in terms of the literacy curriculum in nurseries and schools is that computer games are located within a universe of related products, which include books, comics and magazines. The more successful computer games for younger children are usually linked to television series, videos or films which promote specific characters and narratives. Children thus become keen to acquire certain computer games not simply because of their status as a game, but because it secures their position in the cultural world shared by their peers. That this is a rich intertextual world (Kinder 1991) which is open to commercial exploitation is beyond question and is what the makers of the recent and hugely popular computer game Pokémon have exploited so ruthlessly. As Burkeman (2000: 2) notes: 'the game is only part of the rapidly proliferating phenomenon. Pokémon is also a cartoon series, a movie and a collection of miniature figurines; and a plethora of merchandising tie-ins, magazines, books, comics and fast-food sponsorship deals'. This has led to much criticism of the aggressive marketing of children by these industries and thus exacerbates many educationalists' inherent mistrust of the products.

Some computer games can be played on a personal computer, but the most popular titles are those that can be used on a games console such as Nintendo, Sony Playstation, Dreamcast or a hand-held Gameboy. Games consoles are potent machines which have been developed solely for the use of games. In fact, as Fleming (1996: 180) points out, Nintendo deliberately masked the computing potential of these consoles in order to market them as gaming machines:

> Nintendo's marketing success was in downplaying the identity of their box of tricks as a computer and emphasising instead its identity as a toy. To this day, Nintendo consoles have computer system interface connectors tucked away under a little plastic cover, connectors that would allow them to function as processing units within more elaborate computer systems . . . but Nintendo, except for a few trials in Japan, have not yet decided to market their boxes in this way.

Many children have access to Nintendo, Sony Playstation or Dreamcast games through ownership, or the use of the machines of friends, relatives and neighbours. Class is a defining factor in access to different types of computer; working-class children are more likely to own a games console than a PC (Gaile 1993; Sefton-Green 1999). This means that the games that many middle-class children play on their machines may be the same as, or similar to, those games found on machines in school. It also means that teachers are less likely to be familiar with the games played by working-class children and therefore more likely to stereotype the programs.

Which games are most popular with young children? A recent survey of 6- and 7-year-olds in a multicultural, inner-city school (Marsh and Millard 2000) suggested that the most popular games were:

- Pokémon
- Super Mario Brothers
- Sonic the Hedgehog
- Rugrats
- South Park
- Superman
- Simpsons

Most of these games are part of the territory of pupils' popular culture. As suggested earlier, children have access not just to the computer games, but related comics, magazines, books, toys and household artefacts. Fleming (1996: 102) has suggested that this constitutes a 'narrativisation' process whereby artefacts are collectively linked to one theme to form a broad narrative and relate to each other as different aspects of that narrative. Thus, the satisfaction derived from playing with any one of the commodities is heightened because of the associated meanings derived from other commodities. We have seen how the Pokémon phenomenon has taken advantage of this approach to toys and games for children, but it is not alone. Disney, for example, has similar marketing strategies and the computer games they produce fit seamlessly into this semiotic web of interrelated texts. It is this intertextuality which offers considerable potential for literacy development within the classroom, yet these types of game are rarely mentioned in textbooks aimed at teachers. However, in order to utilize them effectively, we need first to take a closer look at the programs themselves.

The nature of the games

Computer games have developed considerably since the 1970s and 1980s when the first home games appeared. Technological advances mean that more realistic settings have been developed and players can become involved in particular elements of the game. However, the types of game popular with many young children primarily involve the players negotiating a character through specific terrains which contain a range of challenges. Players have to be successful at meeting these challenges before being allowed to move on to a more difficult level. Fleming (1996: 190) has described the pleasure derived from such games: 'Playing Mario well is a wonderful experience. Playing for the first – and second or third or tenth – time can be very frustrating. But when it starts to come right there is a bodily ease combined with a mental alertness that together support one's absorption . . . into the Mushroom Kingdom'.

This absorption into the world of the computer game has alarmed critics, with some suggesting that games are addictive (Griffiths 1993). However, there is little real evidence of this. Studies suggest that there is a wide range of level of involvement in computer games, with some children playing approximately two hours a day and others two hours a week (Funk *et al.* 1997). Children certainly appear to use these games no more often than they watch television (Livingstone and Bovill 1999). Other concerns relate to the undoubted violence, racism and sexism contained within many popular computer games.

Oppressive ideologies

Many computer games involve some level of aggression and violence, although the 'zapping' of inanimate objects found in the most inane games bears little relationship to the graphic violence contained in others. It is this violent element which has caused most controversy. The 'ill-effects' literature has been widely criticized in relation to television violence (Barker and Petley 1997) and it is clear that there is also a lack of conclusive evidence to suggest a direct link between the playing of computer games and subsequent levels of aggression in players. There are no straightforward answers, but teachers need to tread carefully through such highly charged territory. Talking about the issues with children, rather than ignoring them, is a way of ensuring pupils are engaged more critically with the material. This is not to suggest, however, that children's critical faculties are automatically suspended when they play such games.

There is some evidence that boys are more attracted to computer games than girls (Sanger *et al.* 1997). The discourse which surrounds computer games is undoubtedly masculinist in nature. Alloway and Gilbert (1998) outline how the marketing of such games is aimed at boys and, certainly, any cursory glance at computer magazines on a newsagent's shelf would confirm this. The characters within many of the narratives are, primarily, male and the few female characters that exist are steeped in stereotypical iconography. Thus the Tomb Raider series of games does feature a female, Lara Croft, as the main protagonist, but she looks like an electronic Barbie doll and embodies what Connell (1987) suggests is an 'emphasized femininity', in contrast to the hegemonic masculinity embedded within the computer games discourse. Hence, Lara Croft becomes the pin-up girl of the gaming world and her physical attributes take on a significance beyond the world of the computer narrative. Other female characters within the games feature more frequently as victims to be rescued or zapped and lack the agency associated with male characters. This does not appear to deter females from playing the games. Gaile (1993) has suggested that many girls enjoy computer games, though they do not play them as frequently as boys.

The xenophobia and racism within the discourse has been less frequently explored, but is no less apparent. Black and ethnic minority characters are rare and, when they do appear, are often constructed as the villains and given stereotypical attributes. The situation is changing gradually as more manufacturers become aware of the need to reflect the make-up of their prime audiences, but there is still some way to go before computer games represent fairly the multicultural world in which we live. This in itself poses difficulties for many teachers who are now using picture books and fiction texts which reflect a more diverse world. Such concerns could make work on computer games appear to be a retrogressive step. However, as in work on violence and sexism, children can be encouraged to explore issues of racism in computer games, analysing the texts and engaging in dialogue with manufacturers and magazine editors about such concerns.

The anxieties aroused by computer games are similar to criticisms made of many popular cultural texts aimed at children (Marsh and Millard 2000). Some criticisms do have strong foundations and cannot be suppressed, yet simply dismissing these texts will not serve the interests of children, who will ignore such worries and engage with the games anyway. Rather, educators need to explore what benefits can be gained from work which enables children to acknowledge the pleasure they receive from the discourses at the same time as encouraging them to critically analyse the content. In addition, popular computer games cannot be simply dismissed as having little educational value. The next section moves on to examine studies which indicate that children do benefit from their engagement with these games.

The educational value of computer games

Because of their extensive permeation in many children's lives, it is important to examine what skills are developed when children play popular computer games. Research conducted in this area has tended not to separate games into 'educational' and 'commercial', apart from the research relating to the effect of violent games. As suggested earlier, the term 'educational game' is used here to refer to programs which ostensibly aim to develop children's skills in particular areas that are linked to the school curriculum, using a game format. Commercial games are primarily constructed for pleasure; any educational benefits are incidental. It is necessary, therefore, to look at the more general literature on the educational benefits to be gained from playing computer games.

Research has indicated that hand–eye coordination is developed as children manipulate the figures on screen around tracks and paths (Loftus and Loftus 1983; Greenfield 1984; Gagnon 1985). Gagnon (1985) suggests that such games improve spatial skills; children need to be aware of direction, the height and width of the settings on the screen, as well as one object's relationship to another. Other researchers have argued that computer games develop problem-solving skills (Greenfield 1984), although this is dependent upon the nature of the game in question and usually applies to adventure games. However, other types of popular commercialized games such as platform games and 'shoot-'em-ups' demand a certain level of problem solving, as challenges are always posed and particular movements necessary in order to increase scores and move on to the next level. Greenfield (1984) states that computer games develop children's skills in parallel processing – that is, their ability to absorb information from a number of sources at once. She also argues that computer games develop the capacity to 'induce the relations among multiple interacting variables' (1984: 103). It is these two skills, parallel processing and inductive reasoning, which seem to be particularly evident in young children's game-playing and there needs to be further research undertaken in order to explore the transferability of these skills to other areas of learning. It could be argued that children who play computer games regularly might benefit from an improved ability to concentrate on activities for sustained periods of time and may also be more strongly orientated towards independent learning. However, Monteith (1999) also reminds us that collaborative learning is enhanced through the use of computers and, indeed, many children delight in introducing each other to the rules and 'cheats' involved in particular games. In addition, Monteith suggests that:

> it is certainly true that early games playing has produced one fortui-
> tous yet agreeable outcome – children understand high numbers
> much more quickly than they once did . . . Games manufacturers
> tend to put games scores in high numbers. Now very young children
> can tell the difference between their scores and those of other players.
>
> (1999: 141)

It can be seen that computer games do have a great deal of potential in terms of children's learning. Certainly, as the skills needed to interact with televisual texts increase as technological advances develop the medium, one could argue that children who are comfortable with the visual literacy skills needed for computer games have a head start in this area. However, there are less obvious links with literacy skills that relate to the reading of printed text. There may be direct ways in which the playing of computer games relates to reading and writing skills in relation to printed text. For example, improved hand–eye coordination and fine motor skills as a result of playing the games could enhance children's writing skills. Computer games do develop visual awareness and so could develop the skills necessary to read complex textual layouts which include texts and pictures. The games sometimes feature written instructions within their narrative structure and so promote print-reading skills. In addition, the games are accompanied by written instructions and pack-aging which contain a variety of printed text. However, it is more likely that benefits are indirectly linked to literacy. Robinson (1997: 180) has detailed the similarities that exist between reading print and televisual narratives and suggests that:

> it is their understandings of and familiarity with narrative on which
> the children are drawing, rather then any similarities inherent in the
> media. They are learning about narrative from their encounters
> with narrative in whichever medium, rather than being taught by
> television how to read print or vice versa.

Powerful links can be made between the narratives of computer games and those of printed texts (Berger 2000). Nonetheless, it is computer games' place within the 'commercial supersystem of transmedia inter-textuality' (Kinder 1991: 3) that I would argue provides the possibilities for developing children's literacy skills. Children who play computer games may be encouraged to read related books or comics. In a study of 'heavy users' (children who played computer games for more than two hours a day), researchers found that those children who were the heaviest users of computer games also self-reported as being keener readers than other children in the study: 'They also report reading more comics and books, although the latter should be set in the context of the fact that they tend to prefer less demanding material such as picture books' (Roe and Muijs 1998: 190).

In their haste to dismiss the reading skills of these 'heavy users' of computer games, the researchers do not explore the nature of the reading material with which the children were engaged. It is possible that the children were reading magazines and comics related to the computer games they were playing. This kind of reading has been traditionally denigrated as inferior to the reading of continuous prose (as is suggested in Roe and Muijs' final comment), but actually the reading skills demanded by this genre are not insubstantial. It is, simply, not the case that a text which contains pictures is less demanding to read than is continuous prose. Indeed, children's computer magazines present innumerable challenges to readers. Children need to be able to navigate complex layouts and relate text to pictures and diagrams. This type of reading ability is becoming more important with developments in technology (Kress and van Leeuwen 1996). As suggested earlier, it may be the case that children who are comfortable with complex visual layouts, such as the settings used in many computer games, have some advantages in reading material of this type. However, the significance of Roe and Muijs' findings lies in the fact that the children who were deemed the heaviest users of computer games also appeared to be the most avid readers. Many educators have feared that the onset of computer games would lead to the demise of reading, with concerns that some children will spend more time playing computer games than they do reading books. This may be the case (see Livingstone and Bovill 1999), but that does not necessarily mean that children are reading less than they were before the advent of computer games. As it is evident that there has been an increase in book-buying over the years (Hearst 1998), one could argue that children's computer game-playing is replacing other kinds of leisure pursuits, such as playing outside with peers. In addition, these studies usually compare game-playing with the reading of books and fail to address the wider reading diet of children, which includes comics and magazines. It would appear that computer games present numerous opportunities for children to engage in pleasurable reading, even if not the type of reading recognized and valued by many adults.

Computer games in the classroom

How do children's experiences of computers at home map onto their experiences in the classroom? Evidence suggests that for many children, there is a clear disjunction between experiences of a computer in both environments (Sanger *et al.* 1997; Livingstone and Bovill 1999). Some types of game produced for PCs are similar to those which can be played on a Nintendo or Sony Playstation machine, but obviously there is a much wider variety on offer. Certainly the games which are located within classrooms are PC-based and more educational in nature. It is these games which middle-class children's parents are more likely to buy for use within the home. This serves to further increase the 'cultural capital' (Bourdieu 1977) of middle-class children in that they bring to school a ready knowledge of a genre more commonly used within the classroom, which gives them an educational advantage. The work of Giroux (1988), Luke (1993), Gee (1996) and Lankshear *et al.* (1997) has been instrumental in informing our understanding of how the literacy curriculum is located within dominant cultural discourses. I would argue that we see the same processes at work in relation to computer literacy skills. The computer literacy skills of children who are located within dominant cultural groups (i.e. white, middle class) are celebrated within the curriculum, while those of working-class children are ignored, or even derided. Sanger *et al.* (1997) in a study of 4–9-year-olds' experiences with videos and computer games, found that popular computer games were viewed with scepticism and hostility by teachers:

> teachers were disinclined to embrace anything related to commercial, as opposed to educational, hardware and software . . . Games magazines were unknown territory to many teachers (and parents) with whom we talked, although teachers admitted to banishing them from schools without any knowledge of the contents.
>
> (Sanger *et al.* 1997: 39)

It is clear that many educationalists do not value the out-of-school computer literacy practices of most working-class children and opportunities are not provided for children to bring their substantial knowledge of this genre into the classroom. No doubt it is the negative aspects of the genre, which we explored earlier, which deter teachers, yet the games do offer great potential to motivate children and develop literacy skills.

Using popular games in the classroom

Popular computer games can provide a range of opportunities for exciting literacy work within the classroom. Not all of this work involves children playing the games at school; indeed, most does not. However, using the games in school would be a useful means of developing children's speaking and listening skills. Children could be asked to bring in their favourite game and demonstrate it to others, explaining its rules. Children could then be interviewed in depth about that game by their peers. This activity could provide an opportunity for those children who are usually reluctant to talk in front of a group to develop confidence, through the discussion of a topic about which they are particularly knowledgeable.

Table 8.1 Frame for computer game review

Title of game:

Setting:
Characters:
What you have to do to win:
Good features:
Not-so-good features:
Overall recommendation:
Overall rating ⟶1 2 3 4 5 6 7 8 9 10
                 Not very good   Very good

One of the obvious ways in which children can celebrate their passion for computer games is to devise a database which enables them to compare and contrast the types of game played by members of the class. In one Year 2 class, this led to the recognition that computer games were almost as popular with girls as they were with boys. Working with databases encourages children to develop a range of literacy skills as they enter and manipulate data. Databases can be set up which enable children to compare and contrast specific features of computer games. This work could promote children's understanding of the various genres, such as adventure games, fantasy games or 'real-life' scenarios. The types of characters and settings found in each of the genres could be analysed and the narrative structure of the games determined, using similar techniques to those used with fiction texts. For example, children can be asked to sequence the story of a particular game in images and captions, or produce a comic-strip version of the story (see Thomas 1998 for a range of ideas relating to the analysis of narrative structures).

Children enjoy writing reviews of computer games and there are a number of magazines which can provide models for this. The frame shown in Table 8.1 has proved helpful in classrooms of younger children. Frames like this can be placed in a familiar software program which children can access when necessary. Reviews could then be compiled into one booklet that children can access. Adding such reviews to class websites can assure the site's attractiveness to other children.

Children enjoy devising their own computer games. If the relevant software is available, Papert (1993) suggests that children should be taught programming in order to develop their own electronic games. However, games can also be devised in a simple paper-planning exercise. Such a task can develop problem-solving skills as well as extend proficiency in reading and writing as children research characters, develop the setting and provide an overall narrative structure for their game. Even younger children can be encouraged to devise simple outlines for their own games and such activities can motivate reluctant writers (see Marsh and Millard 2000: 132).

Once children have analysed a range of commercial games in terms of their violence, racism or sexism, they could be asked to devise computer games which challenge these stereotypes. In addition, classes could investigate current press scare stories relating to computer games. Responses could include letters to the local and national press, or the organization of a children's phone-in to argue whether Pokémon cards, Gameboys and so on should be banned.

Popular computer games offer the potential for work on a range of genres as children write instructions for games, devise promotional leaflets for their products, develop glossaries of essential terms users must know, create posters which advertise games, develop online 'fanzines' of particular games and so on. All of these activities can be used to stimulate the development of information and communication technology (ICT) skills as children use word processors, desktop publishing software, web authoring tools, multimedia packages, digital cameras and scanners. Such work is to be promoted not because it develops skills that other topics cannot, but because it may provide motivation and stimulus for children who may otherwise feel they are not fully paid-up members of the 'literacy club' (Smith 1988). In addition, incorporating the interests of all children into the curriculum can begin to break down the institutional barriers which exclude the cultural capital of certain groups; however, this is not to make the simplistic suggestion that such an act can, of itself, promote equality of opportunity within the educational system.

Conclusion

Throughout this chapter, I have argued that nurseries and schools need to take account of children's home computer literacy skills if they are to provide learning experiences which build upon the skills and experiences children already have. There is indicative evidence that the introduction of popular culture into the primary literacy curriculum can provide a great deal of pleasure, dialogue and motivation, and orientate children towards schooled literacy practices (Dyson 1996, 1998; Marsh 1999, 2000). Computer games are such an integral part of children's popular culture that they offer more potential than many other texts with which children engage. The consequences for continuing to ignore children's out-of-school computer literacy practices are made more serious by the rapid speed at which technology ensures that such practices will be even more ubiquitous in years to come. If we fail to comprehend the full nature of the literacy experienced by the children we teach, then the texts we offer them within the confines of the classroom will seem increasingly outmoded and uninteresting to them. This is not to suggest that the rich array of children's books in the book corner, built up so carefully over the years, needs to be ripped apart to make exclusive room for Pokémon, Super Mario and Streetfighter, but that the texts offered need to be as diverse as the children we teach, reflecting a range of home interests and creating rich opportunities for dialogue.

References

Alloway, N. and Gilbert, P. (1998) Video game culture: playing with masculinity, violence and pleasure, in S. Howerd (ed.) *Wired Up: Young People and the Electronic Media*. London: UCL Press.
Barker, M. and Petley, J. (eds) (1997) *Ill Effects: The Media-Violence Debate*. London: Routledge.
Berger, A.A. (2000) Arthur's computer (narrative) adventure, *Televizion*, 13(1): 40.
Birkerts, S. (1998) Sense and semblance: the implications of virtuality, in B. Cox (ed.) *Literacy is Not Enough: Essays on the Importance of Reading*. Manchester: Manchester University Press.
Bourdieu, P. (1977) *Outline of a Theory of Practice*. Cambridge: Cambridge University Press.
Burkeman, O. (2000) Pokemon Power, *The Guardian*, 20 April: 2–3.
Connell, R.W. (1987) *Gender and Power: Society, The Person and Sexual Politics*. Cambridge: Polity Press.
Dyson, A.H. (1996) Cultural constellations and childhood identities: On Greek gods, cartoon heroes, and the social lives of schoolchildren, *Harvard Educational Review*, 66(3): 471–95.
Dyson, A.H. (1998) Folk processes and media creatures: reflections on popular culture for literacy educators, *The Reading Teacher*, 51(5): 392–402.
Eagleton, T. (2000) *The Idea of Culture*. Oxford: Blackwell.
Fleming, D. (1996) *Powerplay: Toys as Popular Culture*. Manchester: Manchester University Press.
Funk, J.B. and Buchman, D.D. (1995) Video game controversies, *Paediatric Annals*, 24: 91–4.
Funk, J.B., Behmann, J.N. and Buchman, D.D. (1997) Children and electronic games in the United States, *Trends in Communication*, 2: 111–26.
Gagnon, D. (1985) Videogames and spatial skills: an exploratory study, *Educational Communication and Technology Journal*, 33(4): 263–75.
Gaile, C.W. (1993) Mediated messages: gender, class and cosmos in home video games, *Journal of Popular Culture*, 27(1): 81–98.
Gee, P. (1996) *Social Linguistics and Literacies: Ideology in Discourses*, 2nd edn. London: Taylor & Francis.
Giroux, H.A. (1988) *Schooling for Democracy: Critical Pedagogy in the Modern Age*. London: Routledge.
Green, B., Reid, J. and Bigum, C. (1998) Teaching the Nintendo generation? Children, computer culture and popular technologies, in S. Howerd (ed.) *Wired Up: Young People and the Electronic Media*. London: UCL Press.
Greenfield, P.M. (1984) *Mind and Media: The Effects of Television, Computers and Video Games*. London: Fontana.

Griffiths, M.D. (1993) Are computer games bad for children? *The Psychologist: Bulletin of the British Psychological Society*, 6: 401–7.

Hearst, S. (1998) Television and its influences on reading, in B. Cox (ed.) *Literacy is Not Enough: Essays on the Importance of Reading*. Manchester: Manchester University Press.

Jenks, C. (1993) *Culture*. London: Routledge.

Kinder, M. (1991) *Playing with Power in Movies: Television and Video Games from Muppet Babies to Teenage Mutant Ninja Turtles*. Berkeley, CA: University of California Press.

Kline, S. (1993) *Out of the Garden: Toys and Children's Culture in the Age of TV Marketing*. London: Verso.

Kress, G. (1998) Visual and verbal modes of representation in electronically mediated communication: the potentials of new forms of text in I. Snyder *Page to Screen*. London: Routledge.

Kress, G. and van Leeuwen, T. (1996) *Reading Images: The Grammar of Visual Design*. London: Routledge.

Lankshear, C. with Gee, J.P., Knobel, M. and Searle, C. (1997) *Changing Literacies*. Buckingham: Open University Press.

Livingstone, S. and Bovill, M. (1999) *Young People, New Media*. London: London School of Economics.

Loftus, G.R. and Loftus, E.E. (1983) *Mind at Play: The Psychology of Video Games*. New York: Basic Books.

Luke, A. (1993) *The Social Construction of Literacy in the Primary School*. Melbourne: Macmillan Education Australia.

Luke, C. (2000) What next? Toddler Netizens, Playstation Thumb, Techno-literacies, *Contemporary Issues in Early Childhood*, 1(1): 95–100.

Marsh, J. (1999) Batman and Batwoman go to school: popular culture in the literacy curriculum, *International Journal of Early Years Education*, 7(2): 117–31.

Marsh, J. (2000) Teletubby tales: popular culture in the early years literacy curriculum, *Contemporary Issues in Early Childhood*, 1(2): 119–36 (www.triangle.co.uk/ciec/).

Marsh, J. and Millard, E. (2000) *Literacy and Popular Culture: Using Children's Culture in the Classroom*. London: Paul Chapman.

Monteith, M. (1999) Computer literacy, in J. Marsh and E. Hallet (eds) *Desirable Literacies: Approaches to Language and Literacy in the Early Years*. London: Paul Chapman.

Papert, S. (1993) *The Children's Machine: Rethinking School in the Age of the Computer*. London: Harvester Wheatsheaf.

Postman, N. (1983) *The Disappearance of Childhood*. London: W.H. Allen.

Robinson, M. (1997) *Children Reading Print and Television*. London: Falmer Press.

Roe, K. and Muijs, D. (1998) Children and computer games: A profile of the heavy user, *European Journal of Communication*, 13(2): 181–200.

Sanger, J. with Willson, J., Davies, B. and Whitaker, R. (1997) *Young Children, Videos and Computer Games*. London: Falmer Press.

Sefton-Green, J. (1999) Review article: playing the game: the critical study of computer games, *Convergence*, 5(4): 114–20.

Smith, F. (1988) *Joining the Literacy Club – Further Essays into Education*. London: Heinemann.

Springhall, J. (1998) *Youth, Popular Culture and Moral Panics: Penny Gaffs to Gangsta Rap*. Basingstoke: Macmillan.

TES (2000) Pocket monsters provoke fights, *Times Educational Supplement*, 14 April: 4.

Thomas, H. (1998) *Reading and Responding to Fiction*. Leamington: Scholastic.

Tuman, M. (1992) *Wordperfect: Literacy in the Computer Age*. London: Falmer Press.

9

TALKING STORIES, TEXTOIDS AND DIALOGIC READING

Bob Fox

Introduction: talking stories

'We went to the beach, just Grandma and me...' The speaker is Little Critter, an anthropomorphic furry rodent of indeterminate species, at the start of *Just Grandma and Me*, by Mercer Mayer (1983), which is probably the best known talking book CD-ROM in the world, and perhaps the best loved, if Internet reviews are anything to go by. Little Critter speaks in a child's voice (in American, Japanese or Spanish in the US edition, or English, French or German in the UK version); he is male, and represents 6-year-olds everywhere in his cheerily egocentric assertions about what he did on his day at the beach. As he speaks, the text on the page is highlighted a phrase at a time, and part of his story is enacted in the picture. As soon as the talking is over, a pointer appears, and control is passed to the user who is then in a position to *play*.

Almost any object on the screen can be a target for the mouse-wielding user. You point at an object and click, and if it is a 'hotspot' something happens. There are on average 23 hotspots per page (Lewis 2000). A bird leaves its nest and flies in a circle, accompanied by aeroplane noises; a starfish does a dance; a cloud transforms into an elephant. As the story of Little Critter's day at the beach unfolds, a multitude of little dramas are enacted by the bit-players in the scene. An owl with a fishing rod catches a boot; a female raccoon steps onto the sand and finds it too hot for her feet. Some characters appear on several of the pages, their own stories developing in parallel to the main theme, though they may appear oblivious to it. Some characters seem to have a greater awareness of their context – they are *performing* for *you*: the pelican on the jetty on page 8 turns his head to acknowledge the reader (or viewer) both before and after he performs a neat trick to catch a fish, as if to say, 'Watch this' and 'See?'

Some motifs recur (the starfish, the beach umbrellas), but on each page their actions are different. The reader is thus encouraged to anticipate, speculate and predict, and the pages are not short of imaginative surprises, at least at the first reading. This is a fertile environment for someone's imagination.

The depth of observation of human behaviour is also impressive, as is the impeccable timing of some of the incidental activity. Clicking on a flower on page 1 causes a bee to fly onto Little Critter's hat. When Grandma draws his attention to it, the level and manner of his panic are instantly recognizable and understandable, and Grandma responds as Grandmas do: 'Keep still – you'll frighten the bee'. Little Critter asks nervously if the bee has gone, at which point it flies off, leaving Grandma to reply calmly, 'Yes dear – it's just flown away . . .'

Just Grandma and Me existed as a picture book before the CD-ROM was created. The text of both versions is identical; in general terms the pictures show the same objects, characters and events, though the CD-ROM pages are more elaborate and more densely populated, and the layout has been altered somewhat to accommodate the various animations. Interestingly, the animal nature of Little Critter and Grandma has been reduced on the CD-ROM; they no longer have the clawed hands and feet that were evident in the book. Mayer is a prolific author, and there are many Little Critter books. He is also personally involved in the production of CD-ROMs of his stories.

The animations may be categorized into three headings. First, there are actions or sounds which are directly relevant to the central theme, and enhance or deepen one's experience of it (click on the window of Grandma's house on page 1 and the telephone rings, followed by Grandma's voice saying, 'This is Grandma's answerphone – Little Critter and I went to the beach – talk to you later!'). Second, there are many actions which, though they are completely incidental to the central theme, nevertheless add local colour to the scene on the page. Some characters and motifs, as I have indicated above, actually follow through from page to page, and it can take several readings before even the most astute of readers notices the connections. Third, there are the trivial 'fun' actions like the dancing starfish, which apparently contribute nothing to the main story, but are included simply for their instant amusement value. Lewis (2000: 21) refers to these as 'attractive nuisances'. When teachers raise objections to talking books because of their 'triviality' it is always actions in this third category that they cite. It may be, however, that some of these have an unacknowledged (and probably unmeasurable) value in their capacity to develop anticipation and prediction skills. As the first two categories are not generally commented on, their potential value is unacknowledged.

At the outset (in parallel with the other CD-ROMs in the 'Living Books' series to which *Just Grandma and Me* belongs), you are offered two choices: 'Read to me', in which case the story runs without the added animations, and 'Let me play'. It is hard to imagine that anyone ever made the former choice. After the text on each page has been read, you can click to rerun the text, or click on individual words to hear them repeated, though there is little evidence that users make extensive use of this facility; rather, it often seems as though the reading out of the text is something to be endured before you can get on with the *real* business.

Though the 'Living Books' series has received much praise for the quality of its production, and though innumerable copies have been sold into schools around the world, CD-ROM talking books do not currently gain acceptance as literary artefacts in the way that, say, some picture books do. Of the dozens of papers presented at a recent UK conference on picture book illustration, not a single one made more than a passing reference to CD-ROM stories, and nobody discussed the possibilities of the genre.

This is strange and fairly new territory, poised somewhere between the conventional picture book, the cartoon film or video and the computer game, though with significant differences from any of these. Publishers' blurbs on CD-ROM boxes tend to emphasize the 'learning' aspect of the talking book, presumably to attract parents; whereas when programs begin with the main character addressing the user directly about the options available, the words 'play' and 'fun' are more in evidence.

Teachers tend to regard talking books as trivial, as games, as more appropriate for the home market, as 'edutainment'. Where they are used in classrooms it seems they are almost invariably treated as a means of motivating reluctant readers, or at least keeping them occupied. It is not clear exactly what the terms of reference are by which one might judge if talking books are successful or not. The growing body of research evidence is equivocal, or suggests that talking books can, perhaps, make some slight difference to children's reading performance (Miller *et al.* 1994). Teachers seem to welcome them in general terms, and recognize that they have some potential as part of the range of reading activities on offer, but they often express some unease at the tendency of users to spend all their time clicking on hotspots and almost no time attending to the written text (Lewis 2000). There is even concern about the tendency of children to squabble over the mouse when 'working' in twos or threes. Should we be surprised at this? Perhaps it is more like sharing a sweet than sharing a comic.

Narrative, the literacy strategy and ICT

Narrative, according to Barbara Hardy's much-quoted phrase, is a 'primary act of mind' (Hardy 1977: 12–13):

> For we dream in narrative, daydream in narrative, remember, anticipate, hope, despair, believe, doubt, plan, revise, criticize, construct, gossip, learn, hate, and love by narrative. In order really to live, we make up stories about ourselves and others, about the personal as well as the social past and future.
>
> I set out this long, incomplete, and highly obvious list not simply to point to the narrative structure of acts of mind but to suggest the deficiency of our commonly posited antagonism between dream and realistic vision. Educationalists still suggest that the process of maturation involves movement out of the fantasy-life into a vision of life 'as it is'. Teachers have even constructed syllabuses on the assumption that we begin with fairy tales and daydreams and work gradually into realistic modes . . . There is a widespread and, I suggest, dubious but understandable assumption on the part of wishful believers in life-enhancement that human beings begin by telling themselves fairy tales and end by telling truths.

The years since Hardy wrote the above have seen a sharp rise in our awareness of the significance of story, and an even more dramatic retreat into an instrumental, mechanistic view of language activity. From a casual perusal of the UK National Literacy Strategy (NLS) document, one might be forgiven for assuming that stories exist principally to be analysed in terms of plot, character, use of descriptive language and so forth; and that fiction is useful primarily as a means of sugaring the reading pill to enable the achievement of the required standard of 'reading competence' (which is a far more problematic concept than the NLS makes it appear). The hectic forward momentum of the NLS makes it difficult within a school context to accommodate the experience of immersion in a story; even the end-of-the-day story, the 'three-o'clock Polyfilla' that so many remember with affection, has been put under pressure from the competing interests of other curriculum subjects that have been elbowed out of the morning timetable by the demands of the literacy and numeracy curriculum.

The NLS makes very little reference to the use of information and communication technology (ICT) in general, and none at all in the context of story. This has had regrettable consequences, as thousands of schools have nailed down their literacy policies without giving due attention to new technologies, and without so much as a nod in the direction of the 'new literacies' that they might engender. Almost invariably to date, it seems, attempts to infuse literacy teaching with some ICT have served to reinforce a very traditional view of what literacy is.

So what might ICT do for reading? On the one hand, there is a perspective that views non-linear structures and hypertext as a means of hastening the death of the author. In Lydia Plowman's phrase, interactive technologies are, for some, 'the perfect postmodern playground' (Plowman 1996: 44). On the other hand, articles in newspapers often argue that computers can seriously damage our attention spans, and that excessive reliance on them will eventually render us all incapable of reading more than a short paragraph at a time. There is a real issue here. One can obtain vast amounts of reading material from Internet sources like Project Gutenberg (particularly if one has a taste for nineteenth-century American authors), but who ever read a novel on a screen? Surely we are not expected to print them out – and wouldn't it be cheaper to go out and buy a copy of *Huckleberry Finn* than to print your own? Eventually that line of argument may be outflanked by digital 'smart paper', but for the moment it seems reasonable to assume that the computer screen is not a good (or, perhaps, healthy) medium for 'getting lost in a book'. There are various estimates of the maximum amount of text that people are customarily able to read on a screen at any one time; this may well be no more than a few hundred words.

Early 'reading' software tended to concentrate on drill-and-practice exercises in phonics, fill-in-the-missing-word exercises, or predominantly text-based adventure games. None of these made a significant impact on the primary classroom or on home computer use. Faster processors, better graphics capabilities and the coming of the CD-ROM drive eventually made a difference, and the rapid expansion of the home computer market provided the commercial incentive to invest the time and effort in the production of talking books. A large proportion of talking book CD-ROMs produced for the home market are retellings of fairy stories or classics such as *Treasure Island*. This is not really surprising, and it probably makes good commercial sense to work with tried-and-tested and household names, but all too often what emerges is necessarily a drastic abridgement of the original text, and the storyline itself is impoverished and trivialized. From a literary point of view, many of these renditions are really quite horrible; though, as in other fields of literary and artistic endeavour, that does not prevent them from selling quite well.

Picture books and videos: leaving gaps and filling them

Picture books can be very powerful. A mechanistic view of reading would regard the presence of the pictures as a means of supporting and providing hints for the real business of decoding the written text, and thus as something to be grown out of at the earliest opportunity. This view can sometimes be found reflected in children who are on the threshold of independent reading, who want to be seen with books that do not have pictures, having left that babyish stuff behind. We might view children with this cast of mind as sadly misguided, but we should not be surprised by the attitude, given the pressure we place them under to 'achieve'.

On the other hand, those of us who are parents recognize the power of the picture book as a bedtime resource, a vehicle for intimacy with our offspring (as long as we have not abdicated that role to the television, video, Walkman or computer). We know that it is not simply a matter of getting through the book as quickly as possible so that we can move on to the next level. We know that we will be required to revisit the same stories over and over and over again until we can all recite the text from memory (and woe betide us if we 'get it wrong'!). We know that, particularly with high-quality picture books, we can spend long periods of time poring over the pictures and discussing them. We know that the full reading experience contained in a good picture book requires the presence, and the interaction, of both text and pictures. But we also know that, however earnestly we may wish it to be otherwise, even the most educated and erudite of children sometimes form strong attachments to texts that we might think of as trashy and perhaps tasteless.

Most early years teachers, and many parents, are very familiar with Pat Hutchins' *Rosie's Walk* (1970). The text consists of a single, mundane sentence of 32 words: 'Rosie the hen went for a walk across the yard around the pond over the haycock past the mill through the fence under the beehives and got back in time for dinner'. The pictures tell a far more elaborate story about Rosie and the fox who is pursuing her as she walks, apparently unaware of its presence. The text makes no mention of the fox, whose attempts to catch Rosie always meet with disaster. I cannot improve upon Margaret Meek's (1988) excellent, thorough and perceptive account of what is going on in *Rosie's Walk*, and the reader is referred to that short book for a fuller discussion.

From an early age, children enjoying *Rosie's Walk*, or John Burningham's (1977) *Come Away from the Water Shirley*, or Anthony Browne's *Voices in the Park* (1998) learn to accommodate and enjoy irony, or learn to respect that form of creative tension that Keats termed 'negative capability': 'that is, when man is capable of being in uncertainties, Mysteries, doubts, without any irritable reaching after fact and reason . . .' (Forman 1931: 77). In dealing imaginatively with picture books of this quality, children learn to fill in the gaps in the narrative. Reader response theory informs us that meaning is not merely something held locked within a text for the reader to uncover; rather, meaning is constructed *between* the text and the reader (see e.g. Iser 1989: 5: 'meanings in literary texts are generated in the act of reading; they are the product of a complex interaction between text and reader, and not qualities that are hidden in the text . . .'). Arguably, every reading is different, as the reader brings to bear on the text a slightly enhanced set of life experiences, with perhaps a more sophisticated grasp of intertextual resonances. Good readers know that they use their imaginations to fill in the gaps that authors leave. Most of us are familiar with the experience of watching a television dramatization of a book we have read, and thinking, 'But that's not what she looks like . . .'

It is more than 20 years since Arthur Applebee conducted his research into children's concepts of story and story characters (Applebee 1978). In the intervening years, the charm, innocence and variety of his respondents' answers to questions about where Cinderella lives or what a wolf is like in a story have been largely replaced by a cold, uniform certainty, and it is now effectively impossible to replicate his work. Every child knows precisely what happens in the well-known fairy stories, because they have all seen the video. This is not negotiable territory; children can tell you in minute detail exactly how individual scenes are played out, though they cannot always distinguish who are the main protagonists and who are the extras. Margaret Perkins' (1995: 19) discussion with 5–6-year-olds about fairy tales is not untypical:

> Several of the children remembered Cinderella but claimed never to have read a book about her or heard the story. However, they had all seen the Disney video. One little girl proceeded to give me a blow-by-blow account of the video, remembering even the minutest details. What was significant though was the details that were remembered. She described how the mice ate some crumbs from the floor, where they came from, and where they disappeared to. She knew, however, nothing at all about the fairy godmother; when pushed, she said, 'Oh yes, somebody came and gave her a new dress.'

Though it is futile to rail against the ubiquity of the video, one can nevertheless feel a sense of regret that the consumerization and homogenization of stories through that medium may have done some damage to children's capacity to think imaginatively for themselves (Somers 1995; Gold 2000). There is a simple test you can try on your friends – I find that those who read *Watership Down* before they saw the film pictured real rabbits in their imagination; those who read it afterwards picture cartoon rabbits.

Dialogic reading and textoids

Mechanistic approaches to reading might be effective in developing its surface aspects (which are invariably what gets tested when 'reading competence' is assessed), but they do little to foster the capacity for more literary, critical or aesthetic reading. There is a pressing need to encourage readers to read dialogically, and we need to acknowledge this as an essential component of children's engagement with story from their earliest experiences onwards. I use the term 'dialogic reading' here in the sense that it is used by Hunt and Vipond (Hunt 1996). It implies a level of active engagement or dialogue with the story, a relationship between reader and text that is not simply a one-way transmission of 'meaning' from the words on the page to the brain of the reader.

So what might dialogic reading entail? A very provisional and incomplete list of characteristics might include: seeing (and *expecting* to see) patterns and connections; forming opinions; speculating about what will happen; anticipating events and responses; placing queries, uncertainties, ambiguities and contradictions in temporary storage and recognizing when (or if) they have been resolved; accommodating surprises; acknowledging the 'ring of truth' and detecting the false or contrived; being aware of, and valuing, intertextual resonances; suspending disbelief; and colluding with the author. These are not 'higher-order skills' that can be added to the reading repertoire once a child has grasped the basic business of decoding text; they are among the central skills of interacting with story, and most of us had experience of, and knew something about, all of them before we ever learned to decode. Narrative is a primary act of mind, and we develop our capacity for storying early. As Carol Fox (1993: 193) puts it, our role is 'to lead children into literacy through what they already know and can recognize'.

You can hear parts of the dialogic process at work if you eavesdrop on a small child interacting with a talking book: 'Let's click on this and see what happens – oh look, there's that mouse again – I wonder what the starfish will do this time'. Interactivity is a rather slippery concept. In the context of new technologies, and the Internet in particular, it is taken to mean that what happens next on the screen can be decided (to a certain extent) by the user. This is not, of course, the same sort of interactivity that occurs in face-to-face human discourse. There is a dimension to oral storytelling, for example, which can only come into play if there is direct contact between the teller and the listener: the small nuances and variations in intonation and pace, the gestures and body language, the capacity to *respond to responses*, that make interactivity a genuinely two-way process. Inevitably, something of these characteristics must be missing in any pre-recorded or pre-programmed story, whether on an audiotape, a video or a computer program. In those terms, talking books are not really interactive, though the existence of choices and alternatives, the ability to do things in any order and at your own speed does give the user a far greater measure of control than does the video.

Rosie's Walk as it exists is more or less perfect; without the pictures it would be pointless; a video of *Rosie's Walk* might be entertaining – once or twice – but would leave the reader nothing to do and no alternatives to explore. It may also be that many talking book CD-ROMs have a relatively short shelf-life. Judith Graham (1994: 16), reviewing a 'Living Books' CD-ROM, observes:

For all the inventiveness, in the end I was not being asked to be creative and for all the choice that I was offered, I couldn't actually change anything ... For me that is not a major problem – I like feeling that I am in the hands of a story-teller who has shaped the story in only one way. What I felt, however, is that by exploiting every last ounce of potential in the illustrations, the makers of the program had made it unlikely that I would revisit the text.

Though I do not agree with this conclusion (and anecdotal evidence suggests that children who own 'Living Books' CD-ROMs revisit them quite often), I think there is another potential danger – that showing you in detail *how* events happened tends to close the imaginative gaps, stifle speculation about alternatives and reduce the capacity for irony. On several pages of *Just Grandma and Me* there is ironic tension between what Little Critter *says* he did and what the picture *shows*. Because the CD-ROM version animates the activity, some of these tensions are re-solved, and questions receive a definitive answer, in much the same way that a Disney video annihilates alternative versions. Incidentally, I am not proposing that there should be an interactive CD-ROM of *Rosie's Walk*. Just imagine it ...

The largest research project yet undertaken in connection with talking books is Project LITT (Literacy Instruction Through Technology) (Lewis 2000), which examined the capacity of 'hypermedia-based children's literature' to enhance the reading skills of 'students with learning dis-abilities'. In its first phase, it identified and analysed all talking book materials available in the USA, identifying over 300 titles, which were classified according to a range of criteria including the number of words in the text, the readability level, the type and levels of interaction with the text and graphics (including the prevalence of hotspots), and several other features.

There was considerable variety, in terms of the criteria listed above. There were some clear distinctions to be drawn between those stories intended for home use and those designed for school use. The former were generally less expensive, included a higher proportion of interactions with graphics and tended to feature game activities; the latter were more likely to include 'instructionally relevant features such as glossaries, word-processing activities, and reading skill lessons' (Lewis 2000: 10). Another distinction was that, in the case of some of the texts designed for school use, clicking on the graphic hotspots produced word labels rather than animations. As Matthew (1996) puts it, 'Living Books' wild and zany animation can easily distract the reader from the text ... Pop-up labels found in the illustrations in [other books] help students associate the written word with the object it represents'.

This distinction perhaps characterizes the dilemma – what are talking books for? My heart sinks at the thought of pop-up labels, and the subordination of dialogic engagement with story to the tyranny of 'word recognition'. I am not seeking to deny the importance of decoding skills, of course, but this seems to me to be a singularly inappropriate way of using the medium. Talking books designed for use in school are often the equivalent of reading scheme materials – in Russell Hunt's term, they are 'textoids' (Hunt, 1989, 1993, 1996), texts which exist in order to have something done with them, texts which are always a means to an end rather than an end in themselves. Hunt's point is that children soon learn to recognize textoids, and associate them with the type of 'school learning' that has no direct bearing on their real lives:

> The possibility that the author, like the person across the table telling a story, might be engaged in sharing values and inviting the reader to make points, is obliterated by the fact that the story is in reality the possession of, and is being offered to the student by, the textbook and the teacher – by the educational institution. It is not being offered by its speaker or author. And it's being offered not as an utterance, but as . . . 'an example' of something, a pretext for a test.
>
> (Hunt 1993: 119)

The danger, then, is that in the name of education we might take something that is potentially a good idea and turn it into just another version of school work. Project LITT was geared towards exploring the potential of talking books to produce measurable 'gains in reading skills' among children with learning disabilities, and found that in unstructured interactions children spent most of their time 'interacting with the graphics components' and mostly ignored 'supports within the program such as speech aids and word definitions'. The project also found that children's gains in terms of word recognition were minimal, whereas when there was 'instructional support' and children were required to read the pages aloud, word recognition scores improved considerably (Lewis 2000). What did they expect? Is this really the best way to use a talking book?

Among the talking books commonly available in the UK, the Oxford Reading Tree CD-ROMs (Sherston Software) are self-evidently reading scheme materials, as they complement a widely-used scheme. Perhaps the best-known and most widely-used UK series, the Sherston 'Naughty Stories', though not part of any scheme, nevertheless seem to fulfil a similar function. They are textoids – they do not even appear to have an identified author. For an online example, see www.sherston.com/shocked/edwina.html

The problem with these particular materials is that they are very poor; the pictures generally do no more than illustrate the rather pedestrian text; the single animation on each page is often no more than a movement of a character's arm or leg, with an accompanying sound effect. The stories are mostly trivial and predictable. No discerning child would want to be read one at bedtime. Whatever their efficacy as a means of motivating reluctant readers (Burns 1995), and however much they might appear to improve children's word recognition (Medwell 1996, 1998), they represent such a culturally impoverished version of literacy that in the long term they may perhaps do more harm than good. One cannot dwell in the landscapes they create, or speculate on the motives of the characters. There are no imaginative gaps to fill in, either in the text, the graphics or the interaction between the two.

The point, I suppose, is this: most people would agree that bedtime stories and the accompanying activities and talk can provide an excellent basis for the development of enthusiastic and effective readers. My contention is that the sort of playful activities children engage in when they use talking books at home can also encourage the development of dialogic reading. They are powerfully motivating (I have never met a child who disliked talking books); they can add richness and texture to the story; they can open the eyes of the less imaginative child to a wider range of possibilities. But the fear is that if the text is ignored altogether they can encourage a lazy approach to story.

I believe there is a different place for talking books in the primary classroom, and it has very little to do directly with improving decoding skills (though this may well be a by-product), or sitting children at a computer in pairs and expecting them to 'read' the talking book. The Literacy Hour structure expects that time will be spent in whole-class text-level activity, typically with 'big books'. Teachers fortunate enough to have a large screen or data projector could make very effective use of a talking book in that section of the hour, or failing that they could work with smaller groups and a standard computer screen. The point of the exercise would be to engage children in dialogue about the narrative and metanarrative features of the story – where do you think the hotspots are? What do you think will happen? Why do you think that? Why do you think the author chose to show this in this way? If you were going to design this page, what would you do differently? It would be interesting to place each animation into one of the three categories suggested earlier. Wherever possible, open questions should be used, and genuine and sustained discussion should be encouraged. There would be no squabbling over the mouse, or over whose turn it is. Children's collective experiences would be pooled. Work done away from the computer could include the design of alternative pages, extra animations or hypertext links. Given the level of sophistication of a talking book page, it is relatively unlikely that children would have sufficient time or resources to build elaborate multimedia pages for themselves, though there are software packages (for example, Storymaker, Storybook Weaver) which enable something of the sort to be done relatively efficiently.

What makes a good talking book?

Some stories lend themselves easily to the medium, particularly if their original illustrations are cartoon-like. Dr Seuss classics like *The Cat in the Hat* (1957) or *Green Eggs and Ham* (1962) generally work well, as the jokey, quirky style of the originals anticipates the treatment the stories receive at the hands of the animators. Animators should be careful to resist the urge to 'improve' on the original, as, for example in the case of *Green Eggs and Ham*. Butler (1997: 220) points out that:

> The slight changes in text or illustration are not bothersome until the last page, where someone saw a need to improve on Seuss's ending by adding reciprocity – a blue turkey given back to Sam with a 'try it you'll like it.' Surely young readers get the meaning the first time around – or the second or the third. They don't need the blunt instrument of a social message.

A far more sophisticated and interesting example of the medium, though one which has received relatively little attention, is *George Shrinks*, by William Joyce (1985). The paper version was originally published in 1985. The story explores the imaginative possibilities of a situation in which George, an indomitably positive child, wakes up to discover that he has shrunk. This is in many ways familiar territory; Joyce acknowledges *The Borrowers* (Norton 1952) as a source, and there are obvious parallels with Florence Parry Heide's (1975) *The Shrinking of Treehorn*. The story is very simple. George reads a letter from his parents, which lists a number of tasks he must remember to do. Each page contains a single instruction, with an illustration showing a tiny George undertaking the specified task. In the end, after many adventures and an encounter with a fierce and sharp-clawed cat, George wakes up, restored to his normal size. As with *Rosie's Walk*, the text on its own conveys very little of the 'real' story. Again, this is a picture book that demands to be read dialogically. What would it be like to do the washing up if you could fit comfortably inside a single cup? Joyce's original illustrations are imaginative, and repay close inspection; even without the addition of animation; the CD-ROM version expands the possibilities still further, with a number of hotspots on each page, some continuing subplots that carry across from page to page. A good source of further information is Project LITT, which contains an analysis of all the 300 CD-ROM titles it identified.

Finally, one should mention the much more sophisticated award-winning French story, *Le Livre de Lulu* (translated variously as *Lulu's Enchanted Book*, or *The Book of Lulu*), which was created as a CD-ROM and could not exist as a paper text. This beautiful and complex story is a work of substantial length, and space precludes the detailed description it deserves (but see James 1999).

The CD-ROM talking book is a medium that deserves to be taken seriously. It is quite possible that as broadband Internet access becomes more widespread the CD-ROM as such will cease to be the medium used. There are many talented picture book authors and illustrators currently at work in the UK. It would be interesting to see what, say, Colin McNaughton or Anthony Browne could make of the talking story medium.

Software (CD-ROMs)

George Shrinks: HarperCollins Interactive.
Green Eggs and Ham: Living Books.
Just Grandma and Me: Living Books.
Oxford Reading Tree: Sherston Software.
The Book of Lulu: Organa.
The Cat in the Hat: Living Books.
The Sherston Naughty Stories: Sherston Software.

References

Applebee, A.N. (1978) *The Child's Concept of Story*. Chicago: Chicago University Press.
Browne, A. (1998) *Voices in the Park*. New York: Doubleday.
Burningham, J. (1977) *Come Away from the Water Shirley*. London: Jonathan Cape.
Burns, C. (1995) Talking IT up, *Educational Computing & Technology*, February: 16, 18.
Butler, T.P. (1997) Tale-spinning: children's books on CD-ROM, *The Horn Book Magazine*, March/April: 219–24.
Fox, C. (1993) *At the Very Edge of the Forest*. London: Cassell.
Forman, M.B. (1931) *The Letters of John Keats*. Oxford: Oxford University Press.
Gold, K.J. (2000) Grim tales, *First Things*, 106: 17–19. www.firstthings.com/ftissues/ft0010/opinion/gold.html (accessed Feb. 2001).
Graham, J. (1994) Trouble for Arthur's teacher? A closer look at reading CD-ROMS, *The English & Media Magazine*, 31: 15–17.
Hardy, B. (1977) Towards a poetics of fiction: an approach through narrative, in M. Meek, A. Warlow and G. Barton (eds) *The Cool Web*. London: Bodley Head.
Heide, F.P. (1975) *The Shrinking of Treehorn*. London: Puffin.
Hunt, R. (1989) A horse named Hans, a boy named Shawn: the Herr van Osten theory of response to writing, in C. Anson (ed.) *Writing and Response: Theory, Practice, and Research*, pp. 80–100. Champaign-Urbana: National Council of Teachers of English. www.stthomasu.ca/~hunt/hans.htm (accessed Feb. 2001).
Hunt, R. (1993) Texts, textoids and utterances: writing and reading for meaning, in and out of classrooms, in S.B. Straw and D. Bogdan (eds) *Constructive Reading: Teaching Beyond Communication*, pp. 113–29. Portsmouth, NH: Heinemann. www.stthomasu.ca/~hunt/ttu.htm (accessed Feb. 2001).
Hunt, R. (1996) Literacy as dialogic involvement: methodological implications for the empirical study of literary reading, in R.J. Kreuz and M.S. McNealy

(eds) *Empirical Approaches to Literature and Aesthetics: Advances in Discourse Processes*, vol. 52, pp. 479–94. www.stthomasu.ca/~hunt/igel3.htm (accessed Feb. 2001).

Hutchins, P. (1970) *Rosie's Walk*. London: Bodley Head.

Iser, W. (1989) *Prospecting: From Reader Response to Literary Anthropology*. Baltimore, MD: The Johns Hopkins University Press.

James, R. (1999) Navigating CD-Roms: an exploration of children reading interactive narratives, *Children's Literature in Education*, 30(1): 47–62.

Joyce, W. (1985) *George Shrinks*. New York: Harper & Row.

Lewis, R.B. (2000) *Project LITT (Literacy Instruction Through Technology): Enhancing the Reading Skills of Students with Learning Disabilities through Hypermedia-Based Children's Literature*. San Diego, CA: San Diego State University. http://edweb.sdsu.edu/SPED/ProjectLitt/LITT (accessed Feb. 2001).

McKeown, S. (1998) Barriers to literacy? *Literacy & Learning*, spring: 55–7.

Matthew, K.I. (1996) The promise and potential of CD-ROM books, *SITE96, Proceedings – Technology and Teacher Education Annual 1996*. www.coe.uh.edu/insite/elec_pub/html1996/03readin.htm (accessed Feb. 2001).

Mayer, M. (1983) *Just Grandma and Me*. New York: Golden Books.

Medwell, J. (1996) Talking books and reading, *Reading*, April: 41–6.

Medwell, J. (1998) The Talking Books Project: some further insights into the use of talking books to develop reading, *Reading*, April: 3–8.

Meek, M. (1988) *How Texts Teach What Readers Learn*. Stroud: The Thimble Press.

Miller, L., Blackstock, J. and Miller, R. (1994) An exploratory study into the use of CD-ROM storybooks, *Computers in Education*, 22(1/2): 187–204.

Norton, M. (1952) *The Borrowers*. London: Dent.

Perkins, M. (1995) Never mind the book, I've seen the video, *Sustaining the Vision, IASL 24ᵗʰ Annual Conference, Worcester College of Higher Education, July 1995 – Selected Papers*, pp. 18–21.

Plowman, L. (1996) Narrative, interactivity and the secret world of multimedia, *The English & Media Magazine*, 35: 44–8.

Seuss, Dr (1957) *The Cat in the Hat*. New York: Random House.

Seuss, Dr (1962) *Green Eggs and Ham*. New York: Random House.

Somers, J. (1995) Stories in cyberspace, *Children's Literature in Education*, 26(4): 197–209.

10

SOFTWARE IN ACTION

Carol Fine and
Mary Lou Thornbury

Believing ... that man is an animal suspended in webs of significance he himself has spun, I take culture to be those webs, and the analysis of it to be therefore not an experimental science in search of law but an interpretive one in search of meaning.

(Geertz 1993: 5)

Introduction

This chapter emerges from two strands in our research: the first was a study of early software and the conceptual coherence and pedagogical soundness emerging despite the difficulties with the interface; the second was a professional need to develop a more effective way of evaluating software for use in the classroom – to make the link between a study of the software and its use with a full class in a primary classroom. Learning gains arising from the use of the computer result from the conjunction of technology and curriculum – the coming together of the designer, the teacher and the learner. The balance depends on teachers' perception of their role in the negotiation of knowledge and designers' ability to scaffold learners in their transition to autonomy.

A further element which we identify is the context for this learning. Embedded in the curriculum for language and literacy, the context communicates a version of their culture to the children in the classroom. Global or Eurocentric, humanistic or scientific, élitist or inclusive, the pictures it represents in terms of class and sexual politics will also be conveyed in our teaching. It is not possible for software to be neutral in this, or rather it is not possible for us to think that when we teach with computers we are using a new technology that does not partake of these values.

Take, for example, an early package called 'Maths with a Story'.[1] One program was a colouring puzzle which encouraged thinking skills and oral exploration of problem-solving strategies. Maths programs can make for very focused oral exchanges including, for example, the use of robots (Fine and Thornbury 2000). The documentation accompanying Maths with a Story described how this puzzle had been set throughout the ages and could now be definitively solved by the use of the computer. The documentation did not principally occupy itself with detailed instructions for use, but gave a reason for using the program in terms of a culture of 'thinking mathematically' within a western tradition.

We can take a 'thin' view of the technology (Geertz 1993) and regard it as an artefact, the command of which can be attained through the study of its parts; but we have a curriculum which quite properly asks for the use of the computer to be embedded within it. This further level of understanding, the 'thick' interpretation of the learning and the contribution the software makes to it, is the subject of this chapter.

The generation and use of software

The production and dissemination of software were seen by Wellington (writing in 1985) as the result of a partnership in which teachers were seconded to work with programmers or acted through professional associations to put together curriculum software. We take as examples two pieces of educational software, one developed early on and another more recent commercial product, to discuss the importance of the philosophy behind software production.

However the software is generated, it is the teacher who dictates its use. The model of computer use that teachers bring to their teaching will be based on their philosophy of teaching. Writers looking at software and its impact on learning address a range of learning models, from the behaviourist through to a model of working with children in the light of a philosophy of the 'social nature' of human learning. We suggest that 'the philosophy in action' of the teacher can affect the way they introduce activities with the computer whatever the model implicit in the design of the software.

Somekh (1997) looks at this from the point of view of the teacher and describes teachers' views of computing:

- *The computer as tutor* sees the computer as replacing the teacher in providing adequate explanations to enable the child to learn, and correcting mistakes in such a way as to support further learning.

- *The computer as neutral tool* sees the computer as 'similar to a pencil' – an alternative way of *presenting* material, be it writing, graphs or graphics, but without a change in the style of learning.
- *The computer as cognitive tool* implies that children's learning is enhanced by a tool which changes the style of learning and explores patterns of knowledge not previously accessible to earlier pedagogic technologies.

Somekh found that teachers who were influenced by this last view made the most developed use of the computer.

Software which is used for language and literacy development

Our first software is a multi-language font word processor[2] expressly developed for pupils (not adults in offices) and also developed as an agent of understanding about language and culture. We next take the example of a multimedia CD-ROM talking book, *Payuta*[3] to exemplify three focal questions which we believe offer a framework for analysing the potential of software. These questions may seem self-evident but our argument is that complex paradigms and categorizations can divert attention from the teaching purpose and that a more simple framework is called for in day-to-day teaching.

Educational software cannot be usefully categorized or evaluated without referring to the roles of the teacher, the pupils and their interaction with the programmer via the program. This is why case study research is such a powerful force in enabling enthusiastic teachers to use information and communication technology (ICT) in their classrooms. Case studies bring together all these factors: the context, the roles of the teacher and the pupils, and the adequacy of the software. In our examples we also consider the history of program design and development and its impact on the finished nature and success of the software.

A multilingual word processor

Early educational computer programs which were produced in Britain had no expectation of recouping production costs; their targets were to enrich children's learning through the use of the computer. A prime example was the program Allwrite, produced by the Inner London Educational Computer Centre (ILECC) in the 1980s. Allwrite arose from a keen awareness of the richness of London's languages. At the ILECC, teams of teachers and programmers worked together to produce and pilot educational software. Very early in the 1980s it became clear to London teachers that the word processor could have a positive effect on reading and writing. In the multicultural urban schools of Inner London, teachers quickly identified how fonts and community languages would empower learning for the growing numbers of children in London schools who spoke English as an additional language.

The experience of the script and vocabulary of another language could make children aware of the differences between languages and thoughtful about their own. Young children are especially interested in words, they play with them and learn 'big' words or foreign languages with delight and alacrity. The words allow them to experience the difference of another language, as in the following accounts of teachers working with Allwrite.

Case study 1: the use of the multilingual word processor in the nursery

The teacher began by encouraging attention to the initial letters of the children's names, in both scripts. She then responded to the children's requests for her to write for them:

> the support I gave them was in developing their understanding of writing – the different purposes for writing and who they were writing for. Above all, access to Panjabi gave status to the children's language for it helped them to realise that we valued their knowledge of their home script.
> Watching and listening to the children I began to see how much they knew and wanted to know about *how language worked.*
> (Wheatley 1993: 34)

The teacher later set up a shop so that the children could make up shopping lists on the computer, on their own. Parents also became involved and a new script (in Bengali) was bought to support them in working alongside their children. The most important feature of Allwrite was that it did not rely on having an alternative keyboard. The keyboard was on the screen and the symbols were chosen with the mouse, so that either the keyboard or the mouse could be used (see Figure 10.1).

Schools could purchase a disk with the community languages for their local area. Thousands of hours of imaginative collaboration between teachers, programmers, artists and community linguists resulted in a tool that was used not just by pupils but also by parent groups in the schools. Eventually Allwrite provided some 19 language fonts including Urdu, Bengali, Chinese and Arabic.

A project such as this could not be costed in present day commercial terms; many of the participants gave their time freely, donating their intellectual property for the greater good of the children in the schools. Tools for community recognition and integration were there. They are no longer available.

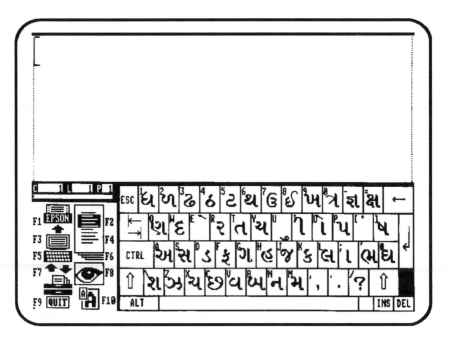

Figure 10.1 The main screen of Allwrite with the Gujarati font loaded

Case study 2: using the Punjabi characters

Each morning children in an infant class learned a new Punjabi word. They learned how it was written and how it could be reproduced quickly via key presses. They looked at the component symbols of that word and learned to pronounce it. These young children gained all the advantages of a bilingual environment: the children whose first language was English and those for whom Punjabi was the mother tongue gained from the explicit unwrapping of the nature of language and its representation in print. They were all beginning to understand the properties of a word and its representation. The pupils could write the English translation of the word underneath and look at the symbols that made up that word (Allwrite had a toggling facility which changed the computer back to English with one button press).

Case study 3: writing and translating in Arabic

In another school with many Arabic speakers the teacher chose a small group of 10-year-olds to compose a story in Arabic. The four children (three boys and one girl) were all Arabic speakers. They were pleased that when the font came up on the computer it began from the right-hand side. They began a discussion about which was the 'best' way to write. They embarked on a description of themselves and it emerged that they had not written or read their language for quite a while. The girl was surest in her decisions about spelling and mostly dictated when the others were unsure. With one key press they were able to change to English and write the translation underneath; this, too, provoked argument as they were mostly fluent enough to disagree about the English as well. Attempts at transliteration revealed the difficulty of translation. Later a parent came in to adjudicate where there were disagreements and to complete the story as a dual text. Dual text books such as this were a feature of class libraries in many schools before printed ones became prevalent, in the late 1980s and early 1990s.

Besides having their sense of belonging in that 'English' classroom strengthened, the children became aware of the nature of translation and the semantic and grammatical constructions of their different languages. The support that this exercise gave to those less fluent in English was evident but also important was their awareness of how they expressed themselves precisely in their own tongue. The advantages of bilinguality are well known for the establishment of the mental structures underlying linguistic understanding on which further language learning is based.

Texts

The multi-font word processor was not seen by the teachers and developers as just an educational tool but also as a cultural agent which gave status to all languages and was a means of valuing each culture and its children. The anthropologist, Geertz, writes: 'The culture of a people is an ensemble of texts, themselves ensembles, which the anthropologist strains to read over the shoulders of those to whom they properly belong' (Luhrmann 2001).

With this definition of texts we can see how access to their own language in writing can be part of the identity of schoolchildren. Empowering them to write texts gives them access to, and integrates them with, their culture. This will apply to children who have a mother tongue other than English: with a recognized identity in the classroom they will have the confidence to take the next step to acculturation in English. Understanding the nature of texts is equally important to the native speakers of English learning to write and to all of us exercising our urge to write. Writing is important beyond its instrumental uses; by writing we all become part of the 'web' and add to the 'meaning'; we share in the making of our 'culture', as defined in the quotation that

introduced this chapter. This is why we write and why it is important
that children be initiated into the wider purposes of writing.

Discussion

The question of updating a program like Allwrite brings into focus the
modern tension between a program which may well change the nature
of the learning environment for thousands of children but has not been
seen as adapting easily to the culture of the National Curriculum in
England, and a literacy strategy with its focus on English as the dominant
culture. Reflecting on Allwrite is useful as a point of comparison for the
other word processors we use with children: in particular the decisions
the programmers made in limiting the pupils to a small number of word-
processing facilities at a time. Some word-processing programs now work
on the same principle of slowly initiating children to the important processes: saving and printing first, then a small range of font changes and
the facility to move text, and so on.

Word-processing programs like Allwrite have sometimes been used to
exemplify the 'computer as neutral tool' but they allow for more than
just printed presentation. The word processor enables ease in realization
of the author's expression and makes possible the exploration of meaning.
The ease lies in the physical facility with which children make letters on
a screen; it also lies in the facility with which they can change those
letters. The decision to change anything written on the screen is a
metacognitive one, based on reflection. The reflection could be about an
alternative spelling, an alternative word, word order or phrase, and in
thinking about any of these the child is exploring the meaning of what
they are writing and the expression of that meaning for themselves and
for their audience – in two languages! The 'tool' is not neutral; it changes
the process of writing.

Translating

The facility of changing to English for translation takes that exploration
of meaning to a further level of linguistic understanding. The examples
we have used draw attention to the role of the teacher in organizing and
designing relevant, creative and challenging tasks with the software. The
power of the computer is realized in the rigour of the software design
combined with the inspiration of the teacher. After the introduction and
an initial period of joint attention by teacher and pupils the role of the
programmer emerges as the 'transitional teacher': the program with
its icons and limited range of editing tools scaffolds learning, not as a
teacher does but within parameters that have already been learned. The

child knows they are negotiating with the computer independently and feels in control of the program.

Frameworks for analysis

There are already a number of frameworks which describe and analyse educational software. Some focus on the software (sometimes confusingly called the computer), which is described separately from a consideration of the context. Such frameworks enable teachers to analyse some qualities of the software and the uses to which it can be put in the primary classroom, but give no indication of its implications for the role of the teaching/learning protagonists. The frameworks allow teachers to categorize but not necessarily to evaluate the contribution of the software to learning relationships.

Wellington (1985) set out the most useful of these frameworks for analysis, using four paradigms based on the work of Kemmis *et al.* (1997): instructional, revelatory, conjectural and emancipatory, on a sliding scale from computer control to learner-centred student control. Wellington foresaw that new software and the greater use of generic software would mean that these distinctions could not so easily be applied in the future and that for example: 'The use of information retrieval programs or packages in allowing pupils to either form their own database or to study a ready-made database is so open-ended . . . It could involve the revelatory, the conjectural or the emancipatory aspects of computer assisted learning' (Wellington 1985: 64).

The multi-font word processor had a range of aspects of use; its purpose was to develop deeper levels of understanding about language.

Evaluating software

Having worked with teachers for many years it became clear to us how some categories and paradigms for software did not actually help them in their teaching. We doggedly questioned teachers, asking them to give examples of 'revelatory' or 'neutral' software. The introduction of the recent ICT curriculum for teacher training has added to these paradigms. It proposes that categorizing the functions of ICT will enhance teachers' ability to use ICT in their classrooms. Therefore another paradigm or framework is proposed, an instrumental one: 'Trainees must be taught how to take account of the functions of ICT and the ways in which these can be used by teachers in achieving subject teaching and learning objectives' (TTA 1998). The 'functions' are detailed as speed and automatic function, capacity and range, the provisional nature of information and the interactive way in which information is stored, processed and presented.

However, neither we nor the teachers understood how this knowledge would improve our teaching. We agreed that focusing on the design of the software through checklists diverted attention from the role of the teacher and the pupil. An active model of software use was needed. Thoughtful teachers can make remarkable use of poorly designed software but some of the best software might be inadequately used by teachers who have not been trained in the use of analytical tools for establishing the curriculum purposes behind the software.

It is the unique circumstance of the presence of the pupils, the teacher and the computer which changes traditional learning relationships. The teacher may not be inspired, the pupil may not be gifted, the program may not be the best, but that grouping offers a new democratization of the learning process. The teacher has knowledge to impart but also shares knowledge acquisition. A superb example of this occurs in Vaughan's (1997) paper in which she explores how far children can go in their understanding of large numbers, supported by interactions with different forms of technology. This understanding went far beyond what was envisaged by textbook or curriculum guidelines and demonstrated how the computer facilitated shared learning and advanced mathematical understanding.

Mercer (1993) applies to all these perspectives the prism of the 'context' of relevant shared knowledge and the shared reflection on outcomes in which metacognition resides. He emphasizes the role of the teacher in providing skilled support and promoting the intellectual sharing of the group. This is a construction which grants the teacher with a class of 30 children a viable role.

A multimedia program

With these issues in mind we set up an experimental evaluation of a new CD-ROM. *Payuta and the Ice God* is a commercially produced program based on an Inuit folk tale. It has the option of three European languages: English, French and German. The folk tale is written clearly on 11 pages and between the pages there are intermediate episodes of animation which elaborate the characters and plot. It is also possible to make jigsaws of the animated scenes and there are other 'games' that involve finding out about Arctic animals, hearing and recognizing animal sounds or completing a game with objects from the story. The sleeve description says: '*Payuta*'s incredible adventure, an interactive story brimming with poetry, emotion and humour, will take you on a journey to the vast icy reaches of the Arctic'. It is a part of Inuit folklore so we look, like the anthropologist, over the shoulders of the Inuit to a reading of one of their texts. The extent to which teaching this story is culturally contextualized will be one of the decisions the teacher will take.

The story and games are fixed. Though the CD is termed 'interactive', no components can be changed. This might mean that the learner is passive but the extent of that passivity will be determined by the teacher and pupil. The CD-ROM is in cartoon style and is attractive, with multi-media text, animation, sounds and music. So how can this interactive storybook be used to enrich children's learning? We introduced the CD-ROM to teachers in two different ways. The first group were to evaluate it on their own with no introduction at all. The teachers gave the CD-ROM between 15 and 30 minutes' attention before indicating that they had formed their opinions. They found the narrator's accent 'difficult', the story too long and slow and very few of them could think of reasons why they would (or how they could) include the CD-ROM in their classroom curriculum. For the second group, we pointed out the narrator's dialect and discussed the dearth of alternative voices in talking books, the need to appreciate other cultures in our classrooms and whether or not this CD-ROM was an adequate representation. We made it clear that to evaluate the CD-ROM with any perception we expected that the teachers would need to work and take notes for at least an hour. We suggested that everyone should think about the images and characters in the story, issues of stereotyping and areas of the curriculum where the use of such software might enrich learning. We also suggested that they work in pairs so that they could discuss ideas and opinions. The response from this second group was very different to the first. Without exception the teachers liked the accent of the narrator. They drew attention to the fact that both the narrator and Payuta were male but they were nevertheless positive about the CD-ROM, finding Payuta's sister 'feisty'. They all had ideas about how they would use the CD-ROM to encourage language, storytelling, geography and social awareness (they liked the inclusion of a deaf character using sign language). They noticed details such as different characters being given a musical motif. Most of their teaching ideas required specific input from the teacher, often as a class activity.

These two sessions could be paralleled to the classroom use of a talking book. They illustrate the important role of the teacher in engaging the insight of the pupil. Here we have an example of multimedia software with considerable potential for drawing the student into the story. However, one student at one computer, with no introduction, led to a rather arid experience. With the second class the context, the roles, the communication and the relationships enabled the CD-ROM to become a catalyst for learning. The teachers identified a number of reasons why they would use the CD-ROM in spite of some of the negative features of the design: they had reservations about gender roles; they thought the puzzles sometimes took attention away from the storyline; they would have liked more emphasis on text, such as the highlighting of words. This is where the programmer or designer needs contact with teachers and educators in the trialling of software, but it is highly unlikely that schools will be asked for feedback on which to base a revised version; there is no process for registering the response of the client audience.

The teacher using new software

Knowing how to use a program is only the first stage to using it in teaching. We approach the learning and understanding of a new software application by learning to control the technology (lower-level technical skills) at the same time as bringing to bear on the software our subject knowledge (higher-level application and analytical skills). The children on the other hand use the program in order to facilitate learning in a subject area; the children will learn how to use the program with a learning purpose. It is the role of the teacher to facilitate direct access, through the computer, to that learning purpose.

The second group of teachers in the *Payuta* example benefited by considering a number of questions which provoked them to make decisions about the best way to use the software in the classroom. Our practice model is in the form of questions based on the presumption that the teacher has tackled the lower-level activities of learning the software and how it works. We have noticed that sometimes teachers tackling a new piece of software interpret the challenge as 'How easy was it to learn how to use this software?' We need to go beyond this to ponder, 'How can this software change the learning in my classroom?' In the *Payuta* example the computer skills needed to use the software are not formidable; it is the curriculum application that is key. The deeper the teacher's knowledge of the development of reading, social skills, classroom management and organization the more profound will be their use of the CD-ROM. Categorizing or 'evaluating' software does not necessarily help the teacher plan for its classroom use or realize its potential.

The classroom practice model

The model we propose, using *Payuta* as the example, is based on three questions, as follows.

How would I introduce the use of Payuta in the classroom? An episode of joint attention

Our teachers agreed on an approach using the CD-ROM to teach story. The software is described as being for ages 4 to 9. However, there is no support for the beginning reader such as the highlighting and speaking of individual words and phrases, so this is a CD-ROM text which might be better used with the age group 8 to 11. It is quite a long and complicated story and there is an expectation that pupils will recognize even unknown words from the narrator's voice-over. The text pages are uncluttered by images; the text itself is straightforward but not artificially simplified and the subtleties of motive and character are elaborated by the voices in the animation. In this context the small amount of text on each screen was a positive advantage and it was felt that discussions on how the story was communicated without text would be of great benefit, revealing the children's awareness of non-textual cues. Two genres are in play in the story: that of the quest and that of the story with a moral, in the context of a mythical explanation for natural phenomena – the seasons. These offer models for children's own stories. There are many supporting characters in the story and children could be encouraged to take on a role and act or write their version of the story.

The first stage of our model requires reflection on the *joint attention* that teachers and pupils will bring to the program. The children's attention is drawn to the story, the characters and the words. At this stage the teacher will make choices about the order or selection of themes. These are choices about which story forms to emphasize, whether to extend the learning towards geography and the Inuit people or whether to focus on parallel folk tales about spring. Not all of these can take place together; one strand will be chosen and others returned to later.

How will the children go on to use the program? The transitional stage

After the introduction the teacher will make a decision about the management of the follow-up. Close analysis of the software is important at this stage as we must identify the extent to which the software supports transitional activities or whether such activities rely more heavily on the teacher. The planning is important; the teacher's intervention does not cease with the introduction. The children will be enabled to work at focused tasks without the presence of the teacher after the context has been established. The models of working relationships will now be pupil, peer and computer programmer or pupil and computer programmer. Programs differ in the degree of help or scaffolding which is supplied. In the case of *Payuta* there is a voice behind the script which points out, for example, the morals that the story illustrates. Also, the animations move the narrative on and give some clues to character.

If the children are working in pairs there needs to be guidance as to how they share and discuss. In the *Payuta* program only the mouse is used and therefore children will plan for alternating with the mouse and following the suggestions of partners. Possible scenarios are that the teacher will ask that each pair read through the story and bring back to the group a question relating to it, a reason for choosing a favourite character or the identification of an important turning point in the story. This is *scaffolded* or *transitional* use of the software.

How will the teacher build on the independent learning of the children? The sharing or democratic stage

At this point the tripartite relationship is different from the first stage; the children bring their learning to the democratic exchange having learned enough to begin to direct the content of the discussion. In a teacher-mediated conversation children will pursue the context of the folk tale, its explanation for natural phenomena or the study of Inuit people. This is not a 'plenary' or summary of the learning; it is another stage. The first two stages have provided the children with new knowledge and sometimes increased ICT skills. Another stage is required to reflect on and process this new knowledge in order to deepen the engagement with the story or branch out into further study.

With the *Payuta* CD-ROM the playing of the games provided within the program will not add much to the children's understanding and the program itself contributes little more than has been described already. It is unlikely that children will need to work much further with this CD-ROM, but they will return to the subject of Inuit life. This is an aspect of the CD-ROM design; software with greater educational input could support further activity related to the learning. The adults who engage with children's learning (parents or teachers) will want to explore the culture offered. They might direct the child to do some research on the web or on another CD-ROM, and introduce the use of a word processor or paint program. The subject would be ideal for a dramatic presentation.

Payuta is a 'thin' program and as such the stages described offer a linear progression of learning. It is also possible to apply the three stages discussed to more open-ended and generic software, like the multilingual word processor, Allwrite. In that situation the children and the teacher will constantly revisit the different stages as their skills develop and as they work to a more sophisticated agenda. This model of joint attention, transitional and independent learning followed by democratic exchange is simple in the context of a talking book. It is more complex in relation to open-ended or generic software.

The notes provided with *Payuta* deal only with the technical instructions for setting up, or turning pages. It would be of help to teachers and parents if some thematic hints were given. We do not want programs bundled with too much print; experience tells us that it is not read. However, for *Payuta* we would have liked an indication of the origin of the story and a sentence that indicated that it was a quest story with a didactic style that points up the morality in people's actions. The other dimension is the mythical dimension which could be followed up in the classroom by reading other Inuit tales or by making a collection from

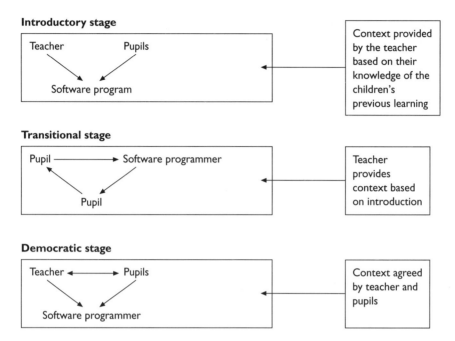

Figure 10.2 The three learning stages and their contexts

other cultures of myths or legends about the seasons. These could be enumerated or website references given.

The model described

Mercer (1993: 30) writes about 'the complexity of the tripartite teaching and learning relationship between teacher, learner and computer (perhaps with its own "hidden teacher" in the software) . . .' He makes explicit the role of the programmer and in allocating the programmer a role implies that their share in the partnership will be based on a knowledge of (and a desire to) promote children's learning. A diagrammatic representation of the three questions above demonstrates that the context for the learning lies outside the tripartite relationship and is governed by the teacher, or the teacher and pupils, with the software influencing, but not directing, the learning (see Figure 10.2).

Conclusion

The emphasis in our model is on the role of the teacher, a role rendered all the more important by the dissociated nature of much of the software which can be used in the classroom. What was distinctive about the older software was that it assumed that the crucial role would be the teacher's, not that of the computer. Older software was sometimes difficult to learn because the learning (of the program) was at two levels, the technological and the educational. It was 'thick' software, with layers of learning and reflection. The documentation often reflected this and probed how the computer could make for different learning; it answered the question 'Why use a computer in education?' by presenting a way of looking that goes beyond what can be done with pen and paper.

Modern educational computer software makes use of enormous technical advances such as full multimedia and virtual reality. Many programs are produced by commercial companies which cannot hope to employ the comprehensive research, planning, piloting and documenting which earlier programs enjoyed. Wellington warned in 1985 that one possibility in the future was that 'software should be produced commercially through traditional publishing houses and new software publishers. Schools, colleges and parents would then pay a commercial price for the CAL [computer assisted learning] materials and the whole system would live or die on a profit and loss basis' (p. 65). Wellington identified a number of problems with this approach, such as the high price of software, 'the lack of innovation and experiment in such a system' and copyright issues. It is this system that seems to have evolved and one result could be that more work devolves onto the teacher. A program like *Payuta* is like a book in the library; it can be read by the solitary reader and returned to the shelf or it can be explored with a whole class and themes developed. CD-ROMs are still too expensive to be used for surface learning: if they have the power to hold children's attention then they also have the capacity to be mined for deeper reflection.

Commercial priorities might cause a blurring of purpose and audience between software for the 'home' market and software for the 'educational' market. Some CD-ROMs are marketed as educational and are technically easy to access. Since they are not specifically intended for the teaching of children in school it becomes the professional concern of teachers to make the use of the program appropriate to the children's learning. The development of writing, the examination of complex spelling patterns, the probing of vocabulary and the elucidation of themes (the 'thick' approach) is down to the teacher.

When the New Zealand government set up their educational web resource they asked the teachers what they wanted on it. The replies indicated that teachers did not want lesson plans or worksheets; they wanted ideas for lessons or for using materials. The lesson plan or the worksheet is always particular to the class and the context; ideas are a springboard for the teacher to develop themes or explore issues. One of the most powerful inspirations for a teacher is other teachers' stories of 'software in action' and organizations such as the Teacher Training Agency

(TTA) in England are asking teachers to write up their experiences. There is already a great source of such stories in the many magazines to do with ICT. By telling the 'stories' of our 'search for meaning' we will refine our analytical tools for making the most of software and for making decisions about what is best for use with children.

Notes

1 Maths with a Story 1 & 2 was a package of investigations developed in the 1980s by Pete Smyth for the BBC computer and made available on 480Z and Nimbus.
2 Allwrite was produced by the Inner London Computing Centre in the 1980s. There were 19 language fonts.
3 *Payuta and the Ice God* (1996) is by Ubisoft, Vantage House, 1 Weir Road, Wimbledon, London SW19 8UX.

References

Fine, C. and Thornbury, M.L. (2000) Children in control, in M. Monteith (ed.) *IT for Learning Enhancement.* Bristol: Intellect.
Geertz, C. (1993) *Towards an Interpretive Theory of Culture.* New York: Fontan.
Kemmis, S. with Atkin, R. and Wright, E. (1997) *How do Students Learn?* Working papers on computer assisted learning. Norwich: University of East Anglia.
Luhrmann, T.M. (2001) The touch of the real: at once cold and concerned, the exemplary eye of Clifford Geertz, *The Times Literary Supplement,* 12 January.
Mercer, N. (1993) Computer based activities in classroom contexts, in P. Scrimshaw (ed.) *Language, Classrooms and Computers.* London: Routledge.
Somekh, B. (1997) Exploring and evaluating how IT can support learning, in B. Somekh and N. Davis (eds) *Using Information Technology Effectively in Teaching and Learning.* London: Routledge.
TTA (Teacher Training Agency) (1998) *Initial Teacher Training National Curriculum for the Use of Information and Communications Technology in Subject Teaching.* London: TTA.
Vaughan, G. (1997) Number education for very young children: can IT change the nature of early years' mathematics education?, in B. Somekh and N. Davis (eds) *Using Information Technology Effectively in Teaching and Learning.* London: Routledge.
Wellington, J.J. (1985) *Children, Computers and the Curriculum.* New York: Harper & Row.
Wheatley, V. (1993) Word-processing in the nursery, in *Developing English Approaches with IT.* Sheffield: NATE.

11

CHILDREN, LITERACY AND THE WORLD WIDE WEB: HOW CHILDREN ACCESS AND MANIPULATE INFORMATION FROM THE INTERNET TO SUPPORT THEIR LEARNING

Tatiana Wilson

Introduction

In recent years the UK government has invested millions of pounds to enable schools to be linked to the Internet. Training opportunities for existing teachers and raised expectations for trainees have contributed to higher expectations of information and communication technology (ICT) instruction in schools. Alongside these developments, the Internet brings opportunities to gain up-to-date information on any topic that might interest both pupils and teachers. Schools, with this new access to electronic information, are faced with the issue of how to enable pupils to use it to 'best effect' to support their learning, and teachers to support their teaching.

What is actually meant by 'best effect' is an interesting question. Tensions between enabling pupils to pursue their own interests and lines of enquiry *and* fulfil the requirements of the National Curriculum continue to exist. The role teachers must play in this process with the learner(s) is crucial and one I will return to later.

Other issues, including the need to protect children from unsuitable material on the Internet, a lack of staff expertise and problems with network installation, have meant that schools have struggled to embrace these new developments. Indeed some teaching staff have questioned the high status given to computers in education by the Department for Education and Employment (DfEE) in the UK and by other governments elsewhere.

Over the space of two terms I looked at children's views of the Internet and investigated how they accessed and used Internet texts. I wanted to find out whether they were able to use and apply the strategies they had learned in their classroom time on literacy (in England the Literacy Hour), using information texts, in this new electronic context. I felt this project was important as it not only involved ICT skills and National Literacy Strategy (NLS) objectives but also had cross-curricular relevance for teaching and learning.

Research approach

The project involved a small-scale action research study that focused on my work with a group of six children: three girls and three boys, aged 9 or 10 years. For most of the time the group worked collaboratively although they were given opportunities to choose with whom they wished to work. Throughout the project I kept detailed field notes and used this material as well as semi-structured interviews to build up a body of data for analysis.

The children I worked with had limited Internet experience. Some had never accessed it before. Others had used the Internet with a family member to help them but did not feel any degree of independence or competence about this usage. One child, Ricky, had started to use the Internet by himself at home but still did not feel he was able to use it with any degree of success.

The current ICT policy of the particular school where I was working enabled the entire staff to have termly ICT skills training linked to teacher INSET (inservice training). The purpose of the training was to ensure that all teachers learned how to use and teach the full range of ICT tasks as required by the National Curriculum. At the time of the project only three computers in the school had access to the Internet although there were plans to connect the school's network so that a whole class could be taught together.

Children's preconceptions

At the start of the project I interviewed each of the children (using a semi-structured interview approach) and asked them about their previous computer experience. While I wanted responses to similar questions I was aware that the children might need these questions to be phrased differently or that I would need to encourage them to expand on what they had said. Each week throughout the project we discussed as a group what had already been done, and the next step. In doing this I wanted to enable the children to feel a part of the research and for them to find the experience empowering. It was therefore agreed between us all that at the start of the project I would interview each of the children individually. I asked them some general questions about their reading, the books they enjoyed and also what ICT experience they had – what they could *do*. I also wanted to find out whether they had access to a computer at home.

Interestingly, all the children said they had learned most about how to use computers from male family members: fathers, brothers and grandfathers. One child, Simon, explained how his uncle taught his dad who then taught him. Most of the children said they enjoyed using computers. When I asked Ricky what he did, he did not seem to have clear strategies or methods in the way he worked: 'I just mess about at home on the computer and sometimes I find information'. When I later asked him to show me what he did he was unable to open the computer programs independently and it became evident that he relied on additional help to set up the programs he wanted to use.

One of the difficulties that emerged from my initial interviews with the children was that they had few, if any, strategies for finding material on the Internet and most were unaware of how to manipulate the information they retrieved from it. In particular, the children who had used the Internet before did not seem aware of the need to refine their searches or how to use a number of key words to help them. They clicked on the link pages and hoped that the information they wanted would appear. With such an approach they had only limited, and somewhat random, success.

Some of the children reiterated the pleasure of 'playing' on the computer without a sense of purpose. However, when they wanted to find more specific information many children asked a more experienced person to help them. Harriet told of how she asked her brother to research things for her: 'I asked him how to do it and then he did it for me and I just read all the stuff that I wanted to know'. All had experienced some success in using CD-ROM encyclopedias but often found the information very dense and uninteresting. Ricky found research on the Internet frustrating: 'When I'm just playing about on the Internet it's quite easy, but when I'm trying to find some information it's quite hard'. These children had limited experience in terms of independent use and only Ricky had had much practice using the computer without support.

Table 11.1   The EXIT model: stages and questions

Process stages	Questions
Activation of previous knowledge	What do I already know about this subject?
Establishing purposes	What do I need to find out and what will I do with the information?
Locating information	Where and how will I get this information?
Adopting an appropriate strategy	How should I use this source of information to get what I need?
Interacting with text	What can I do to help me understand this better?
Monitoring understanding	What can I do if there are parts I don't understand?
Making a record	What should I make a note of from this information?
Evaluating information	Which items of information should I believe and which should I keep an open mind about?
Assisting memory	How can I help myself remember the important parts?
Communicating information	How should I let other people know about this?

Linking book-related activities to the Internet

I concentrated on showing the group how the strategies they had already learned when using information in books could also be used when researching texts on the Internet. The underpinning rationale for this approach is that we learn by making links with what we already know (Anderson 1977; Anderson and Pearson 1984; Lave and Wenger 1991) and build on this knowledge either by challenging our preconceptions or adding further detail, thus extending and refining knowledge, skills and understanding.

The EXIT model (Extending Interactions with Texts) was developed out of a desire to enable children to work in meaningful and purposeful contexts with information texts. Influenced by the work of Tann (1988), among others, and her discussion of approaches to teaching through topic work, Wray and Lewis (1997) developed her ideas and appropriated them for the English curriculum. They organized their model into ten main 'stages' which could be summarized in terms of process or rephrased as questions which children could use to guide their thinking (see Table 11.1).

The EXIT model (Wray and Lewis 1997) was used as a framework for teaching to extend children's interactions with text in more meaningful ways which do not involve copying, or in the case of the computer, printing reams of indigestible text. The model is also one familiar to all primary school teachers in England, as it is incorporated into Module 6 ('Reading and writing for information') of the training materials supporting the implementation of the NLS (DfEE 1998). I hoped that by making links between Literacy Hour lessons and ICT lessons focusing on Internet use, the children would be able to extend their previous understanding of information retrieval and processing.

Wray and Lewis (1997) also advocated three key inputs teachers should offer their pupils in order to develop their skills: modelling and demonstration, joint activity and independent activity. This scaffolded approach to learning was advocated explicitly in the Literacy Hour training materials that all primary schools in England received when the NLS was first launched. Many schools still rely heavily on published reading schemes and reading skills are often taught out of context – the very approach Wray and Lewis were trying to discourage. Learning new skills outside any meaningful context does not help embed these skills, and if children have not been given the opportunity to make connections with their prior knowledge they are less likely to retain what they have learned.

A KWL grid (where K = what I know, W = what I want to find out and L = what I learned) was first developed by Ogle (1989) as a teaching strategy that takes children through the steps of a research process and also records their learning. Wray and Lewis (1997) then adopted it as one of the approaches to their EXIT model. A KWL grid is useful because it is a simple framework for organizing learning.

At the time I started the project the children were learning about the Blitz in the Second World War, so I linked my work with them to this focus. We revised what they already knew and considered what they wanted to find out using a KWL grid (see Table 11.2). From this the children then agreed on key words that they felt would be useful in their search for information. The grid offers a logical support that seems useful to children as scaffolding for their learning when they are unfamiliar with strategies to search for new information.

At the outset the children used the contents and index pages of books to locate pages of information and then skimmed down these to find key sentences. The children all did this well although I was aware that they were reluctant to discard books that didn't have the information they needed. We talked about this and of the importance of not wasting time when researching. As the session progressed they became more confident of their own skills.

Having used books to answer some of their questions the children then tried to retrieve information from the Internet. I modelled how to use a search engine, giving them a list of key tips for refining searches as well as showing them how to search within the BBC website. First we listed all the words we thought might be relevant to our search and

Table 11.2 KWL grid on the Blitz

What I know	What I want to find out	What I learned
The Blitz happened in the Second World War	Where did the Blitz happen? Was it just in London?	
It was about bombing	What were German bombs made of?	
One bomb was called a Doodlebug	What were other bombs called?	
Children had to be evacuated to the countryside	Where were children evacuated?	
Some people who were evacuated are still alive	What were conditions like for them? Who did they live with? What did it feel like to be evacuated?	
The war was between England and Germany. Other countries were also in the war like France, Holland and the USA		

tried to link them so that we could refine the search to answer specific questions. We used the + symbol to do this; for example, when we were trying to find out about evacuees we typed in 'evacuee + "Second World War"'. (By putting quotation marks around the phrase 'Second World War' the search engine searches for the whole phrase and not Second + World + War.)

The children could locate the web pages quite easily but were barred from accessing them because of the filter that was in place. A filter is an optional screening device that is used to prevent children accessing inappropriate material: it bars access to websites containing key words so that children do not access undesirable sites. Filters are often used by schools as a 'safety net' but can be problematic. Some key words that might be inappropriate in one context (e.g. bombs – how to make them) might be legitimate in another (e.g. bombs – their use in the Second World War). It is often difficult to override the barrier of a filter and teachers can find that materials they access on a computer at home cannot be accessed in school. In this project some soundbites retelling evacuees' experiences were not available, even though this was a BBC education site, because some of the key words describing the web pages included 'abuse' and 'slavery'. This was frustrating as having prepared the work at home I had not envisaged these problems.

Clearly there are implications for teachers regarding the need to plan their Internet work at school where filters are in place on each networked computer. Teachers need to know about the restrictions on research areas they are thinking of using.

I gave the children the opportunity to select a topic of their own that they would like to research. They all chose to find out about different television programmes and used a KWL grid in order to identify their questions and key words. All but one of the children was then able to access the website they had decided would answer their questions. Although Fiona was able to access the web page she found that her questions were not ones to which she could find answers. I was again reminded of the importance of teaching pupils to ask the right kind of questions when teaching them how to research using the Internet. This is a strategy which can be taught away from the computer.

Ricky wanted to find out how the makers of the Cartoon Network's television programmes came up with their creative ideas. The filter prevented access to their website directly. However, when Ricky tried to find the information using the search engine Alta Vista he found an excellent website that explained clearly the different arts involved in the creative process and the people connected with it. The filter the school used seemed very effective at the start of an Internet search, however, it seemed less able to bar access as the children worked through hypertext links, surfing from one page to the next. Teachers need to be aware that children can access some information by using a more circuitous route.

Marking texts

In a later session we used the KWL grid to generate some questions about the Victorians, the children's new history topic. Having only just started the topic they knew little about it so our focus was on Queen Victoria herself. The children felt confident using the BBC website and found all the information they needed in the History Zone there. I noticed how the children used their fingers to help them scan down the text on the screen, identifying key words. They seemed to be mirroring instinctively what they had been taught to do on the pages of books, using their finger to help them speed-read through the web page until they identified a key word. They reported that they found this an easier way to look out for the important bits. When they found a key word they then went back to read the sentence.

From the information they read they were able to fill in the L column (what I learned) of the KWL grid and generate some further questions they wanted to answer. As a group they were particularly interested in the inventions of famous 'local heroes' and we printed off the biographies of a selection of them. One of them was Joseph Adamson who invented the first flushing system for toilets and the other was Marc Isambard Brunel who was responsible for the construction of the tunnel underneath the

Thames between Rotherhithe and Wapping. When we looked at the text on the computer screen they all found it very dense and hard to read. The printed versions were still quite challenging to read and the children needed supporting strategies to understand them.

On paper the children were able to colour code important parts of the text using a series of categories. First they read through the text in groups of three and then agreed what the key points were. From this they were able to reread the text a paragraph at a time and code it. This was a time consuming activity and the children needed a good deal of encouragement to keep on task. It is the type of activity that would work well in a guided group context.

When they had finished this piece of work they told each other what they had found out and thought of ways they might want to present this information to others. The girls who had been finding out about Victorian flushing toilets wanted to draw a poster with key facts on it. The boys wanted to draw a series of cartoons telling the story of Brunel's tunnel project and the different disasters that befell it. Both groups were excited by the information they had found out and keen to present it to the rest of the class. When I next visited the school the children presented their work and answered questions from their peers.

Using children's own interests

As a final activity I gave the children the opportunity to work independently on a self-chosen research topic. Ricky wanted to find out about Tottenham Hotspur football team, to know who was being transferred, if they had a junior team, and what the current training strip for them looked like. In contrast, Fiona wanted to find out some background information about the Tweenies (early years television characters). Harriet wanted to find out about archaeology and the British Museum, while Neil and Simon both wanted to discover more about Pokémon cards and strategies for playing with them. One child was absent.

Fiona and Ricky, who were the more confident members of the group, did not use the KWL format in its pure form. Instead they listed only the questions they wanted to answer. Both said that they felt they didn't need to use the grids anymore and wanted to focus on accessing and recording information. Interestingly they still used elements of the grid format to help them. They did not bother to write down what they already knew but instead wrote down the questions they wanted to ask and a list of key words they might find helpful in their searches.

KWL grids are a form of scaffolded support for children and like all scaffolding the hope is that it is removed when it is no longer needed. Fiona and Ricky seemed to be demonstrating a move towards independence, having previously been enabled to do something new with support.

With practice they should all become increasingly confident and independent in the way they manipulate information texts.

Losing the K column (what I know) in some ways is a disadvantage for the teacher as it means that it is harder to identify the pupils' misconceptions. Talking with pupils about their understanding and preconceptions is an important element in enabling children to maximize their learning. By talking things through with pupils, teachers can identify whether the questions children are asking are in fact ones they need to know the answers to, or if they are time wasting by not stretching themselves to discover anything new.

The theoretical underpinning of the EXIT model is that of scaffolding. The structured support the children were given enabled them to access the information from a variety of websites in a way they had not been able to before. As children become more confident and independent in the way they manipulate information texts they are able to use this structure in a more fluid way.

None of the children had any difficulty finding what they considered to be appropriate websites, although many of the websites took a long time to download, and when they appeared on the screen had little relevant information. Having said this, Harriet found few obvious answers to her questions about the British Museum and had to use a dictionary alongside her site map to help her understand which collections were in it. She thought of accessing the vacancy pages to find out if they employed any archaeologists and when she didn't find any found little additional material in the BBC's History Zone, which up until then had been a really accessible resource.

The two boys finding information about Pokémon cards found that most of the information they wanted came in a chart that detailed the relative strengths of the characters. The boys had little difficulty in interpreting the chart, probably because they already had a secure understanding of the topic.

At the end of the project I re-interviewed the children and asked them about what they had learned, what advice they might give others and whether they thought the Internet was a worthwhile thing to use in school. Again I used a semi-structured interview as I felt this would be most effective. Ricky did not want to be taped this time so instead I wrote detailed notes as he talked to me. From these interviews a number of important issues emerged, each of which will now be discussed.

Initial anxiety about using the Internet

The entire group spoke of how they found aspects of using the Internet stressful. Most of them found the procedures they needed to follow in order to access the Internet hard to remember at first and felt that pupils needed reassurance at these moments in order to build confidence. Fiona commented that 'It's scary sometimes when this thing comes up like cancel "yes" or "no" and you don't know which one to press. Sometimes it pauses and I think I've done something wrong, and it gets quite scary . . . if you don't know what you are doing', while Simon said 'Sometimes it goes blank and I'm like, oh no what have I done?' This was especially the case at the start of the project. Teachers need to be aware of this and give children sufficient time and opportunity to consolidate their learning. It is also important that teachers ensure that pupils are sufficiently supported at the beginning of an activity so that they can continue working independently with greater confidence.

Value of collaboration

All the pupils reported that they benefited from working in a small group context. They were able to give and receive help and found working together more enjoyable than working alone. Simon said that 'If they [other pupils] know they'll show you and then you know and then you show other people'. Group work using ICT is also useful as it means that teachers can make use of work done on the computers in different contexts. Using a computer text in a guided reading session for example supports both literacy and ICT and helps pupils transfer their skills more easily to different contexts.

Importance of formulating questions

The group I worked with found Wray and Lewis' (1997) KWL grids supportive and usable. This may be because they were able to transfer skills they had already practised in the Literacy Hour to this new context. By making connections with previous knowledge the children found it easier to extend their understanding of information retrieval and processing using books to include computer texts. The grids enabled them to tap into their prior knowledge of a subject and from that formulate questions they wanted to find answers to. I introduced a further step, which was to brainstorm key words linked to the questions, and the children found these really useful when using search engines. When the children had researched a topic they could then record their findings concisely on the grid as well as generate new questions for another time. Recording the websites visited was also useful as sometimes the bookmarks left on the computer had been deleted when the children returned to use them again. The KWL grid, while a useful starting point, needed additional modification to include a place to note key words and link these together to enable the children to be more precise in their searching (see Table 11.3).

Table 11.3 Internet research grid

What I know	What I want to find out	Search words (using +, " ", ñ,*)	What I learned	Where I found the information (websites)

It is also important for children to be taught how to use search engines to full effect. For example: using quotation marks around a phrase, linking several words using the + symbol, blocking out specific words with the ñ symbol and using the * symbol for words they are not sure how to spell. By using these tools pupils are more likely to refine their searches effectively and retrieve the information they are looking for. Having said this, the children I worked with found the BBC website the easiest and most accessible one to use. This was because of the clear way it was organized, the links with familiar television programmes and the clear language that was generally used.

Frustrations of using Internet texts

The language of many websites was quite dense and inaccessible for the children in terms of reading. The biography work was quite hard for the children to sustain and they would have found it difficult to do without the structured support and encouragement I could give them. Sometimes printing a copy and doing colour-coded text marking activities helped, while at other times the children found it hard to engage even a little with the text. Anyone can set up a web page and therefore it is important that pupils are aware that the texts they read might be biased or inaccurate – perhaps to an even greater extent than the books they have in school. Using a base site such as the BBC or Channel 4 websites is one way of addressing this, as the hope is that the links from these sites will be more reliable. Teachers also need to be careful to monitor children's engagement with a task and not let them get too frustrated.

National Curriculum versus interest-led research

The Internet is a valuable resource in terms of storing up-to-the-minute information. The children spoke of how they were keen to use the Internet when they were doing other research in class as they felt it offered additional information that the school could not otherwise provide. At times however they found it hard to access information linked to their classwork because the filter prevented access to certain websites. The children all reported there was equal value in doing interest-led research that was not explicitly linked to the National Curriculum. They recognized the important skills they were developing and thought that they were transferable irrespective of the topic: 'You need to know how to use the Internet anyway and it doesn't necessarily have to be school work'; 'It all seems the same to me 'cause it's all like pictures and writing so they're all the same'.

All the children enjoyed using the Internet and computers in general. Because the network was timetabled for the school and shared by 14 classes, this limited access may have been a contributing factor to their enjoyment of the project. Only Helen said 'Sometimes it's more frustrating than fun, but most of the time it's more fun'. Because of this high enjoyment factor it makes sense for teachers to tap into children's enthusiasm and incorporate Internet text into children's reading repertoire.

Fostering links with home

Many children have access to the Internet at home and one-to-one support from family members. Therefore schools should also consider fostering home-school links through ICT. For children in Key Stage 2 who may be reading less at home than they were in previous years, varying the contexts in which they read to include Internet texts might be a useful means of encouraging their continued progress in reading. Using the Internet can take up a lot of time, and this is another excellent reason for encouraging children to use computers they have access to out of school. By doing this pupils can share website addresses and resources, and support peers in school. Obviously schools need to provide additional support and opportunities for pupils with less access to computers out of school. Many schools already run successful computer clubs and valuable initiatives such as these give children more time to practise their skills.

Implications for class development

The Internet is a valuable resource for teachers as pupils often consider it a high interest subject. Skills from the Literacy Hour's emphasis on using information texts can be transferred to ICT work. Indeed, Internet skills can be developed within the guided group and independent work contexts of the Literacy Hour.

Some children are more able to transfer book reading skills to a computer context independently, while others need to be shown this explicitly. From the evidence of working with my group of children it would appear that getting children to activate their prior knowledge on a subject needs to be considered an important precursor to formulating the questions they want to answer in their research. When they have done this, children then need to be confident in the different ways they can retrieve information from the Internet and benefit from having a list of key words and phrases to support their searches.

Building children's confidence in the way that they use the Internet is a key factor in their success. Children then need to be encouraged to skim and scan texts so that they can locate the information quickly. Once the information is located there are a variety of ways in which children can record and present it. By changing the way the information is presented to others (e.g. by making a poster) the children engage with what they read, process it and are therefore likely to remember more.

References

Anderson, R.C. (1977) The notion of schemata and the educational enterprise, in R.C. Anderson, R.J. Spiro and W.E. Montague (eds) *Schooling and the Acquisition of Knowledge*. Hillsdale, NJ: Lawrence Erlbaum Associates.

Anderson, R.C. and Pearson, P.D. (1984) A scheme-theoretical view of basic processes in reading comprehension, in P.D. Pearson (ed.) *Handbook of Reading Research*. New York: Longman.

DfEE (Department for Education and Employment) (1998) *National Literacy Strategy. Module 6: Reading and Writing for Information*. London: HMSO.

Lave, J. and Wenger, E. (1991) *Situated Learning*. Cambridge: Cambridge University Press.

Ogle, D.M. (1989) The know, want to know, learn strategy, in K.D. Muth (ed.) *Children's Comprehension of Text*. Newark, DE: International Reading Association.

Tann, S. (1988) *Developing Topic Work in the Primary School*. Brighton: Falmer Press.

Wray, D. and Lewis, M. (1997) *Extending Literacy: Children Reading and Writing Non-fiction*. London: Routledge.

12

VISUAL LITERACY: FROM PICTURE BOOKS TO ELECTRONIC TEXTS

Jon Callow and
Katina Zammit

Introduction

Open a magazine, read a newspaper, log on to the Internet and you are faced with an array of texts – written, spoken, still and moving images. Changes to the way we read and the texts we read are occurring rapidly as we enter the new century and the explosion of the information age. We read and create written, visual, aural and live texts in a range of contexts. Hence, one has to be literate in a range of meaning systems, or modes of representation, in order to participate fully in today's (and tomorrow's) society. One has to be 'multiliterate' (The New London Group 1996; Cope and Kalantzis 2000).

Literacy used to be considered as a set of discrete skills to be learned for the reading and writing of printed paper-based texts (Christie 1990). Today it is acknowledged that literacy also involves learning about social practices (Graddol 1994) and includes knowledge of different roles as a reader (Freebody and Luke 1990) and control of the genres of a society (Christie and Misson 1998). As the texts that we engage with become more complex, so does the notion of what counts as literacy and what it means to be a literate person. This leads to the realization that traditional literacy definitions are not enough any more (Goodman 1996; Downes and Zammit 2001). In addition, the focus has historically been on language to the neglect of other semiotic modes of meaning (Kress 1997, 2000).

Nowadays, the term 'literacy' is linked to a number of other knowledge areas – computer literacy, scientific literacy, visual literacy, technological literacy, information literacy to name a few – as we attempt to redress this imbalance and focus attention on other forms of representation and ways of creating meaning.

With the advent and increased use of technology in schools and workplaces there has been a renewed interest in visual literacy. It must be acknowledged that images are playing a greater role in conveying information within educational and technological texts (Goodman 1996; Kress and van Leeuwen 1996; Kress 1997, 2000; Horn 1998; Raney 1998. Even within the public sphere of communication there has been an increasing dominance of the visual medium. Over the years, there has been a shift in the role of images from merely illustrating to showing important elements of information. As Kress (1997: 65) states: 'Information that *displays* what the world is like is carried by the image; information that *orients* [our emphasis] the reader to that information is carried by language'.

In the information society of the twenty-first century, the screen is fast becoming the new page (Kress 1997). The texts found in computing environments, digital and electronic texts significantly employ the visual mode to convey information. They use a diversity of visuals, such as animations, photographs, videos, graphs and diagrams, to represent and convey information to the reader. Even the written texts are highly visual. Hence, being visually literate is becoming essential. As Kress and van Leeuwen (1996: 3) state: 'Not being "visually literate" will attract social sanctions. "Visual literacy" will be a matter of survival, especially in the workplace'.

So what can assist children to understand visual texts? A metalanguage, which incorporates semiotic theory and also provides tools for children and teachers to be critically literate is in order. The seminal works of Kress and van Leeuwen (1990, 1996) and O'Toole (1994) have begun to meet such a need by taking systemic linguistic theory (Halliday 1985, 1994; Halliday and Hasan 1985; Martin 1992) and adapting it to visual images. At the same time, further work needs to be done with this theory to accommodate the use of sound, animation/video, navigation and movement within the types of hypermedia texts that are being produced today.

This chapter is an attempt to explore the links between visual and written texts, from picture books to digital and electronic texts. It will introduce a number of tools drawn from functional semiotic and sociolinguistic theories to assist with the reading of visuals, including a metalanguage called *visual systemics*. These tools will be exemplified by the use of a range of images, from picture books to screens from electronic and digital texts to demonstrate how images might be read and what messages are conveyed by their content, composition and layout.

Beginning school: images in picture books

The face of a large animal fills the page, confronting the reader with his conniving presence. With teeth gleaming, small beady eyes staring and hairs of fur slashed across the page in the way that only school coloured pencils can, there can be no mistaking this fearsome figure – the big bad wolf!

Michelle and her Year 1 class of 6-year-olds have been completing a series of lessons on fairytales, which incorporated not only the written text but also visual images (Early Literacy Initiative 1997). Her children were encouraged to read pictures and text, learning how to discuss and interpret not only the written meanings but the visual meanings. One particular area of exploration was how the distance used in an image could have an effect on how a viewer related to someone in the image. A close-up shot could make the viewer feel scared of a character. A long shot might make them feel more distant towards that same character. Michelle had her children sort images of people from magazines into long, medium or close shots, discussing the effect. A digital camera was used, allowing children to take photos of themselves, choosing the shot distance for the desired effect.

Having explored these and other aspects of the images they were viewing, the class decided that their drawings of the big bad wolf would look much scarier if they drew him in a close shot, making him really quite threatening to the viewer. This choice demonstrated not only a growing knowledge of the cultural representation of particular fairytale characters, but also an understanding of how those representations are created in a visual form. Impressive work from 5- and 6-year-olds, many of whom were learning English as a second language. Yet, this beginning work in school with text and image (both print and electronic) really needs to be an everyday part of literacy learning in our schools.

Picture books, which have a time-honoured place in all primary classrooms, are an ideal way to introduce children and teachers to a richer view of visual literacy. All texts, visual or written, are created within particular historical and social contexts where their authors are engaged in relations of power. Any text, from a picture book to a web page, needs to be considered in its cultural, situational and authorial context and the intended audience recognized (Graddol 1994). With the advent of improved colour printing at the beginning of the twentieth century, the picture book has evolved from simple moral tales and nursery rhyme illustration into a variety of genres and styles, many reflecting a postmodern and self-reflexive position, which engage young children and adults alike (Anstey and Bull 2000). The sophistication of the stories is reflected in the interplay of both the written and visual texts, which in turn requires quite a rigorous understanding of how both text and image work.

The Stinky Cheese Man and other Fairly Stupid Tales by Scieszka and Smith (1993) is a satirical look at fairytales, where the narrator of the story not only addresses the reader directly, but has major disagreements with characters in the story. Older children, familiar with fairytales, enjoy the satire and bizarre nature of the interplay, which is reflected in the text and images (see Figure 12.1). The written text follows on from an

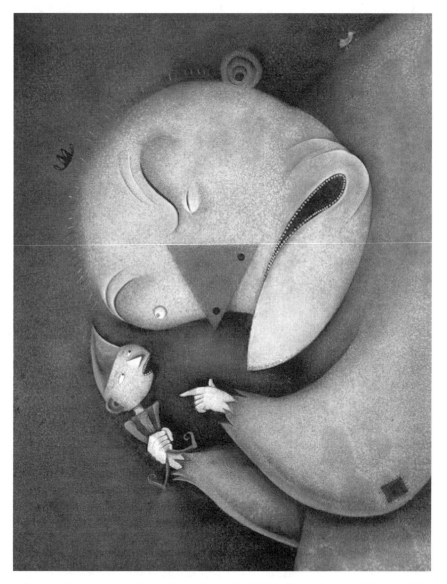

Figure 12.1 Jack and the Giant from *The Stinky Cheese Man and Other Fairly Stupid Tales* (Scieszka and Smith 1993, reprinted with permission)

altercation that Jack (who is the narrator of the whole book) has had with the Giant. Jack criticized the Giant's attempts at a story, so the Giant has retaliated, demanding a better story. Even the typographic sizing of the text is used here as a visual feature to accentuate the action and humour.

In terms of the visual text, let's consider what actions and relationships are being constructed here. The comic slapstick of the text is both paralleled and enhanced by the image. The clenched fist of the giant, squeezing the body of Jack to an impossibly thin state, the accusatory pointing finger, the sparse spiky hair and the eyeball to eyeball contact create a humorous yet aggressive interplay. The strong lines of the Giant's mouth, arms and eyebrows all draw the viewer to the character of Jack, the centre of the Giant's actions. The use of a triangular nose suggests a surrealist feel to the image, as does the tiny hat on the giant's head and the white dotted teeth of both the characters. The viewer is confronted by the closeness of the action, feeling the anger of the giant by his proximity to us, through the use of a midshot – his bulk fills most of the frame as we look on at eye level with the characters. The image is sepia in colour, which is consistent with the rest of the book and gives it a strangely old feel, like that of parchment. Combined with the surreal nature of the images, this further builds the absurdist and satirical atmosphere.

In the same way that the children in Michelle's Year 1 class were beginning to articulate the design of the images they were viewing and producing, so older children reading *The Stinky Cheese Man* can begin to build even more sophisticated readings of images. Here we have used some of the functional semiotics framework to draw out some of the meanings in the text. It would be essential to place any reading of this text in the cultural context of fairytales – where they come from, what purpose they originally served and the purposes for which we read them now. Teamed with this would be the idea of satire, helping children to understand the nature of this sophisticated literary tool. At the individual image level, the previous description of the Jack and the Giant included three aspects:

- the experiential nature of the image – what is happening, the events portrayed and the use of lines to emphasize these actions;
- the interpersonal aspect – how the viewer relates to the image in terms of the social distance (close-, mid- or longshot) and the use of colour;
- the textual aspect – how the page is laid out, what the most dominant or salient elements in the picture are and where these are positioned.

These aspects (or metafunctions) can be combined with discussion of the overall meanings and social context of the story, including a critical approach to the possible interpretation of the story. For example, how does this story represent the traditional hero (Jack) and the villain (Giant) compared to other fairytales? What is the significance of Jack (who is also the narrator of the whole book) being attacked by another character, who demands a 'better story'? The question of metafictive texts, where the reader's attention is drawn to the constructed nature of the text, then arises from a seemingly simple fairytale (Anstey and Bull 2000: 9). By drawing on a theoretical framework to interpret images, both teachers and children can participate in much richer and more critical readings of a text.

Comparison of texts is also a very helpful tool to promote critical readings. Comparing this text with the more traditional versions would allow children to discuss what dominant readings are being suggested by mainstream images of fairytales, such as those in the Disney cartoons, or the more traditional and naturalistic versions of Grimm's fairytales. This could also lead to a discussion as to why the author might have chosen to parody or satirize particular characters. What might they be commenting on by doing so? What views of narrators/heroes/villains do each of the texts present, both through the written text and the pictures? Which ones do you find entertaining, stereotypical or even offensive? Picture books are an ideal source for entering into visual literacy activities, for children from kindergarten to secondary level. However, they are just one part of the image culture that we inhabit.

The place of visuals in electronic texts: the Internet

Allan's upper primary class of 11-year-olds are learning about rainforests and people's impact upon them. They are engaged in learning about the topic through paper-based and electronic sources – books and Internet sites. Their task is scaffolded through the completion of a webquest (guided Internet search), with the final product being a PowerPoint presentation around the key concepts of the unit. During the information gathering and scaffolded learning about PowerPoint, the teachers, the classroom teacher, the teacher-librarian and the information and communication technology (ICT) co-ordinator draw children's attention to the construction of the electronic Internet sites.

To scaffold the children's learning the classroom teacher deconstructed the Greenpeace site with small groups, because it would be difficult for the whole class to see the small computer screen (the session would have been improved if the school had possessed a data projector so that the whole class could see the Internet site at once and share their ideas). The questions that guided the discussion of the site's homepage were:

- What is the purpose of this site?
- How is this conveyed in the construction of the screen you see?
- Can you 'read' the whole page on the screen or do you need to scroll?

- How does scrolling influence the way you read the screen?
- Can the way the page is made influence where you go?
- What texts (visual or written) are used on the home page?
- What information do they provide?
- Where are they placed and why?
- What type of images are used? Photos? Cartoons? Drawings? Abstract? Scientific? Naturalistic?
- Why do you think these were selected?
- What is the background like? Why might this have been chosen as the background?
- What colours are used? Why do you think these were chosen?
- How does the site draw your attention to it?

Discussing the construction of the home pages as individual entities, or comparing the sites, provided the children with an initial way to talk about the visuals of Internet sites. From this general beginning, Allan can then introduce the children to a language about visuals – the visual grammar. By being more articulate about the construction of a site, children can begin to have insights into the hidden meanings of the design and the way sites position the user in relation to the information. Children can then use this knowledge in the construction of their own work; for example, a PowerPoint presentation about rainforests.

To further explore children's visual literacy language we now consider some aspects of the visual construction of the 'Volcano World' home page (see Figure 12.2), which can be found at http://volcano.und.nodak.edu In the deconstruction of the Volcano World page we focus on the textual aspect of layout and composition, the accompanying visual grammar terms and some areas of the interpersonal aspect.

Volcano World is promoted as 'The web's premier source of volcano info'. As such, it presents information about volcanoes for the user to access. Most of the page is visible on the screen, so that the user does not have to scroll down very far to see the entire contents. The information on the site is categorized into sections, listed down the right-hand side of the page. This home page presents the parts of the whole site to the user. It also includes an image of 'Rocky' the volcano waving at users, welcoming them to the site. In terms of what the page is about (the experiential nature of the page), the lines between written and visual texts blur here. Although the cartoon-like volcano image is a narrative, engaging in an action, the whole screen is more conceptual. This links to the main purpose of the site: to provide information about volcanoes.

Volcano World is quite unusual in its layout. Most Internet sites place the contents of the site on the left-hand side of the page (known as the *given* side in visual systemics[1]), with the rest of the page containing the main image and/ or information. Volcano World's layout places the 'sections' navigation bar as 'new' information (that is, on the right-hand

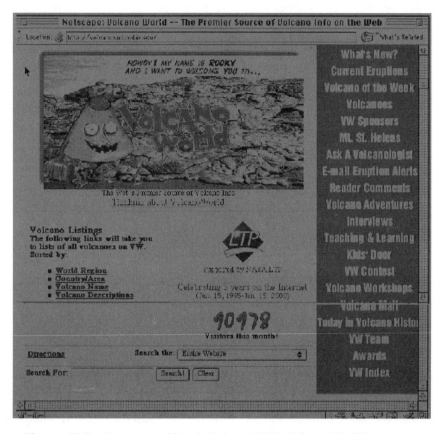

Figure 12.2 University of North Dakota (UND) *Volcano World* home page

side of the screen). The 'sections' part of the site is placed in the most prominent position on the screen. This importance is emphasized by the background colour, which contrasts with the white writing, additionally highlighted by the shadowing of the words. The user is also drawn to this part of the page by the choice of colour and the framing of the table. Additionally, each section changes colour to a bright blue background as the mouse cursor is moved over it, highlighting it with an almost surreal use of colour.

The other dominant element on the page is the image of 'Rocky' the volcano, which is placed in the ideal position – that is, at the top of the page. In terms of top and bottom organization of the visual elements in western-style images, what has been placed at the top can be said to represent the 'idealized' part of an image, while what has been placed at the bottom represents the 'real', more down to earth or everyday position. On this web page, Volcano World and its unknown knowledge are given prominence at the top. 'Rocky' engages the user directly by making eye contact, demanding our attention. The cartoon uses full colour, making it appear larger than life, almost 'unreal'. It also engages the reader personally by 'speaking' to them: 'Howdy! My name is Rocky and I want to welcome you to . . . Volcano World'. The addition of the direct speech amplifies the engagement of the user with the image and hence the site. The Rocky image can change the next time the site is visited but it remains in the same position.

The use of cartoons in science texts is not unusual. The technique is used to appeal to younger audiences, to portray the content as fun and to engage the reader's attention. As the child views the Rocky image, the framing lines in the background, combined with the title of the page, draw their attention to the table of contents, again focusing their subsequent actions on this side of the page.

So far we have looked at static images, in paper and electronic forms. But visuals can also be dynamic, moving as the child interacts with them or as the image is activated. In the next section we consider the literacy demands of electronic multimedia texts that also involve some form of movement.

Reading for information: images in CD-ROM programs

Unlike current web pages, CD-ROM programs have the advantage of being able to store large video, sound and animation files, which can be accessed instantly. Thus there is the possibility for more creative combinations in a multi-modal electronic text. Children can be assisted to find information using CD-ROM materials by knowing how they are constructed, including the visual composition and purpose of the construction and its relation to information presentation and gathering. This knowledge can provide guidance and support for information skills.

Teresa's composite class of 9-, 10- and 11-year-olds are working on the topic of machines. They are focusing on learning about a specific machine of their choice and creating a written and visual explanation of how their machine works. The teacher initially works with a small group scaffolding their learning of the program *The Way Things Work* (v. 2) (Dorling Kindersley 1996). Teresa draws the children's attention to the construction of the program. Her discussion focuses on the particular way that the designer has constructed the layout of the program to assist children with their information searches.

The Way Things Work contains information about a variety of machines. We are introduced to the program by its designer/author, David Macauley, as he takes us through to the main screen, explaining what can be found in the program. The main screen (see Figure 12.3) is divided vertically into the narrow program navigation bar on the left and the much larger

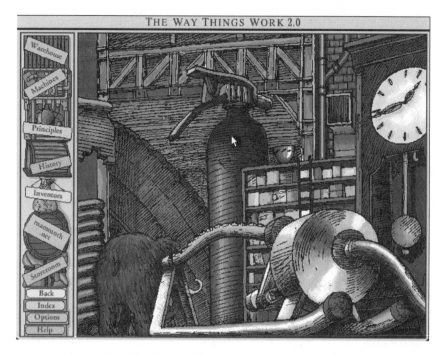

Figure 12.3 *The Way Things Work* main screen (Dorling Kindersley 1996, reprinted with permission)

information screen (here showing a large warehouse) on the right. This means that the viewer focuses on the 'new' information being presented on the right side of the screen (i.e. the warehouse), as opposed to the static or 'given' navigation bar on the left. The larger size and right-hand side positioning of the information screen mean that it is tempting for children to interact with this side of the screen first. However, if they are looking for specific information, entering into the program via this screen may not be the most efficient way of finding what they want. Accessing the program via the warehouse takes the user on a random tour of machines. Using the index in the navigation bar, however, will enable the user to search for a specific machine.

Using written text, images, animations and diagrams, *The Way Things Work* provides examples of how things work: the principles of science behind each machine, when they were invented, who invented them and how they relate to each other. Each section is visually different, but the static navigation bar is constantly on the left-hand (given) side. The 'History' section is a timeline, with hotlinked dates to the corresponding information screen. The 'Inventors' section is a 'book' from A–Z, organized according to the surname of the inventor. It looks like an address book. The 'Principles of Science' section is a map, with labels of the different

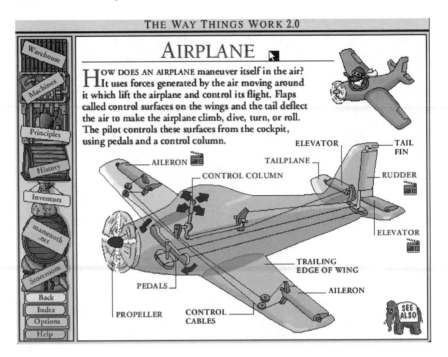

Figure 12.4   *The Way Things Work* airplane screen (Dorling Kindersley 1996, reprinted with permission)

principles, an image of a machine that uses each principle and 'people' walking around the streets. These are linked to a machine screen by the action of clicking on that section while viewing the information screen. For example, while viewing the airplane screen (see Figure 12.4) a user can click on the Inventors' navigation icon and the program will show the page with the inventor of the aeroplane. The same applies to the Principles of Science; an overlay screen appears showing 'Related principles of science' and a list of pictorial icons to choose from. All information – whether it is written text, images, hotlinked words or images, or animations – is presented on the right (new) side of the screen, which is also the larger section.

Once the children are familiar with the program's navigation structure and sections, the next step is to build up their knowledge of the composition of the information screen. During this and other scaffolded viewing sessions, the teacher considers the screen's construction and the interaction of the elements with the user. In addition, they discuss the relationship of the overlays and animations to reading the information.

The information screen on airplanes (note the American spelling due to the American authorship) will be used to exemplify the points made about the screen. Within this screen, and other similar information pages, the image dominates. It is the most salient element. It is also placed in the bottom half of the screen, representing the reality or 'what is' section. The written text is placed in the top, the ideal position, here representing the knowledge to be gained and valued. This written knowledge is demonstrated by the visual text, its hotlinked sections and animated movements. Only two of the labels in the visual text are mentioned in the written text: the control column and pedals, as they manipulate the control surfaces on the plane. These labels are not elaborated upon in the written text but they are part of the visual explanation. Where the user's eyes are initially drawn to and where they travel on an image (the reading path) becomes quite complex here. Where does the user start to read this explanation?

The user's eye may be drawn to the arrows by their colour and size. But the hotlinked words on the right side (elevator and rudder) are placed in the 'new' position and may influence the user to go there first. In addition, both have 'movie clips' signalled with the 'clapperboard' icon. The organizational structure of the information screen is more a centre-margin layout, where the image in the centre is most important, with the labels, text and animations supporting this image. However, when the user clicks on the arrows, the small aeroplane in the top right -hand corner, which is the most highly valued section of the screen, actually moves. This demonstrates what is 'happening' when these parts of the plane move – how to go up, go down, turn left or right. The diagrammatic changes illustrate the effect of moving the control column on parts of the plane. This complex variety of visual and interactive possibilities is rich with possibility but also with confusion for a young researcher.

Most of the machine information screens in this program seem to be representative of a science book, offering the reader information. The images, such as that of the aeroplane, are diagrams and are scientifically orientated. The selection of colours, particularly the use of red, high-lights those sections and parts of the diagram that children need to focus on and engage with to build up their understanding of how the machine works. With the aeroplane, the captions provide information about a given part of the plane, while the movement demonstrates (not just illustrates) how the plane works. Younger or inexperienced users need instruction on the viewing of the screen – which elements and movements are related and what this means in the explanation. In addition, the reading of the screen, with regard to both the written and visual texts, needs to be supported in the initial learning stage, in the same way we would scaffold the shared reading of factual books.

Many factual CD-ROM programs segment information into visuals with supporting written text. This layering of information can be read in any order by the user, but to get the whole picture they need to interact with all the sections, the technical vocabulary and the moving images. Such programs provide bite-sized pieces of information or 'information chunks' to assist the user to understand the information. However, teachers cannot assume that children are able to put these pieces together. As with information books, it is a good idea to provide experiences for children to learn how to read these information screens. Through shared viewing activities, children can learn how to use, interact and read the visual and written information.

Conclusion

How to learn to learn is important in any learning environment, be it paper-based or electronic. Given the range of texts that are part of a child's school experience we cannot assume that children can expertly read all the different forms. The use of visual and multi-modal texts as resources within the classroom is going to increase and we need to provide children with opportunities to learn about, as well as from, these texts. Providing children with a language to talk about visual texts and engaging them in critiquing such texts can form the basis of teaching and learning through them.

Note

1 In written English, given information usually comes first, followed by new information which is not already known (see Halliday 1985: 274). For example: 'The Australian kangaroo is *a type of marsupial*'; 'London is *the capital city of England*'.

Websites and software

Dorling Kindersley (1996) *The Way Things Work* 2.0. DK Multimedia.
University of North Dakota (UND) *Volcano World*. http://volcano.und.nodak.edu (accessed June 2000).

References

Anstey, M. and Bull, G. (2000) *Reading the Visual – Written and Illustrated Children's Literature*. Sydney: Harcourt.
Christie, F. (1990) *Literacy for a Changing World*. Melbourne: ACER.
Christie, F. and Misson, R. (1998) *Literacy and Schooling*. London: Routledge.
Cope, B. and Kalantzis, M. (eds) (2000) *Multiliteracies: Literacy Learning and the Design of Social Futures*. Melbourne: Macmillan.

Downes, T. and Zammit, K. (2001) New literacies for connected learning in global classrooms: a framework for the future, in P. Hogenbirk and H. Taylor (eds) *The Bookmark of the School of the Future*. Boston, MA: Kluwer Academic Publishers.

Early Literacy Initiative (NSW Department of Education & Training) (1997) *Visual Literacy* (video tape). Sydney: OTEN, NSW Department of Education & Training.

Freebody, P. and Luke, A. (1990) 'Literacies' programs: debates and demands in cultural context, *Prospect*, 5(3): 7–16.

Goodman, S. (1996) Visual English, in S. Goodman and D. Graddol (eds) *Redesigning English: New Texts, New Identities*. Buckingham: Open University Press.

Graddol, D. (1994) What is a text? in O. Boyd-Barrett and D. Graddol (eds) *Media Texts, Authors and Readers: A Reader*. Clevedon: Multilingual Matters.

Halliday, M.A.K. (1985) *An Introduction to Functional Grammar*, 1st edn. London: Arnold.

Halliday, M.A.K. (1994) *An Introduction to Functional Grammar*, 2nd edn. London: Arnold.

Halliday, M.A.K. and Hassan, R. (1985) *Language, Context, and Text: Aspects of Language in a Social Semiotic Perspective*. Geelong, VIC: Deakin University Press.

Horn, R. (1998) *Visual Language: Global Communication for the 21st Century*. Washington: MacroVU Inc.

Kress, G. (1997) Visual and verbal modes of representation in electronically mediated communication: the potentials of new forms of text, in I. Snyder (ed.) *From Page to Screen: Taking Literacy into the Electronic Era*, pp. 53–79. Sydney: Allen & Unwin.

Kress, G. (2000) Multimodality, in B. Cope and M. Kalantzis (eds) *Multiliteracies: Literacy Learning and the Design of Social Futures*. Melbourne: Macmillan.

Kress, G. and van Leeuwen, T. (1990) *Reading Images*. Geelong, Vic: Deakin University.

Kress, G. and van Leeuwen, T. (1996) *Reading Images: The Grammar of Visual Design*. London: Routledge.

Martin, J.R. (1992) *English Text: System and Structure*. Philadelphia, PA: John Benjamins.

O'Toole, M. (1994) *The Language of Displayed Art*. London: Leicester University Press.

Raney, K. (1998) A matter of survival: on being visually literate, *The English & Media Magazine*, 39(autumn): 37–42.

Scieszka, J. and Smith, L. (1993) *The Stinky Cheese Man and other Fairly Stupid Tales*. London: Puffin.

The New London Group (1996) A pedagogy of multiliteracies: designing social futures, *Harvard Educational Review*, 66(1): 60–92.

INDEX